More Human than Otherwise

Selected Papers

Irwin Hirsch

More Human than Otherwise

Selected Papers

Irwin Hirsch

IPBOOKS.net
International Psychoanalytic Books

International Psychoanalytic Books (IPBooks)
New York • http://www.IPBooks.net

International Psychoanalytic Books (IPBooks)
Queens, New York
Online at: www.IPBooks.net

On the Cover: Image Copyright © David Newman, Reeds, 2014, oil on paper and wood panel, 16 x 20 inches, davidnewmanpaintings.com

Interior book design by Lawrence L. Schwartz, IPBooks

ISBN: 978-1-949093-12-4

PERMISSIONS

Chapter 1: Hirsch, I. (1983). Analytic intimacy and the restoration of nurturance. *American Journal of Psychoanalysis.* 43:325–343, reprinted courtesy of *American Journal of Psychoanalysis.*

Chapter 4: Hirsch, I. (1993). The ubiquity and relativity of narcissism. In: J. Fiscalini & A. Grey (Eds.), *Narcissism and the Interpersonal Self.* New York: Columbia University Press. pp. 293–317, reprinted courtesy of Columbia University Press.

Chapter 6: Hirsch, I. & Roth, J. (1995). Changing conceptions of unconscious. *Contemporary Psychoanalysis.* 31:263–276, reprinted courtesy of *Contemporary Psychoanalysis.*

Chapter 10: Hirsch, I. (2009). On idealism and soberness: Founding and maintaining an analytic institute. *Contemporary Psychoanalysis.* 45:330–345, reprinted courtesy of *Contemporary Psychoanalysis.*

Chapter 14: Hirsch, I. (2016). Reflections on Ferenczi: Analytic subjectivity and analytic hierarchy. *Contemporary Psychoanalysis.* 52:383–390, reprinted courtesy of *Contemporary Psychoanalysis.*

Chapter 16: Hirsch, I. (2018). From familiar and familial repetition to the anxiety of living differently. *Contemporary Psychoanalysis.* 54:290–298, reprinted courtesy of *Contemporary Psychoanalysis.*

Chapter 3: Hirsch, I. & Kessel, P. (1988). Reflections on mature love and countertransference. *Free Associations.* 12:60–83, reprinted courtesy of the journal *Free Associations.*

Chapter 8: Hirsch, I. (1998). Analytic intimacy, analyzability and the vulnerable analyst. *Free Associations.* 42:250–259, reprinted courtesy of the journal *Free Associations.*

Chapter 5: Hirsch, I. (1994). Interpersonal perspective: The analyst's participant-observation with the special" patient. In: P. Buirski (Ed), *Contemporary Schools of Analytic Therapy.* Northfield, New Jersey: Jason Aronson. pp. 107–137, reprinted courtesy of Jason Aronson.

Chapter 7: Hirsch, I. (1997). The widening concept of dissociation. *Journal of the American Academy of Psychoanalysis.* 25:603–615, *Journal of the American Academy of Psychoanalysis,* reprinted with permission of the *Journal of the American Academy of Psychoanalysis.*

Chapter 9: Hirsch, I. & Hirsch, C. (2000). *Seinfeld's* humor noir: A look at our dark side. *Journal of Popular Film and Television.* 29:116–123, reprinted courtesy of the *Journal of Popular Film and Television.*

DEDICATION

*To my grandchildren: Dilan, Theo, Ana,
and Aurelie, and to their parents.*

ACKNOWLEDGEMENTS

With much gratitude to my dear and patient wife Willa for all the weekend hours spent alone, while I was holed-up, in strictly enforced silence, writing the stuff in this volume, and more. And as well, for reading, criticizing and proofreading every single word produced.

And a different quality of gratitude to my patients, for it is they who taught me how to productively work psychoanalytically, especially those who stuck with me when I wasn't working particularly effectively. I thank them too, for helping me evolve as a more tolerant and accepting person than I had been in my younger years.

CONTENTS

INTRODUCTION

Of course, my title is taken as part of a quote from Harry Stack Sullivan (1953), for it was Sullivan's portrayal of the analyst as a participant-observer that began to reduce the hierarchy between what had been the view of analysts as objective participants and patients as subjective participants. Indeed, also implied in most pre Interpersonal and traditional psychoanalytic models, is a picture of the analyst as inherently less flawed than the patient, a myth also exploded by Heinrich Racker's (1968) assertion that psychoanalysis is decidedly *not* a relationship between a well therapist and a sick patient. I have always assumed, or I like to think, that Sullivan's awareness of himself as a person with a deeply troubled life history helped him recognize the inevitable existence of more emotional symmetry between analyst and patient and as well, the inevitability that the idiosyncratic person of the analyst will always play a role in analytic interaction. For me, "more human than otherwise" has never meant that we are all alike in our emotional fingerprints, but that each unique fingerprint is characterized by unique emotions that influence all perception and all interpersonal interaction.

What is now generally accepted by most contemporary analytic "schools"—psychoanalysis as a relationship between two subjective co-participants, took quite a long time to settle into the corpus of psychoanalytic theorizing. It has been very difficult for many analysts to give up their stature as an objective scientist in the context of a human relationship, where objectivity and the alleged ability to stand outside of a personal relationship often creates emotional safety for both parties. Yet in spite of lip-service acceptance of analysts' subjectivity, a medical model of psychoanalysis still dominates the profession, even given the fact that most psychoanalysts are no longer medical doctors. Our literature is dominated by references to diagnostic categorization, with particular ways both to understand the life historical development of people placed in these diagnostic categories and specified methods to treat each of these distinct categories of people. Clear lines of hierarchy simplify the inherent confusion and complication of an intense human relationship, albeit a professional and fee-for-service human relationship. In spite of an inherent asymmetry in any professional relationship, the unique individual properties of each analytic participant in the dyad should carry more weight than any prescribed methodology.

The establishment of undue hierarchy and its potential ill effects is a theme that runs through most of my writing. I compare the more human and flawed subjective analyst with models of analyst as scientist, doctor, nurturing mother and benign empathic father. Though the scientist and the doctor appear to be a more directly hierarchical position, the view of the analyst as a good enough parent can be equally so. When adult patients are viewed either as ill, deficient or as a child, the analyst naturally devolves into being a scientist/doctor or a good and better than original parent. In this context, the adaptive resilience of our patients maybe minimized and their weaknesses emphasized. Infantilization, condescension and even pity may readily lead to iatrogenic solutions with those patients who are compliant and/or are comfortable being *less than* and/or excessively dependent on their analyst.

So much of my affinity for the Interpersonal tradition reflects my personal sensitivity to excessive hierarchy and as well, to infantalization. These went hand in hand for me while growing up. I do not want to indulge in too much memoir mode or autobiography but I was raised in a way that encouraged some awe and acceptance of those who had more status and power than my own family. When I allowed myself to look more closely, however, this power was often vacant and unwarranted, much like the empty suit of the Wizard of Oz. I came to life by being defiant and by challenging undeserved power and ultimately by defining my own strengths. What had made it natural and easy for me earlier in life to be overly respectful to designated authority was the low esteem that my parents unfortunately felt in relation to themselves and transmitted to me. Coupled with having been overly protected and infantilized by frightened and cautious people, I could have been a living wreck had I not become rebellious and disrespectful of those who I deemed undeserving of the power granted to them. Throughout my professional writing there is a skepticism, much in the vein Harold Searles (1979), toward colleagues who present themselves not only as thoroughly good parental figures but as selfless and purely altruistic. Invariably, their *less than* ideal human being patients must fall far below these standards. To me, "more human than otherwise" means more uniquely subjective than otherwise, which adds up to more idiosyncratically flawed than otherwise. We are more poised to help our patients when embracing our flaws both in and out of our professional lives—our patients need not be either less loving people or more troubled than are we. We can be useful to them either way as long as we are not self-deceptive about our subjective, more human than otherwise participation.

REFERENCES

Racker, H. (1968). *Transference and Countertransference.* New York: International Universities Press.

Searles, H. (1979). *Countertransference and Related Subjects.* New York: International Universities Press.

Sullivan, H.S. (1953). *Conceptions of Modern Psychiatry.* New York: Norton.

Prologue to Chapter 1:
ANALYTIC INTIMACY AND THE RESTORATION OF NURTURANCE

This chapter is the third psychoanalytic paper I published and reflects a theme that runs through much of my writing and prevalent in many of the papers in this volume. The tone for this theme was set in my first published article, "Authoritarian aspects of the psychoanalytic relationship"[1], where I attempted to outline the normative prevalence of unwarranted hierarchy between psychoanalysts and their patients. For much of my life I have been sensitive to issues of social hierarchy, though I will not elaborate here the familial and sociocultural origins of this sensitivity. In my primary and secondary school years this took the form clownish behavior, mocking those teachers whose arbitrary authority did not match their skills as educators. Though I was often admired by my peers for what they perceived as a kind of disinhibited bravery, I too often suffered significant negative consequences like deflated grades and placement in classes that were below my intellectual abilities. In spite of these consequences this quality persisted intermittently all the way through my psychoanalytic training and well into my career as a psychologist-psychoanalyst, whenever I believed that my existence was impinged upon by authorities that I deemed undeserving of their power. I was almost fired from more than one early career job, was actually fired from another and most significantly damaging, was denied strongly sought after promotion within the institute where I trained and that represented my primary professional affiliation. This last experience, which I have written about[2], hurt me deeply enough to lead to efforts to channel my critical eye into the written word and into papers like this and others throughout this volume.

In this paper I focus my critical eye on what at the time was the emergence in the USA of two psychoanalytic traditions, Middle School British Object Relations and American Self-Psychology. I argue that both these perspectives situated the analyst as a nurturing parent to the adult patient, perceived less as an adult than as a deficient child. Implicit

---

[1]Hirsch, I. (1980–1981). Authoritarian aspects of the psychoanalytic relationship. *Review of Existential Psychology and Psychiatry.* 17:105–133.

[2]Hirsch, I. (2014). Emerging from the oppositional and the negative. In: Steven Kuchuck (Ed.), *Clinical Implications of the Analyst's Life Experience: Where the Personal Becomes Professional.* New York & London: Routledge. pp. 49–64.

in this configuration was an affirmation of the analyst as a sufficient adult providing doctor-patient like tender care to someone less developed. This hierarchy was viewed by its proponents as more loving and benign than the Classical Freudian hierarchy that situated the analyst as a scientific and objective observer and interpreter of the patient's instinctually dominated subjectivity. I suggest that neither position sufficiently respects the patient as a peer chronological adult, independent of the problems in living that they present to the analyst. In these configurations, fully respectful and potentially intimate peer relatedness is precluded. That is, neither an allegedly objective scientist nor a benign parent can engage without excessive hierarchy to a patient, who by definition is seen as *inherently* less capable of mature adult rlatedness than is the analyst. I further suggest that the newer Object Relations and Self-Psychologists offer the illusion of intimacy based on their view of the patient as a wounded and deprived child in contrast to the traditional Freudian view of the patient as a sexual and aggressive instinct dominated child. I argue that as long an analyst presumes or implies adult maturity for themselves and inevitable child-like immaturity in all patients, the relationships has too much hierarchy to qualify as an ideally intimate psychoanalytic engagement.

Chapter 1

ANALYTIC INTIMACY AND THE
RESTORATION OF NURTURANCE*

"The wilder manias of pseudointimacy which serve as a desperate camouflage (for hopelessness) could also be seen as desperate gambits to retrieve what has never been gained. It cannot be denied that the strained smile, or the joyous laughter that often substitutes for friendship at a dinner party, bears some relation to the giggling of a hebephrenic or the grimace of catatonics."[1] To retrieve what has never been achieved is a sad and futile quest. The psychoanalytic relationship can never replace what was absent in the past. It can provide a new relationship and life experience and can clarify what was missing and may still be missing in the life and life historyof the patient. This viewpoint is not shared by many analysts, particularly those who attempt to work with more severely disturbed patients. The analytic interaction often takes the form of a parent-child relationship with the explicit aim of providing to the patient what was missing from childhood. Some refer to simple nurturance and others talk of building structures where there once were structural deficits within the patient.

My primary thesis is that the analyst's promotion of parent-childness in the analysis of adult patients may appear as a form of analytic intimacy but is more often too hierarchical in nature to be either considered intimate or genuinely respectful. That is, the effort to be a better parent to the patient can seem benevolent but, as Farber suggests, may be a camouflage for any number of other problems in the analytic relationship.

Analytic Intimacy

As Farber puts it, "Intimacy is two people presenting themselves or being present."[2] Wolstein speaks of a process wherein both participants present their unique selves.[3] There is no hierarchy or a sense that one person (the patient) is there simply to receive supplies from the other person (the analyst). According to Wolstein, experience is "shared." Despite the coparticipants' being there for different purposes, there is an equality that comes from both the analyst's and patient's

*Hirsch, I. (1983). Analytic intimacy and the restoration of nurturance *American Journal of Psychoanalysis* 43(4):325–343.

undefensively showing their innermost reactions and being open to each other's presentations

Existential philosophy is evident in the background of many analysts who write about intimacy as representing a sense of equality and of "thereness" in the interpersonal dyad (see, e.g., Singer).[4] Martin Buber writes of "I–Thou" relatedness as requiring mutual confrontation and genuine dialogue.[5] The notion of both participants' being "fully in it," without withdrawing or holding back relevant thoughts, challenges some analytic tenets that emphasize the analyst as the sole judge of when the patient is ready to hear certain reactions. Farber refers to the language of science as "scientisms" and as being dominated by professional jargon, instead of consisting of "straight talk."[6] He uses Buber's term *interhuman* to refer to two people engaging without the defensive intermediary of jargon or metapsychological concepts. Schafer has recently devoted a volume to this very matter of metapsychological language as a barrier to open dialogue.[7] I have discussed the use of professional language and concepts as a defensive effort to build a comfortable but stymieing hierarchy between patient and analyst and to promote for the therapist, the security that comes with certainty.[8]

Ehrenberg, in writing of "the intimate edge," describes both parties in the analysis as "observing participants."[9] Intimacy is reflected by both patient and analyst being the objects of mutual study. This includes the examination of the distortions each brings to the relationship. As Wolstein had described earlier, the analyst's vulnerability to the patient is markedly increased when one works in this manner.[10] In another article, Ehrenberg suggests that the firm establishment of the analyst's own selfhood and boundaries make being truly intimate with another person (and thus more vulnerable) a greater likelihood.[11] Wilner, along similar lines, refers to intimacy with oneself, which then may be shared by the analyst.[12] One of the aims of psychoanalysis is, therefore, to help patients find and define their own unique selves. Implicit in this notion is that the self is present in the patient and does not have to be built or developed by the analyst. The analyst's ability honestly to be present helps patients reveal the aspects of their selves that they do not normally show to themselves or to others. This begins the process of self-definition and self-acceptance.

Levenson describes the changing concept of psychoanalytic "cure" as evolving from "you must learn not to distort me" or "to distinguish fantasy from reality" to the present, "you must learn to use as authentic and real whatever your response to me is. It is a reflection of who we are together, what it is like to experience each other frankly, with awareness and without the pressure to change it into something else or something better."[13] The exposure of the self of the analyst and the self of the patient reflects analytic intimacy. "Being oneself" has become a therapeutic aim in and of itself. Levenson goes on to say, "Intimacy has now become an openness to the other person as he is." The intimately relating analyst must make interpretations as subjective observations coming from the subjective self. There is little objectivity outside the two relating, subjective selves struggling to be their authentic selves.

Nurturance in Psychoanalysis

The prevailing psychoanalytic literature divides the patient population into neurotic and character disorders. Members of the former group have been considered "the good analytic patients," and some of the latter group have only recently been viewed as analyzable by the psychoanalytic mainstream. Some analysts feel that nurture (in contrast with analysis) is necessary with neurotic patients, but most analysts are opposed to this. The more severely disturbed group, however, by and large is seen as having early deficits that must be repaired before the usual sort of psychoanalytic work can begin. Others feel that psychoanalysis proper can never be considered with many of these severely disturbed patients and that the only viable aim is the provision of supplies that were missed in childhood. Stolorow and Lachmann outline this dichotomy between neurotic and deficient (more seriously disturbed) patients and recommend two distinct phases of treatment.[14] The early stages are primarily concerned with filling in deficiencies and the later ones with traditional conflict analysis. Indeed, the issue of oedipal or conflict analysis versus pre-oedipal or deficiency analysis is perhaps the hottest current controversy in the field.

Interpersonal analysts, by and large, have not been embroiled in this dispute, since sharp dichotomy between oedipal and pre-oedipal analyses, traditionally, are not made. Even the concepts of oedipal and pre-oedipal are usually not used, just as the metaphor "structural conflict," implying structures of the mind, is not in accord with interpersonal psychoanalytic thought. The controversy lies primarily between classical (conflict) analysts and object relations (deficiency) analysts. Though interpersonal analysts lean more toward object relations analysts in their theory of development and their rejection of Freudian metapsychology, they tend to be more compatible with the classicists in their views on analytic gratification and nurturance. What follows is a sample of issues that address the matters of psychoanalytic nurture, gratification, and intimacy.

The concepts *therapeutic alliance* and *working alliance* have stirred much controversy among classical psychoanalysts. Essentially, the proponents of these concepts suggest that, for a period (usually early) in the analysis, the aim of the analysis is not to analyze but to establish a positive, working relationship. Furthermore, this is recommended not only for patients with character disorders, but also for traditional neurotic analytic patients.

Spitz[15] is acknowledged as a forerunner to this notion. He views the analyst-patient relationship as bearing enormous similarity to the mother-child relationship. Specifically, he speaks about the relative helplessness and passive dependence of the infant upon the mother. He believes that the regressive pressures of the analytic setting generate movement back to the earliest stages of object relatedness. He emphasizes the anaclitic aspects of the patient's relatedness, toward which the analyst usually responds with support. This is comparable to the response of the mother to the infant as the infant moves toward the end of the anaclitic phase of development. Gitelson elaborated, noting that patients in the beginning of analysis often relate in a symbiotic manner.[16] He suggests this is not pathological and should be met with the same attitude as a good mother meets her infant at that developmental stage.

Zetzel states quite clearly that she views the early mother-child configuration as the basic psychology of the analytic situation.[17] She promotes a "therapeutic alliance" by establishing a "positive mother-child tie," brought about by a protecting and mothering attitude. Transference is to be overlooked until the point when the patient feels safe, as with a good mother. She views the early analytic interaction as similar to the fundamental organismic distress suffered by all young children whose needs are not met. The analyst must respond as a good mother lest a therapeutic impasse occur. Further, she continues this line of thinking by drawing parallels between the whole course of analysis and the developmental vicissitudes of the child.

Greenson's[18] *working alliance* is a modified version of Zetzel's *therapeutic alliance*. Greenson advocates an early period in the analysis where the building of the "positive" relationship takes precedence of the analyzing function of the analyst. Although he does not concentrate on parent-child analogies, he does continue Zetzel's line of thinking of an early supportive phase prior to the analysis proper. Stone, like Greenson, attempts to cultivate the positive transference, which he calls the "mature" transference.[19] Both he and Greenson wish to use the patient's cooperation (I would say, compliance) as a lever to weather the negative transference. In order to insure this positive alliance, the analyst must be ready to nurture; that is, to be a good parent so that the patient will not become angry and disrupt the relationship. They imply, though they do not state it as explicitly as Spitz, Gitelson, or Zetzel, that the analyst's good early parenting will instill in the patient a spirit of cooperation toward the analyst. This will bypass the more angry and hateful feelings provoked by the patient's less-than-perfect parents.

A somewhat less controversial viewpoint in the psychoanalytic literature is espoused by Loewald.[20] In a sense it represents "analyst as good father" in contrast with "nurturing mother." Identification with the "new parent"/analyst is seen as the vehicle for analytic cure. The analyst is viewed as a real figure plus a transference object, and his "real" ability to provide undistorted reality and beneficial interpretations is internalized by the patient. The patient identifies not only with the analyst but with the entire analytic process. It is rather clear here that the emergence of the patient's own unique self is not viewed as the primary goal. The patient is dependent on the relationship with an analyst who provides the patient with not just a new experience but with a better (than original) parent. Harris also tries to demonstrate that introjection of the mature qualities of the analyst is a primary source of the patient's improvement.[21] He compares the parental and the analytic relationships and suggests that empathic abilities of the analyst, in a sense, remind the patient of parental empathy. The analyst's often greater (than the parent's) empathic abilities provide the patient with an improved object for identification.

Langs is critical of the classical analytic emphasis on pure interpretation and of the classical analysts' relative ignoring of the analyst as a person in the relationship.[22] He views functions such as the establishment of a secure frame and the availability for incorporative identifications as at least as important to effective analysis as are accurate interpretations. Modell similarly views the analyst and the analytic setting as providing a vessel ("cocoon") for the patient until the patient feels the security to move on to new experience.[23] This strong and secure frame is something more than what the patient experienced as a child. The analyst who provides it is, therefore, a stronger figure for the patient and one with whom the patient does well to incorporate or identify. Langs (as Loewald) believes that it is important that the patient identify with the analytic process and that correct interventions lead to positive identifications with the analyst. It is important that the analyst not make errors or, if errors are made, that they be corrected, lest the flawed analyst be a less-than-ideal introject for the patient.

Analysts who emphasize the security of the therapeutic frame as a representation of a stable family (e.g., Langs, Modell) have developed many of their ideas from the seminal work of Winnicott and his concepts of *good enough mothering* and the *holding environment*.[24] [25] Winnicott came to psychoanalysis from a background in pediatric medicine. Beyond that, he was apparently a man of great largesse, very secure within himself and willing to give generously to others. From anecdotal reports, he appeared as an example of the benevolent tradition of the English upper classes. He actively strove to educate and help those less fortunate than himself and was kind and infinitely patient in so doing. These qualities probably made him a marvelous children's doctor and a very warm and supportive child psychoanalyst when he switched fields. As is widely known, he was strongly influenced by Melanie Klein, who, in her work, emphasized the very early developmental issues of the child. Winnicott was softer and less instinct oriented than his mentor. With this combination of personal, cultural, and professional influences, however, he did talk about his work with adults as others might about their work with children.

"But in the part of our work as analysts that I am referring to there is nothing we do that is unrelated to child-care or to infant-care."[26] Despite Winnicott's obeisance to the importance of interpretive work, it seems clear that, for him, the essence of psychoanalytic cure lies in the relationship between the analyst and the patient. Specifically, the analysis hinges on the ability of the analyst to be empathic and establish a relationship that will evoke enough trust so that the patient will expose his or her most vulnerable aspects ("true self"). The empathy and the concern provide a "holding environment" for the patient until the patient gradually begins his thawing-out process. The analyst thus serves as a "transitional object" between secure holding and exposure to the threatening world. If the patient is adequately held by the "good enough mother"/analyst, the early maternal issues may be compensated and the patient may be better able to continue development.

Winnicott does distinguish between patients according to the severity of developmental conflict. The above configuration applies to those patients who suffer from the mother's failure to "hold" and to provide basic supplies. He acknowledges that these patients need "management" until they are ready, if ever, for analytic work. This is in contrast to others who have "oedipal problems" and are ready to receive traditional conflict analysis. Though he makes clear distinctions among three types of patients and the techniques associated with each of them, careful reading suggests that a nurturing attitude pervades his work. Examination of some of the now everyday terms associated with Winnicott's name (e.g., *holding, transitional object, good enough mother, unfreezing of the true self)* shows an overriding involvement with psychoanalysis as an essentially parent-child relationship. It is possible that he did work with some patients in a traditional classical analysis, but his heart belonged to a relationship characterized by being a substitute mother to the developing child. He was an English gentleman, patrician, and pediatrician ministering to his poorly mothered adult patients.

Balint,[27] Winnicott's contemporary and colleague, is best known for his views on the importance of regression in psychoanalysis. He manifestly subscribes to the traditional verbal psychoanalysis for so-called neurotic patients and preverbal analysis for patients with developmental deficiencies. With the latter category, Balint believes that the traditional therapeutic methods of interpretation and promotion of awareness are not meaningful. He tries to facilitate regression to what he calls the "basic fault," the preverbal point where the patient's core problem began. The analyst's love for the patient, conveyed nonverbally and usually not physically, helps the patient repair the trauma or fault and start on a "new beginning."

As with Winnicott, though Balint speaks of two categories of patients (deficient and nondeficient), the impression is that his preferred way of working with most patients is via regression to the basic fault. Balint views the analyst as both need-recognizing and need-satisfying. Since any sensitive analyst usually wishes to be need-recognizing, the area of controversy is the matter of need-satisfying. Balint has come out very strongly against need satisfaction for itself, that is, satisfaction that does not lead directly to inner change. He is fairly clear, however, that during the extremes of regression he is readily able to feel love for and to give love to the patient. This is usually, as noted earlier, conveyed attitudinally. It may also be conveyed by touching, holding, hugging, rocking, or other forms of non-erotic nurture normally associated with mother-to-child displays of love.

One of the questions provoked by Balint's and Winnicott's work is the meaning of the analyst's desire or preference for working with patients in their possible childlike states. They would say that this is the only way to analyze down to their "schizoid core"[28]; to get to the deepest root of the patient's ills. It must be also considered, however, that the analyst may have a personal need to work with adults as children or to work in an adult-to-relatively-helpless-child configuration.

Two contemporary authors (Khan[29] and Kohut[30][31]), from different sides of the Atlantic, attempt to grapple with the concept of the *self*. Khan descends directly from Winnicott and Balint, while Kohut represents a divergent voice in American classical psychoanalysis. Khan like his two mentors, is involved with the protection of the self. He sees character defenses as warding off a fear of annihilation of the self. Patients who have serious early deprivations are more threatened by their dependency needs and are most reluctant to give in to them, lest they "surrender to resource-less dependence." The less abundant the early supplies, the more the analysis is involved with "holding" patients while they slowly regress to the position they most fear. The analyst is a satisfying object. He likens the experience to what Winnicott calls "being alone in the presence of the mother." In shorthand, the patient becomes a child again and this time around is in the presence of a more self-facilitating mother. The patient is "in the analyst's care" and verbal interpretation matters little. The *true self,* though Khan does not use that term, exists at moments of regression and dependence and later develops within the holding of the analyst and analytic situation.

The controversial work of Kohut bears much similarity to the British theorists. Kohut does not write about regression or analysis down to the most vulnerable core. On the contrary, he tries to avoid regression and is often satisfied to terminate his analyses at a point viewed as less than complete by some of his critics. Kohut converges with Winnicott et al. in his emphasis on empathy and his effort to provide an environment wherein his patients can develop "structures" that were never developed by the original set of parents. Kohut, like Winnicott and Khan, readily acknowledges errors in empathy and the ensuing "objective anger" on the part of the patient. His effort is toward optimum empathy and the provision of an atmosphere that is never challenging or confronting. Here too he differs with Winnicott, who openly deals with analysts' hateful feelings toward patients. Kohut tries to respond differently from the patient's parents. He attempts to provide the empathy that was deficient as well as the admiration and object for identification that were also insufficient. In Kohut's system the analyst tries to make the patient feel good. He does not "hold" his patients during their regressions, but holds them throughout until they develop the absent internal structures and are ready to go forward in life.

On a technical level there are numerous differences among the British analysts and Kohut. On a nonverbal level, however, both emphasize the distribution of supplies to the patient as the primary road toward further development. Both "hold" the patient while absent experiences develop internally, and both seem to strive consciously to be good enough mothers or, at least, better parents than the originals. They do not view their patients as fully formed and see the role of the analyst as a developer.

Perhaps the most concentrated degree of nurturance in the field occurs with those patients diagnosed as schizophrenic. One practical reason is that much of the analytically oriented treatment of such patients occurs in a hospital setting where caretaking is the tradition. Another reason is that most psychoanalysts do not believe that schizophrenic patients can be treated with anything approaching the usual form of analytic procedure. They feel free to modify technique to a point where it barely resembles anything analytic. Those individuals who do attempt to work in an analytic mode with schizophrenic patients fall into two broad categories. Members of the first group attempt to conduct the analysis as closely as possible to the usual way they proceed with better functioning patients. Representative of this group are Fromm-Reichmann,[32] Searles,[33] and Boyer and Giovacchini.[34] Members of the second group of analysts couple their usual form of interpretive work with an effort to "reparent" the patient. Examples from this group are Milner,[35] Rosen,[36] and Sechehaye.[37] Most psychotherapists who work with schizophrenic patients do not use psychoanalytic technique at all. In recent years the use of medication has replaced most efforts to explore deeply the psyches of psychotic individuals. Most hospitals that used to train psychotherapists to do long-term analytic treatment with these patients have changed their policies and now teach drug therapy, supportive therapy, and various forms of directive and behavioral therapies. Many psychoanalysts, indeed, work with schizophrenic patients in the latter modes while working with all their other patients in an analytic manner. For the purpose of this article, I will focus only on nurturant and gratifying interactions in a psychoanalytic context.

Searles describes the tendency among schizophrenic patients to ask others to satisfy all their needs and to offer nothing tangible in return.[38] They often ask others to provide unvarying love and protection and assume the total guidance for their living. He goes on to describe a common historical experience of the patient who had unrelated, narcissistic parents who did not satisfy his basic dependency needs. Indeed, most current clinicians who discuss the genesis of a schizophrenic resolution to life focus either on the early absence of sufficient supplies or on the presence of profound parental intrusion. The latter interferes with the development of virtually any autonomy, and the former leaves the patient in a perennial search for parenting.

With regard to the hungry and obviously deprived schizophrenic patient, the most natural response (aside from backing away) is to attempt to meet the needs. Certainly this appears, on the surface, as the most human response. Analysts such as Milner, Rosen, and Sechehaye base the bulk of their method on becoming new and better parents for their patients. Other analytic therapists (e.g., Bellak)[39] back away from intense personal involvement and supply their patients with drugs and directives. Milner and Sechehaye use the extensive case study approach to detail how they re-raise the child from infancy to adulthood. They entirely discount their patients' adult properties and relate to them only as infants or rejected children. They use extreme delicacy, permissiveness, and caution to avoid causing patients to feel the hurt they experienced as children. They try to be perfect mothers, as much opposite to the real mothers as possible. The therapist's own feelings of frustration, anger, resentment, despair, etc., are suppressed, and only kindness and love are displayed. At times they may be strict and limit setting, but they are usually indulgent and allow the patients to do pretty much what they please. In this atmosphere of total acceptance and love, these analysts hope to raise new children.

Rosen, on his farm/institution in rural Pennsylvania, accepts patients with the idea that they will be there for many years and remain in the community for a period of time after discharge. For the most part these patients are to sever relationships with their families of origin or are to keep those relationships to a bare minimum. Rosen trains professionals and paraprofessionals to be surrogate parents for the patients. The entire milieu is the treatment, and the patient is viewed as a child in an extended family. Contrary to Milner and Sechehaye, acceptance and kindness are not the only responses by the therapist. The milieu is encouraged to react authentically to the patient and to be angry or not forthcoming if that seems to be the best way to respond to the child/patient at any given time. The program does not provide an atmosphere of total love but tries to approximate all the feelings involved in childrearing on the part of the child's extended family (the staff). Most of the patients seem to begin the program as infants regardless of whatever maturity they may have developed in their lives.

Criticism of the Nurturant Position

All the approaches outlined in the previous section in some way try to aid the patient in retrieving what was not developed during earlier periods of development. My own view, corresponding with Farber's, is that this quest is in part a defense against hopelessness.* I speak about the hopeless feeling that one cannot reach the patient or have any effect on the patient's life. The patient as is, in adult form, may appear as if he or she were someone who cannot be helped. The patient may be too angry and destructive, too passive and repressed, or too disorganized and confused. When the analyst is faced with this adult person who may be acting in part or in whole like a child, the task of relating to the patient on a "here and now" level can easily cause the analyst to back off and search for other ways of entering the patient's world. Entering through the patient's childishness is a common solution. As a child, the patient is not only a nicer person but less of a formidable opponent in the analyst's pursuit of analytic change. In a childlike state the patient is seen as not fully formed. Conceptualizations of deficiencies or absent structures give theoretical rationale to this viewpoint. The analyst's rage related to feelings of impotence is tempered, as it is more difficult to experience such feelings toward a deprived childthan toward a stubborn and intransigent adult.

In the process of escaping from feelings of hopelessness about helping the patient in the here and now of adulthood, the analyst becomes a loving parent to the patient as child. Thus, the fact that the patient is chronologically an adult results in the loss of a co-equal relationship, i.e., two selves relating to each other as they are at any given moment. In accordance with my discussion of intimacy in an earlier section,

---

*I will not here deal with the possibility that certain analysts, due to their own unresolved personality difficulties, need to relate to their patients in a superior way.

analytic intimacy is lost and the relationship is established with patient as child and analyst as nurturing adult.

Zucker,[40] Basescu,[41] Levenson,[42] and Gill,[43] among others, have written about the value of meeting the patient in his current life situation and respecting that as representing who the patient is at any given time. A developmental model (see Levenson)[44] of psychoanalysis tries to place the patient in a time period corresponding to an assessed level of maturity and to relate to the patient as if he were that age (level of maturity). Integral in this viewpoint is the notion that a highly immature person is deficient in contrast to the sufficient analyst, who is, indeed, relating as an adult in his work with the patient. Dealing with the patient as the patient is at the moment does not imply an ahistorical approach. The patient's history is examined as a way of helping both analyst and patient to see how the patient became the way he is. This knowledge of personal history serves as an integrating force for the patient. It can help the patient account for the sometimes confusing and puzzling current situation by linking the present with causal antecedents.

Giovacchini[45] proposes that nurturance is not the true expression of the love or intimacy of the analyst toward the patient. He describes analytic love and intimacy as helping the patient understand things never before seen or integrated. This analytic work conveys to the patient a sense that he is worth understanding and that there is a self to understand. He views analytic nurture as counter to seeing the patient as having a self, albeit a very trouble and fragmented self. Also, analytic nurture can be a tease, and it can promote the idea that the analyst is omnipotent. Giovacchini goes on to describe, in the analysis of schizophrenic patients, that to analyze is, in and of itself, a declaration of respect and dignity toward the patient. It is a statement that there is a core that is worth analyzing and the patient is not simply a human tragedy. In underlining the value of treating the patient as an adult, Giovacchini states: "Mother's milk is no longer an adequate nutrient though the patient might not know it." He states that gratification does not fill the gap in the psyche or correct the early traumas. He goes on to say: "Any attempt to give the patient something he didn't have in childhood is relating to him as if he is still really a child." Finally, the same author argues that there are no patients without a self, though there are many patients who do not acknowledge themselves.

The analytic position that each person has a self and that the true intimate analytic relationship is characterized by a meeting of this self as it is is further advanced by Searles. Though both Searles and Giovacchini write primarily about schizophrenic patients, their points of view apply to the analytic relationship with all patients. I refer to them extensively because they both offer a counterpoint to the nurturant positions of Milner, Rosen, and Sechehaye in their work with schizophrenic patients and to the object relations analyst's inclination to treat many patients as children. Furthermore, these two analysts are among the very few who write about the strength and resilience of even the most "broken down" patients.

Searles,[46] in writing about analytic infantilization, wonders what patients think when the analyst is so benignly tolerant and unswervingly kind. He knows that this attitude cannot be trusted because a truly authentic analyst cannot possibly convey such an unbalanced warm and giving attitude. Searles describes a totally benign attitude toward the schizophrenic (or any) patient as pitying and condescending. The patient is viewed as a child, or as helpless, or as egoless. The analyst is there to develop the patient, take care of him, or to lend or build ego. The view that the patient has no ego, or as Giovacchini puts it, no self, is seen by Searles as unconsciously sadistic on the analyst's part. He feels that the patient's strength, essence, and adulthood are all defensively obliterated by holding such a notion. Searles holds the belief, similar to that of Giovacchini and Levenson, that it is crucial to appreciate the patient's illness and not just to try to cure it. All three theorists view the clarification of the self as a more important goal than the changing of the self. An appreciation of who the patient is moves the analyst off the position of responsibility for effecting change and places that burden more on the patient. The patient is thus viewed as an adult with the capacity to choose, just as the analyst views himself as an adult who, in many ways, is not necessarily stronger than the patient. Searles feels that when an analyst is parental and all-nurturing he gives the impression of a greater distance than truly exists between patient and analyst. Searles views a more meaningful and helpful vision of analysis as the experience of a mutual exploration of the reactions of both parties, not as a rescue mission. He sees, as do Giovacchini and Fromm-Reichmann, psychosis and sanity as points on a continuum and not as radically discrete processes. He points out that analysts with little experience in working with schizophrenic patients often exaggerate differences, based on their fear of and their defensive reactions to feelings of hopelessness and futility. Further, analysts often shy away from a more co-equal analytic relationship because of a fear of discovering that they are too similar to their patients.

"The therapist's major task is not to make-up to the patient for past deprivations, but rather to help the patient to arrive at a full and guilt-free awareness of his dependency needs."[47] Fromm-Reichmann[48] describes her early tendency in working with schizophrenic patients to try to make friends and turn the relationship into a pseudosocial one. At that time in her career she worked with extreme delicacy, permissiveness, and caution so that the patient would never feel rejected. She then began to recognize that she addressed the rejected child too much and the grown-up person too little. Her work had a major impact on Searles, Otto Will, and others who specialized in analytic work with schizophrenic patients. Her influence was limited, however. Most analysts do not feel that schizophrenic patients can possibly benefit from psychoanalytic treatment.

Kernberg[49] reviews the British object-relations school as well as the work of Kohut.[50] Though there are many differences between them, he upbraids both of them for not dealing with the totality of the patient. The British analysts (both the classical Kleinians and the Winnicott, Balint, and Khan group) are criticized for overemphasizing the childlike aspects of the patient. Though Winnicott, Balint, and Khan do not focus on the instincts of the first year of life, they do tend usually to wind up talking about the patient's deprivation during infancy. They are inclined to be warm and supportive and to facilitate profound regression by an attitude that can be interpreted as maternal or paternal. They appear to be most comfortable when dealing with adult patients as children and themselves as good enough mothers, holders, stoic fathers, transitional objects, and suppliers of nonverbal and, at times, physical love. Melanie Klein was a child analyst and Winnicott a pediatrician, and though both made enormous contributions, they could not get too far beyond relating to children.

Kernberg points out two other factors in British object-relations thinking that promote a parent-child analytic relationship. One of these is a tendency toward objective, "you" interpretations in contrast to subjective "I think" interpretations. The other is a relative lack of concern about the current issues in the patient's life and an unbalanced involvement with early childhood material. With regard to the former, the tone of the analytic interaction tends toward a dichotomy between one party who knows for certain and another party who either receives or rejects. The analyst seems convinced that he operates from a logical base wherein the child/patient is embedded in irrational subjectivity.

The phrasing of interpretations in an explanatory, didactic, or declarative way leaves little impression of error or of uncertainty. There is very little sense of two people's exploring together in order to find some answers. This represents a more coparticipant or co-equal analytic model that would promote what was earlier described as analytic intimacy. The notion that the patient and the analyst come from different places, each having his own perspective, is somewhat alient to the more nurturant analyst. The analyst is benevolent (for Winnicott and his colleagues) but cool and correct. The analyst's observations are "objective" and controlled by reason in contrast with the patient, who is dominated by regressive pull. This kind of dyad may provide security (holding) for the patient since it can feel good to have one's doctor be so certain and secure. It does, however, indeed detract from what I refer to as the intimacy of two subjective selves presenting themselves.

Analytic focus on early childhood material at the expense of current life problems can give the impression that the patient's adult life is relatively inconsequential. This is quite similar to an earlier point criticizing object-relations theorists for promoting regression and seeming to feel more comfortable as parents vis-a-vis a regressed child. The message that one's analyst wishes to hear little about current life issues (or future aspirations) tells the patient that the only road to resolution lies in returning to childhood (in analysis) and redeveloping. The analytic notion that clarity and acceptance of one's past can solidify a sense of self without necessarily starting from a new beginning is not generally considered. In this situation, patients are inclined to discount many of their adult aspects and respond to the analyst's request to become a child once again.

Kohut's analytic technique, in due respect to all of his progressive theoretical advances, is predicated on the assumption that the patient is structurally deficient. One of the roles of the analyst is to supply the patient with good feelings never received in sufficient quantity from the parents (mirroring). Another analytic function is to facilitate the patient's sense of self by becoming an idealized figure and thereby serving as an object of identification. Kohut is quite clear in his belief that narcissistic (and other) patients do not have a "self" and that the analyst supplies the patient with goods from the outside. He does not believe that these patients can tolerate confrontation with themselves (there is no self) or face their deprived past histories. The analyst operates under great restraint in an effort to be optimally empathic, while recognizing that total empathy is not humanly possible. At times, the analyst can even be inauthentic, suggesting a degree of admiration for the patient that does not genuinely exist. The patient's grandiosity is fed. The analyst's anger is swallowed (see Epstein)[51] lest it interfere with the giving of birth to the self.

Though Kohut has significantly furthered the evolution of classical analysis by eschewing drive theory and viewing psychopathology as caused by people, he falls into the object-relations configuration of conceiving the analyst as a parent/developer. He is explicit in his view that patients suffer from deficiencies, that they cannot squarely face their lives and take stock of what was and/or is missing, and that the analyst supplies the nourishment with which to grow. The analyst is viewed as a sufficient object of identification, and the patient is in a position similar to Winnicott's child though, in this instance, not regressed. Kohut's patients receive and give little in return (see Searles).[52] This passive reception of kindly analytic supplies places the patient in a situation where he dare not be too angry or aggressive. How can one be so angry toward an analyst as empathic and giving as Winnicott or Kohut? Patients' healthy aggression is often suppressed as they wait for holding to provide security or the empathy to fill up the empty inner spaces. Searles[53] (1979) notes the guilt-producing effects of patients feeling such rage toward analysts who are so saintly. He suggests that to experience such fury leads the patient into feeling like a beast in contrast to the analyst. Finally, what indeed can be further from analytic intimacy than feelings on the part of the analyst that can be essentially inauthentic "for the good" of the patient?

Somewhat similar criticisms have been directed toward the work of Spitz, Gitelson, Zetzel, Greenson, and Stone for their writing on "alliance" and toward the work of Loewald for his suggestion that identification may be the primary curative factor in psychoanalysis. Greenacre views the substitution of nurturance and oversensitivity (perennial empathy) for analysis as working against analysis.[54] She feels that overdone kindness is often the analyst's countertransference defense against analyzing material that may be too disquieting. She seems to be in harmony with Giovacchini's sentiments that the most truly nurturant form of analytic love is good analysis. That is, the best gift we can give our patients is to be there forthrightly as psychoanalysts and to share what we see for the sake of clarification and the search for truth. Acting kindly to achieve a particular effect, when not genuinely felt, represents a sidestepping of the patient.

Rangell[55] concurs, viewing a truly "humane" analytic attitude as genuinely trying to understand the patient and interpret what is seen.

He believes that a mother-child configuration is not as humane because it provides only a temporary good feeling. This, he believes, is not as enduring as the benefits of analyzing the patient-analyst interaction. Arlow and Brenner[56] view Zetzel's and other mother-child analytic configurations as transference gratification. They see the mothering attitude as an acting out of the material arising in the transference and a loss to the analysis of what the analyst is best equipped to do, i.e., forthrightly pursue the clarification and the meaning of experience. They refer to a "genetic fallacy" in discussing Zetzel's idea that the patient-analyst relationship is a mother-child relationship. They note that because there are properties in common between mother-child and patient-analyst, everything that bears on one does not correspond with the other.

Loewald's[57] and Langs's[58] emphasis on the importance of the patient's identification with the analyst captures the essence of many of the difficulties I see in the analyst's self-placement in the parental position. For one, present again is the inequality of a parent-child relationship. The assumptions are that the analyst is more mature in most every way (see Wangh)[59] and that all the incorporations should be in one direction. Also implicit is that the analyst has properties that are worth identifying with and that the patient does not have properties that the analyst may covet. Also, it suggests a benevolence and all-nurturing attitude on the analyst's part in that there is a willingness to allow the patient to incorporate. What appears as kindness, however, as discussed earlier, can be a defense against analyzing certain material, a defense against hopelessness that the patient can be successfully analyzed, or a grandiose defense against the possible meaning of a truly intimate, co-equal relationship with the patient. The analyst who promotes identification is in a defensively superior position. It is implicitly, if not explicitly, assumed that the patient does not possess a self and needs to incorporate aspects of the analyst's superior self (see Singer).[60]

A falsely nurturant position is a pseudointimate one. A truly intimate analytic stance is represented by an effort to help patients consolidate their own selves, that is, as Singer puts it, to establish their own identity and not to identify with someone. The need to identify with someone implies that the patient is still an unformed child, and a mutual or intimate adult-to-adult analysis is, therefore, precluded.

Summary

I have tried to distinguish between intimacy and nurturance in the adult psychoanalytic relationship. Intimate relatedness refers to a coparticipation in the relationship, with both parties presenting their experience and opening themselves to the other. A nurturant analytic relationship is characterized by a parent-child configuration in the analysis. The patient is often seen as not formed or not possessing a self and the analyst's task is to provide the sort of nurture that will help the patient develop a self. This can overlook whatever self the patient has developed and work counter to the formation of a solidified identity and a sense of autonomy.

Crucial to the central thesis is the view that past deficiencies cannot be retrieved. The effort to make up for early deficiencies by providing a new parental experience is sometimes a defense against the hopelessness that patients can come to grips with their lives as they are. An intimate analytic inquiry can help patients see and accept who they are and where they have come from. Judicious use of the analyst's self can aid patients in relating intimately, recognizing in the process that they have a self that they, with the analyst's help, can integrate and put to more fruitful use.

End Notes (References)

[1] Farber, L. H. *The Ways of the Will*. New York: Basic Books, 1966.

[2] Farber, L. H. *The Ways of the Will*. New York: Basic Books, 1966.

[3] Wolstein, B. Individuality and identity. *Contemp. Psychoanal.*, 10:1–14, 1974.

[4] Singer, E. *Key Concepts in Psychotherapy*. New York: Basic Books, 1970.

[5] Buber, M. I and *Thou*. New York: Charles Scribner's Sons, 1958.

[6] Farber, L. H., *Ref.* 1.

[7] Schafer, R. *A New Language for Psychoanalysis*. New Haven: Yale University Press, 1976.

[8] Hirsch, I. Authoritarian aspects to the psychoanalytic relationship. *Rev. Existent. Psychol. Psychiatry*, in press.

[9] Ehrenberg, D. The intimate edge in therapeutic relatedness. *Contemp. Psychoanal.*, 10:423–437, 1974.

[10] Wolstein, B. Countertransference: the psychoanalyst's shared experience and inquiry with his patient. *J. Am. Acad. Psychoanal. Dyn. Psychiatr.*, 3:77–89, 1975.

[11] Ehrenberg, D. The quest for intimate relatedness. *Contemp. Psychoanal.*, 11:320–331, 1975.

[12] Wilner, W. The nature of intimacy. *Contemp. Psychoanal.*, 11:206–226, 1975.

13 Levenson, E.A. Changing concepts of intimacy in psychoanalytic practice. *Contemp. Psychoanal.*, 10:359–369, 1975

14 Stolorow, R. D., and Lachmann, F. *Psychoanalysis of Developmental Arrests: Theory and Treatment*. New York: International Universities Press, 1980.

15 Spitz, R. Transference: the analytic setting and its prototype. *Int. J. Psycho-Anal.*, 37:380–385, 1956

16 Gitelson, M. The emotional position of the analyst in the psychoanalytic situation. *Int. J. Psycho-Anal.*, 33:1–10, 1952.

17 Zetzel, E. R. The analytic situation. In R. E. Litman (Ed.), *Psychoanalysis in the Americas*. New York: International Universities Press, 1966, pp. 86–106.

18 Greenson, R. R. *The Technique and Practice of Psychoanalysis*. New York: International Universities Press, 1967

19 Stone, L. *The Psychoanalytic Situation*. New York: International Universities Press, 1961.

20 Loewald, H. On the therapeutic action of psychoanalysis. *Int. J. Psycho-Anal.*, 41:16–33, 1960.

21 Harris, H. D. Dreams about the analyst. *Int. J. Psycho-Anal.*, 43:151–158, 1962.

22 Langs, R. *The Therapeutic Interaction Volume II*. New York: Jason Aronson, 1976.

23 Modell, A. H. The "holding environment" and the therapeutic action of psychoanalysis. *J. Am. Psychoanal. Assoc.*, 24:285–308, 1976.

24 Winnicott, D. W. *The Maturational Processes and the Facilitating Environment*. New York: International Universities Press, 1965

25 Winnicott, D.W. *Through Paediatrics to Psycho-Analysis*. New York: Basic Books, 1975.

26 Winnicott, D. W. *The Maturational Processes and the Facilitating Environment*. New York: International Universities Press, 1965.

27 Balint, M. *The Basic Fault*. London: Tavistock Publications, 1968.

28 Guntrip, H. *Psychoanalytic Theory, Therapy and the Self*. New York: Basic Books, 1971.

29 Khan, M. M. R. *The Privacy of the Self*. New York: International Universities Press, 1974.

30 Kohut, H. *The Analysis of the Self*. New York: International Universities Press, 1971.

31 Kohut, H. *The Restoration of the Self*. New York: International Universities Press, 1977.

32 Fromm-Reichmann, R. Some aspects of psychoanalytic psychotherapy with schizophrenics. In D.M. Bullard (Ed.), *Psychoanalysis and Psychotherapy: Selected Papers of Freida Fromm-Reichmann*. Chicago:

University of Chicago Press, 1959, pp. 176–193.

33 Searles, H. F. *Collected Papers on Schizophrenia and Related Subjects.* New York: International Universities Press, 1965.

34 Boyer, L. B., and Giovacchini, P. L. *Psychoanalytic Treatment of Schizophrenic, Borderline, and Characterological Disorders.* New York: Jason Aronson, 1980.

35 Milner, M. Aspects of symbolism in comprehension of the Not-Self. *Int. J. Psycho-Anal.*, 33:181–195, 1952.

36 Rosen, H. N. *Direct Analysis.* New York: Grune and Stratton, 1953.

37 Sechehaye, M. A. *A New Psychotherapy in Schizophrenia.* New York: Grune and Stratton, 1956.

38 Searles, H. F., *Collected Papers on Schizophrenia and Related Subjects.* New York: International Universities Press, 1965.

39 Bellak, L. The concept of psychoses as a result and in the context of the long-term treatment modalities. In C. Chiland (Ed.) with P. Bequart, *Long-Term Treatment of Psychotic States.* New York: Human Sciences Press, 1977, pp. 47–62.

40 Zucker, H. *Problems of Psychotherapy.* New York: The Free Press, 1967

41 Basescu, S. Anxieties in the analyst, an autobiographical account. In K. Frank (Ed.), *The Human Dimension in Psychoanalytic Practice.* New York: Grune and Stratton, 1977, pp. 153–164.

42 Levenson, E.A. A perspective on responsibility. *Contemporary Psychoanalysis*, 14:571–578, 1978.

43 Gill, M. Psychoanalysis and Psychotherapy: 1954–1979. Paper presented to The New York University Postdoctoral Program, 1979.

44 Levenson, E.A., ref. 42.

45 Boyer, L.B., and Giovacchini, P. L., ref. 34.

46 Searles, H., ref. 33.

47 Searles, H.F. *Countertransference and Related Subjects.* New York: International Universities Press, 1979.

48 Searles, H.F., ref. 33.

49 Fromm-Reichmann, R., ref. 32.

50 Kernberg, O. F. *Internal World and External Reality.* New York: Jason Aronson, 1980.

51 Kernberg, O. F. *Borderline Conditions and Pathological Narcissism.* New York: Jason Aronson, 1975.

52 Epstein, L. The therapeutic function of hate in the countertransference. In L. Epstein and A. H. Feiner (Eds.), *Countertransference.* New York: Jason Aronson, 1979, pp. 213–234.

53 Searles, H.F., ref. 47.

54 Searles, H. F., ref. 47.

55 Greenacre, P. The role of transference. *J. Am. Psychoanal. Assoc.*,

2:671–684, 1954.

[56] Rangell, L. Recent history of the Pan-American Psychoanalytic Congress. In R. E. Litman (Ed.), *Psychoanalysis in the Americas*. New York: International Universities Press, 1966, pp. 9–15.

[57] Arlow, J. A., and Brenner, C. The analytic situation. In R. E. Litman (Ed.), *Psychoanalysis in the Americas*. New York: International Universities Press, 1966, pp. 86–106.

[58] Loewald, H., ref. 20.

[59] Langs, R., ref. 22.

[60] Wangh, M. Discussion of E. R. Zetzel: The analytic situation. In R. E. Litman (Ed.), *Psychoanalysis in the Americas*. New York: International Universities Press, 1966, pp. 126–130.

[61] Singer, E. Identity vs. identification: a thorny psychological issue. *Rev. Existent. Psychol. Psychiatry*, 5:160–175, 1965.

Prologue to Chapter 2:
THE REDISCOVERY OF THE ADVANTAGES OF THE PARTICIPANT-OBSERVATION MODEL

A second significant theme throughout this volume reflects my identification with the Interpersonal psychoanalytic tradition. Trained in an era of classical Freudian hegemony in the USA, there were few alternatives other than what was then considered by the psychoanalytic majority as a fringe movement, more social psychology than psychoanalysis per se. Because the Interpersonal perspective did not view instincts and the defensive compromises against these instincts as the primary building blocks of personality, this *school* was deemed superficial, lacking in depth and fearful of exploring instinctual primitiveness. Some referred to Interpersonal psychoanalysis, in a derogatory way, as the "cultural school", cultural referring to emphasis on exogenous life experience in contrast to the more profound dilemma of how to adapt to inborn primitive drive states.

Exposure to Interpersonal psychoanalysis was originally non-existent outside of its homes in New York and Washington, D.C. When it's founder Harry Stack Sullivan moved to New York and joined with Clara Thompson, Erich Fromm and a few others in the late 1940's to form the William Alanson White Institute, New York became virtually the only the home of this perspective. In the early 1960s a number of psychologists from the White Institute founded the Postdoctoral Program in Psychotherapy and Psychoanalysis at New York University, where I began to train in 1970. Along the way, the journal, *Contemporary Psychoanalysis* became the voice of Interpersonal psychoanalysis, though virtually no one outside of the above two institutions read this journal. Reciprocally and with a rebellious attitude, most of us identified as Interpersonal refused to read the journals reflecting the classical Freudian point of view. There was a romance attached to being part of what felt like a liberal and liberating iconoclastic way of thinking, the mainstream thinking being linked with a rigid and overly conservative, establishment orthodoxy. At the NYU Postdoctoral Program, there existed outright contempt and war between faculty and candidates identified as Freudian and those identified as Interpersonal.

When I graduated this program in 1975 and I started to have teaching responsibilities, I began to expose myself to some of the Freudian literature, especially what could be called the more liberal Freudian

literature. As the 1970s evolved into the 1980s I was finding more classical analytic literature that was veering close to what I'd always known
as the heart of Interpersonal psychoanalysis, Sullivan's shift away from
viewing the analyst as an objective blank screen to a view of the analyst
as an inherently subjective co-participant. This had always been known
as the participant-observation model, emphasizing, in contrast to the
Freudian position, that no human being can be exclusively an observer
while engaged in a two-person field. Of course, one can see how the
increased study of countertransference flowed from this, i.e., if both
parties in the analytic dyad were participating with at least unconscious
affect, the analyst is obliged to try to become aware of his or her influence on the patient. I was finding an increasing volume of literature
penned by classically trained writers that were referring to analysts'
unwitting participation in the process and sometimes actually even using
Sullivan's term, participant-observation, without referencing Sullivan or
any other Interpersonal literature. Since I did not think that these
Freudian analysts were plaigerizing, it seemed to me that they were
rediscovering on there own, the advantages of this model in priority to
their traditional variation of a blank screen model of the analytic relationship. At the time of the writing of this prologue, there are few who
would deny that an analyst cannot, not participate with his or her irreducible subjectivity.

Chapter 2

THE REDISCOVERY OF THE ADVANTAGES OF THE PARTICIPANT-OBSERVATION MODEL*

As Harry Stack Sullivan implied, we are what we do. If you want to know someone's philosophy, watch his behavior. What one does tells more about basic attitudes than what one claims to believe. In psychoanalytic work, emphasis on the here and now of the transference highlights *how* the patient is being with the analyst. This is often more revealing than what the person says, i.e., the verbal content. Bergmann's (1976) observations reflect this point for the analyst. He views an analyst's "way of working" (I prefer this to "technique") as more characteristic of his theoretical position than any exposition of that theoretical position. If we know how someone participates in the analytic dyad, then we know his philosophy, though this may differ from the publicly stated theoretical position.

Sandler (1983), in a recent article, discusses this very distinction between what he calls private and public theories. He observes that analysts, without realizing it, often do not do what they say they do and that their actions or private theories state what they really believe. He suggests that public theories have much to do with political allegiance whereas in the privacy of the office an analyst's real theory emerges through his mode of participation. Unfortunately, Sandier notes, this is often kept private for fear of deviating from the public theories of professional colleagues. Sometimes, however, an analyst may make capital of the private theory he discovers when observing himself at work, and this accounts for the development of expansions in psychoanalytic theory and practice.

In another recent article, Hoffman (1983), a colleague of Merton Gill, comments about what he sees as a growing convergence in the field around the philosophical issue of the relativity of knowledge (perspectivism) and the model of the analytic relationship known as participant-observation. He sees analysts from apparently divergent theoretical and technical backgrounds writing about their thinking in a sympathetic manner, while simultaneously not acknowledging these stark similarities.

---

*Hirsch, I. (1985). The rediscovery of the advantages of the participant-observation model. *Psychoanalysis and Contemporary Thought* 8(3):441–459.

More specifically, he documents that a significant number of prominent classical analysts, in adopting a theoretical position of relativity, are implicitly or explicitly suggesting that they are working within a participant-observation framework and not in a blank-screen paradigm. They have veered away from a blank-screen model toward relativism and participant-observation through an examination of their own private theories. Many of the analysts Hoffman cites have not necessarily abandoned their classical psychoanalytic theory of development, although they may place less emphasis on biological drives and more emphasis on actual interpersonal experience. The question of whether belief in the Freudian theory of universal psychosexual stages which are instinct-based is compatible with a participant-observation method of therapy is an interesting and difficult question but will not be tackled in this essay. Hoffman lightly proposes a new "school of participant-observation." He believes that this way of working is a more meaningful statement of its adherents' philosophy than the variety of theoretical positions to which they may publicly claim allegiance.

Gill's (1982) volume on transference (but really on theory of therapy) represents the primary point of focus of the reemergence of participant-observation as a psychoanalytic model. Writing just prior to the significant volumes of Schafer (1983) and Spence (1982), he anticipates these works by linking philosophic relativism, the analytic model of participant-observation, and the technical significance of concentrating on the here and now of the transference. I shall henceforth refer to this constellation as the "new triangle," in some contrast with the long-assumed theoretical prominence of the old triangle, the Oedipal triangle. This new triangle with participant-observation at the head signifies the *public* reemergence of a tradition initiated by Harry Stack Sullivan and reaches its logical extreme in the work of Levenson (1972, 1983), Participant-observation has been rediscovered without reference to Sullivan by those classical analysts who represent the liberal wing of that school. Gill, Schafer, and Spence are the trio I will focus upon, although the works of Lipton (1977, 1983), McLaughlin (1981, 1982) and Sandler (1976) are also worthy of note. They have all arrived at a way of working, through their own classical pathway, which most interpersonally trained analysts find familiar and compatible. Another prominent contributor, Kohut (1977), also from an orthodox analytic background, has built an interpersonal theory of therapy and of development (minus some of the relativistic bent of the other theorists), also without reference to the interpersonal and object relations analysts he resembles in so many ways.

The lack of reference to Harry Stack Sullivan and other interpersonal theorists who have openly worked as participant-observers for forty or so years does not represent plagiarism or malevolence. Most classically trained analysts were schooled to ignore the interpersonal literature as something antianalytic or simply outside the domain of psychoanalysis. Sullivan's work (e.g., 1953) made much more of an impact on psychiatry than it did on either American or international psychoanalysis. In a personal communication, McLaughlin stated that he was thoroughly unaware that much of what he was writing pertaining to the psychoanalytic relationship was in perfect harmony with an already clearly articulated interpersonal position. He further stated that his training was such that he was never encouraged to read outside the orthodox analytic literature and that, as a quite middle-aged man, he still had not. Gill (1983), in an article comparing the interpersonal and classical paradigms, stated that he also had not been aware, until his recent work became so popular, that his theory of therapy was in such accord with the interpersonal literature. He acknowledged this in the above article, written after he had received a variety of letters and comments referring to the similarity between his work and that of many interpersonalists. To an interpersonally trained analyst it seems most remarkable that an important theorist could develop a stated model of participant-observation in a major contribution to the literature and make no referential link to Sullivan and those who followed in his tradition.

In an effort to account for how participant-observation could gain prominence in some classical circles independent of interpersonal psychoanalysis, one must look at the psychologies of the different theoretical schools and the personalities of their leaders. Sullivan's introduction of the term "participant-observation" grew out of developments in the physical and social sciences of the 1930s and 1940s in the United States. Einstein had explicated his relativity theory and Heisenberg had made public his principle of uncertainty. Scientists influence what they observe and they cannot stand outside of their observations. The dominant schools of anthropology and sociology were trying to demonstrate the impact of culture on personality and how changes in sociocultural conditions can reverse social pathology. Sullivan was developing a theory of psychiatry in sharp contrast to Freud's, emphasizing the impact of the external environment on human development. He thoroughly rejected

Freud's theory of biological drive dominance and posited a theory wherein real interpersonal experience is at the center of human development. Participant-observation as a theory of therapy naturally developed out of this difference. That is, the observer analyst cannot be a blank screen since, by definition, he cannot stand outside his object of study, the patient. Casting aside the illusion of objectivity, Sullivan studied how his participation could be used toward salubrious ends. He arrived at the position of "expert in interpersonal relations," a psychiatrist who could teach the patient how his interpersonal patterns, derived from expectancies based on past experience, were causing difficulties in the present. He attempted to provide a new relationship for the patient which was more benign than the earlier ones and participated as an expert, teacher, and accepting father figure. He aimed to reduce anxiety. It took Sullivan's closest colleague, Thompson (1950) to weave this into something more clearly psychoanalytic. Thompson is rarely given sufficient credit for taking Sullivan and both placing him in a historical context in psychoanalysis and integrating his theory into psychoanalytic theory.

Sullivan, of course, was neither analytically trained nor was he analyzed. As well, he was not a psychoanalytic scholar. Thompson was analytically trained and had a thorough knowledge not only of Freudian theory but of the ideas of the renegades Adler, Jung, Rank, Reich, and Ferenczi and was a close colleague of Fromm and Horney. Thompson also was a far better writer than Sullivan. She made interpersonal theory into a psychoanalytic theory and not simply a theory of development and *psychiatric* technique. Thompson saw clearly how the meanings of the concept of transference, countertransference, and resistance were changed by using a model of participant-observation in contrast to the blank-screen model. Gill's current ideas had their precedent in Thompson's observations that the analyst's personality and moods influenced the transference and that it is therefore essential to bring them into the analyst's awareness. Her thinking encouraged the beginnings of the study of countertransference in America. The analyst as participant must come under study as well as the patient, and not because this participation is necessarily a function of psychopathology (see Epstein and Feiner, 1979). The latter notion had been the classical position on countertransference. Thompson also saw resistance not as simply related to the recovery of repressed memories but as directed toward the analyst as a dangerous figure trying to enter the patient's world and effect frightening changes.

Thompson's efforts to integrate Sullivan, the psychiatrist, into psychoanalysis failed. Sullivan's strongest influence was in analytic work with schizophrenic patients, where his renegade theory was not in direct competition with classical theory, which had traditionally ignored that population. Fromm-Reichmann (1950) and later Searles (1965, 1979), like Thompson, tried to carry Sullivan's work with schizophrenics forward and also integrate it further into psychoanalysis. Both had more success in gaining access to organized psychoanalysis than did Sullivan, the developer of the now popular participant-observation model. The interpersonal analysts made the unfortunate mistake, though it was based on survival needs, of developing their own school and their own journals outside of organized international psychoanalysis. On the one hand, they were not accepted into international psychoanalysis so they did not have much choice. On the other hand, they developed so far outside of the dominant classical school that they were simply never read by the classical analysts and often, they themselves never read the classical literature. With their own school and their own literature which almost no other analysts read, they had no influence and were easily dismissed. They were referred to as "culturalists," i.e., not interested in the inner life. Nothing could be further from the truth, but so few knew better. The interpersonalists were stereotyped, and there was little conflict in the mainstream classical school about ignoring their output.

The personalities of Sullivan and Erich Fromm, the cofounders of the interpersonal school, probably did not help their cause. Sullivan was a loner. He was a peculiar man who was ill at ease with most people and very difficult to get to know. He probably had at least one schizophrenic break, was most likely alcoholic, and was homosexual at a time when that had little acceptance. He was abrasive to most people other than his patients. He was trained in medicine in something akin to a diploma mill, had little formal education, and no analytic training or personal analysis. It was not difficult to dismiss someone with those credentials. Fromm, an outspoken Marxist, was brazenly critical of Freud. His writing, which brought him great fame with the educated public, was more social-psychological than psychoanalytic. His impact as an analyst was more private and he was not identified as a psychoanalyst by most people.

In contrast, Freud and most of his loyal followers were respectable family men and women. They were more traditional in their education and in their ways and their problems of living were less glaring and against the grain than those of the likes of Sullivan. Only when his followers deviated from Freud were their aberrations emphasized (e.g., Rank, Ferenczi, Reich). Most of those who stayed loyal to Freud were like the respectable, conservative bankers of the psychoanalytic profession. They inspired more confidence than the wild analyst Fromm and the peculiar Sullivan.

Ironically, on the other side of the Atlantic, in the 1930s and 1940s, Klein (1964) and Fairbairn (1952) were developing theories also at odds with classical theory. Klein's thinking was quite different from Sullivan's, and she saw herself as extending Freud, not as challenging him. Despite this she served as a transition between drive theory and what is known today as object relations theory. Fairbairn's ideas were quite compatible with Sullivan's (though neither of them knew it) and broke sharply with the drive and instinct model, moving to an interpersonal theory of human development. Klein and Fairbairn were rejected by the British Freudian group, which was led by Anna Freud, but nonetheless managed to stay within the mainstream of international psychoanalysis. How this occurred would make an interesting study in itself. One feature which can partially account for it was the decision of the British analysts to retain much or some of the language of drives and the American interpersonalists to reject both drive theory and its language as well. Klein maintained a drive language, and Fairbairn rejected much of it but kept some. Winnicott (1958, 1965), their most significant descendant, saw himself as a bridge between their thinking and classical thinking, and he and his students have always maintained an allegiance to classical theory, technique, and language while simultaneously developing their own (see Greenberg and Mitchell, 1983). The object relations analysts differ from classicists at least as much as the interpersonalists. Their retention of some of the language and just as significantly, their not developing their own schools and journals have kept them far better recognized by classical analysts than their interpersonal counterparts. The best example of this is the most widely read psychoanalytic journal, *The International Journal of Psycho-Analysis*, which, essentially, is shared by the classical and object relations group, just as their British institute is divided between them.

To put it succinctly, the interpersonalists, led by their easily rejected co-founders, began to speak a different language, and they were the only ones who listened. It took classical psychoanalysis operating in the mainstream of American psychoanalysis to reintroduce the concept of participant-observation (e.g., Gill), to also reject the theory of drives, its language, and structural theory (e.g., G. Klein, 1976), to emphasize the relativity of experience (e.g., McLaughlin, 1981; Schafer, 1983; Spence, 1982), and to view interpersonal experience as the center of human development (e.g., Kohut, 1982).

Interpersonal analysts will argue that everyone is a participant-observer and that the only difference is whether or not it is acknowledged (see, e.g., Singer, 1977), Gill (1983) and Lipton (1977, 1983) extend this argument in discussing the blank-screen model and the "silent technique" as extreme forms of participation in and of themselves. Everything an analyst does or does not to reflects participation, and if this is denied, the analyst's advantage of becoming aware of his stimulus value is lost. Interpersonalists have long believed that classical analysts had an inordinate need to hide behind a screen for fear of losing the protection of scientific objectivity. If, as Schafer (1983), Spence (1982), McLaughlin (1981), Levenson (1983), Wolstein (1964), Tauber and Green (1959), Racker (1968), and numerous others posit, scientific objectivity is thoroughly impossible in this field, the blank-screen model becomes an anachronism.

The origin of the blank screen is dated to 1897, with Freud's most significant theoretical shift, the understanding of childhood seduction. Instead of viewing childhood difficulties as a function of real seduction (actual experience), he shifted to seeing them as projections of the child based on its own wishful fantasies. Psychoanalysis became a science designed to study drive-based fantasies as they are projected onto the blank-screen analyst. Interpersonal relationships and their effects on development became secondary to drives. Masson's (1984) recent book discusses at length the current question as to the meaning of Freud's monumental shift from an interpersonal to a drive-based, fantasy theory of human development. His discussion reflects other current hypotheses (e.g., Levenson, 1981) to the effect that Freud's turn away from actual experience represented a response to his own fear of his actual feelings toward some of his patients and of his father's actual life history and relationship to the younger Freud. Had Freud stayed with the original seduction theory, he would inevitably have recognized that the analyst's feelings, blank-screen attempt or no, must be known by the patient in the same way children know how their parents actually feel toward them. He also would have realized that analysts' feelings toward patients are ever-present, that these feelings inevitably affect the patient, and that these feelings are harmful largely when unrecognized by the analyst.

A participant-observation model is far more compatible with Freud's original theory of actual experience, whereas a blank-screen model fits well with a drive-based theory. If the heart of human development is primarily a function of actual experience with others (see Barnett, 1983), then the acknowledgment and examination of the analyst's actual participation clearly seem in order.

Thus, according to generally accepted interpersonal thinking, classical analysts developed a tradition where their actual participation was not acknowledged and accepted. This could only logically hold for so long if the primary focus of the analytic experience was the recovery of the patient's lost memories and the reliving of close to an exact replication of early experience in the transference. The key to the analyst remaining purely a screen for distortions from the past is the belief that the past is actually reconstructed, i.e., psychoanalysis as archeology. The belief that psychoanalysis recovers absolute truths from the past and that transference is pure projection and distortion have been the cornerstones of the maintenance of the blank-screen ideology. Any notion that suggests that the materials elicited from our patients about their past or in the form of their transferences are inevitably related to the analyst's actual personality, theoretical orientation, or some particular aspect of the unique dyad destroys the whole basis of the blank screen and immediately converts it into participant-observation. This is what has been occurring in the psychoanalytic literature in very recent years and what has led to a rediscovery of the latter model.

Three widely respected classical analysts, Gill, Schafer, and Spence have each published a book since 1981, and each of these books takes clear issue with the blank-screen paradigm. These volumes have caused considerable stir in orthodox analytic circles, somewhat parallel to the ferment provoked by Kohut in his 1977 book. I cannot review all three works extensively but will try to capture the essence of how they underscore a participant-observation model of psychoanalysis.

Gill sees the core of analytic change as the reliving, in the here and now of the analysis, some similar *pattern* of relationship to those significant ones of the past. Part of the analyst's role in this relationship is to clarify the patterns as they are occurring, through transference observations and interpretations. Contrary to seeing transference as a distortion, he sees the analyst as indeed living out many of the things which the patient is claiming. He believes that patients have significant capacity to observe their analysts accurately and that there is significant plausibility in what was formerly thought of as distortion. Of course, because of their particular histories, some people may be more sensitive to some qualities of the analyst than to others. Gill rejects the notion of distortion entirely, saying that the patient's observations are plausible and that truth is so indeterminable that the analyst cannot possibly know if the patient is "wrong" or "right." To say that the patient is distorting implies that the analyst knows the truth, a suggestion which Gill finds defensive and hierarchical. If absolute truth is not knowable, distortion and reality testing are irrelevant concepts and transference refers to the totality of the patient's subjective experience about the analyst. The analyst is viewed as a subjective participant and as having considerable influence on the patient, especially if this influence is not constantly monitored. Thus, Gill always wants to know how the patient is experiencing him so as to make such participation explicit and forestall inadvertent influence and transference cures.

Gill acknowledges that every analyst's personality and psychoanalytic theory exert tremendous influence on the patient and that a focus in the here and now controls this to some degree. He does not believe that exploration of the past leads to discovery of absolute truths about the past and notes that all to often, such genetic insights lack emotional impact and reflect psychoanalysis as an "explanatory art." He is less strict than in his earlier writings in his concern about what an analyst should or should not do, as long as the analyst analyzes the effect on the patient of what he did. He does not encourage or recommend extraanalytic activity of any kind but admits that it often unwittingly occurs and does not destroy the analysis unless it is unexplored with the patient. Thus, unlike Freud, Gill probably would not give herring to his patient. If he did, he would be sure to examine the patient's reaction (see Lipton, 1977).

The triangle referred to above—the relativity of truth, participant-observation, and transference analysis in the here and now—are articulated by Gill more clearly than by anyone else I have come across. Gill bears uncanny similarity to contemporary interpersonal theorists such as Levenson (1972), and Wolstein (1975) as well as considerable similarity to many others. For one familiar with the interpersonal literature, it is jarring to find someone supposedly outside of it representing the core interpersonal point of view, without first reading the interpersonal literature. Gill has come upon all of this through a classical psychoanalytic path and has rediscovered participant-observation.

Schafer stays more allied to the classical viewpoint by maintaining his allegiance to its developmental point of view (but not to the drive theory or the structural theory). After paying that significant obeisance, there is little remnant of what most interpersonal analysts and, I am sure, most classical analysts, would call "classical." Schafer, by examining his own private theory, has rediscovered not only participant-observation but existentialism.

Most interpersonal analysts have an existential strain. Patients are seen as active participants in their present and future. The psychological workings of people are not seen as based on drives and on biologically determined uniform stages of development based upon drives. Sullivan's notion of "dexterity in living" refers to the patient's willful strength and efforts to negotiate a difficult early environment. Even the most severely disturbed patients (see Searles, 1979) have fought long and hard to arrive at where they are, though this position may not seem like advanced development to an outside observer. Everyone, from the best functioning to the worst, actively resists change as well as actively strives for change. Schafer, like many interpersonal analysts, sees the analysis of "resisting" (Schafer's term) in the here and now of the analytic interchange as the focal point of psychoanalysis. Schafer states that he will always opt for this sort of material over any historical or extratransference content. The patient's active attempt to resist analytic penetration in his own characteristic manner and the meaning of that manner, represents the heart of the analysis and is always more important than what he calls "seductive content."

Once establishing himself as a phenomenologist through his view of the patient as an active and willful agent operating on his present and future, Schafer further allies himself with the interpersonal-existential viewpoint by emphasizing the thoroughly subjective nature of both participants in the analytic exchange. His view of the analytic enterprise as an interchange between two subjective selves removes him as a subscriber to a blank-screen model, where by definition, the analyst is relatively objective. The following quotes (Schafer, 1983) are illustrative:

> One cannot distinguish sharply what the analyst finds and what the analyst introduces as a narrative organization; no absolute distinction between analytic subject and object is tenable; all perception is interpretation in context . . . [p. 184].

Analysts with different points of view on theory and technique employ different narrative strategies, and so they develop analytic histories of different types and more or less different content [p. 194].

The here and now is a condensed, coordinated and timeless version of the past and present. What is past (reconstructed) cannot be distinguished from the present. The unconscious is timeless [p. 197].

The analyst tends to engage in the analytic work in a manner that can be taken to express the same problems or characteristics that are under analytic scrutiny at that moment [p. 197].

... [D]ifferent analytic approaches based on different assumptions produce different sets of life histories that support these assumptions [p. 205].

Facts are silly to dispute. The "facts" depend upon the different systems of interpretation. There are no theory-free observations or method-free observations [p. 276].

It could not be stated more clearly: the analyst's life history and psychoanalytic theory thoroughly influence his perception. There is no theory-free or personality-free observation. The patient's experience is interpreted according to the analyst's own "storylines." Schafer's own "storyline" or theory is Freudian. His patients will understand their lives through that particular structure just as any other theorist will convey his own theories to his patient. The here and now is a productive arena because it is least influenced by theoretical presupposition, but there is nowhere really to go to learn the absolute truth. Patients in analysis do not learn about the facts of their past but about a mutually developed narrative about the past.

It remains to be seen whether Schafer can continue to balance his existential and participant-observer position with his Freudian view of development. This phase-specific view of development places less significance in interpersonal influence than in the unfolding of universal psychobiological processes. The significant others in the developing child's life are given less centrality than in the interpersonal and object-relational developmental theory. Schafer still rests, as Greenberg and Mitchell (1983) note, within the "drive structure" model. The therapeutic method, however, may be in discord with the developmental theory. Schafer's theory of therapy is one of thorough co-participation and mutual subjectivity, whereas his developmental model minimizes the impact of the significant others in the child's life. It seems more logically consistent to conclude that if the other person (the analyst) has such a primary effect on the patient, so do the significant others in the patient's early life. A developmental theory emphasizing actual interpersonal experience as the primary developmental variable would help make Schafer's "analytic attitude" more harmonious.

Spence (1982) and Schafer reinforce each other. Both are thoroughly in the participant-observation mode since they both view truth as indeterminable and thereby see analytic understanding as a fiction arrived at by both participants in the relationship. Spence's initial point is that free association is impossible since the listener always supplies the background assumptions, context, and the variety of missing pieces. There is no nonparticipatory listening and the less the material is clearly logical the more the listener supplies from his own context. He goes on to show that subjective interpretation or constructions (as opposed to the more objective reconstructions) begin to be seen as absolute truths instead of a mutually derived fiction (or narrative truth). This may supply both patient and analyst with the security of certainty and serve to remove both parties from feeling the anxiety of not knowing. Patients quickly learn what their analysts wish to hear and waste little time before relating their lives and life histories according to the analyst's preferred theory. The analyst does not intend this but his theory and personality influence everything that is heard. The analyst's interpretations, especially about the bygone past, can never be disproved or proved, and acceptance of these essentially countertransference-based constructions is always tempting.

Spence's solution to the problem he and Schafer both so clearly outline is, again, in accord with solutions arrived at by interpersonal analysts. Spence suggests that we accept that "reality" is psychic reality, i.e., a subjective rather than an objective reality. He sees a good interpretation as a creative experience. We never can determine whether it is true but if it fits well and makes esthetic sense, we can call it a narrative truth and be none the worse for it. He refers to Viderman's (1979) notion of the analyst as a poet as opposed to a historian. If the creative truth fits, illuminates, and leads to an effective chain of associations, it is useful and productive. A veridical view of the past is impossible. This countertransference-based participant-observation model of psychoanalysis is in stark contrast to the archeological tradition of classical analysis. Spence sees this far more ambiguous model as the successor to the archeological tradition: "Because the treating analyst must always be a participant in the discovery process, it follows that any analysis of the text alone, without his participation, is an exercise in half truths" (1982, p. 285).

McLaughlin (1981, 1982) has not published a book and his work has not been disseminated as has Schafer's or Spence's, but he is another classical analyst whose views have evolved to a participant-observation model which appears to be in perfect harmony with the interpersonal point of view about psychoanalysis. McLaughlin objects, for example, to the distinction between transference and countertransference. He sees this dichotomy as a hierarchical effort to protect the analyst from his own subjective participation in the process. He views the analyst as fully capable of transference as the patient and with no greater claim on objectivity, reality, or truth than the latter. He sees the analyst and patient as influencing each other and analysis as "an investigation through participant-observation" (without any reference to Sullivan). He underscores what the other authors argued, i.e., that the analyst strongly influences the data and that the "observer and the observed cannot be separated." Like Gill, Schafer, and Spence, he views emphasis on the here and now of the transference as the most productive force in the therapeutic process. He, like the others, sees this as more alive than the futile search for truth that can never be proven as such. He sees the transference as at most, an inexact repetition of the past though inevitably reflecting the unknowable past.

Conclusion

"The analyst is a participant-observer and not a mere receiving and reflecting mirror" (Blum, 1983, p. 609). This recent assertion by the editor of the *Journal of the American Psychoanalytic Association* captures my main thesis: participant-observation has been rediscovered. Of course, over the years, in orthodox circles there has been frequent reference to the analyst not being a *pure* reflecting mirror. This is only an ideal and impossible in fact. The use of the renegade Sullivan's term, however, marks the new development. In the past the term itself, so intricately associated with the maligned or ignored interpersonal school, was never used. Its use by Blum and other orthodox analysts cited here suggests that at least that aspect of Sullivan's theory is now being integrated into the American mainstream. That aspect of Sullivan's theory, however, is really the heart of his theory. Participant-observation is more than a theory of therapy. It reflects a theory of development which emphasizes interaction with others, in contrast to the unfolding of drives, as the essential force in human development. The model of therapy and of development go hand in hand and together constitute what is the most significant interpersonal contribution to psychoanalysis. To restate the issue, if development is primarily a participatory interaction between people, the psychoanalytic relationship follows suit.

The most recent trend in the psychoanalytic literature reflects a theoretical convergence, with the blank-screen paradigm waning and the participation-observation model growing. To return to one of the opening comments of this essay, one's analytic technique probably says more about one's philosophical position than the stated position. The rediscovery of participant-observation is a forerunner of an even more significant movement away from drive theory and structural theory. Many orthodox analysts have already veered away from drive theory and moved toward some more participatory developmental position, e.g., self psychology, object relations theory. Other orthodox analysts maintain the Freudian drive theory, the developmental theory, or both but are adopting a therapeutic position close to participant-observation. As the era of the gods (Mitchell, 1979) or great psychoanalytic leaders ebbs, more and more analytic participants bring forth their private theories.

REFERENCES

Barnett, J. (1983). Narcissism and dependence in the organization of personality. Presented at colloquium, Manhattan Institute for Psychoanalysis, New York, NY.

Bergmann, M. (1976). Notes on the history of psychoanalytic technique. In: *The Evolution of Psychoanalytic Technique*, ed. M. Bergmann & F. Hartman. New York: Basic Books.

Blum, H. (1983). The position and value of extra-transference interpretations. *J. Amer. Psychoanal. Assn.*, 31: 587–617.

Epstein, L., & Feiner, A. (1979). *Countertransference*. New York: Jason Aronson.

Fairbairn, W.R.D. (1952). *An Object Relations Theory of Personality*. New York: Basic Books.

Fromm-Reichmann, F. (1950). *Principles of Intensive Psychotherapy*. Chicago: University of Chicago Press.

Gill, M. (1982). *Analysis of Transference*, Volume I. New York: International Universities Press.

——— (1983). The interpersonal paradigm and the degree of the therapist's involvement. *Contemp. Psychoanal.*, 19:200–237.

Greenberg, J., & Mitchell, S. (1983). *Object Relations in Psychoanalytic Theory*. Cambridge: Harvard University Press.

Hoffman, I. (1983). The patient as interpreter of the analyst's experience. *Contemp. Psychoanal.*, 19:389–422.

Klein, G. (1976). *Psychoanalytic Theory: An Exploration of Essentials*. New York: International Universities Press.

————(1964). *Contributions to Psychoanalysis, 1921–1945*. New York: McGraw Hill.

Kohut, H. (1977). *The Restoration of the Self*. New York: International Universities Press.

————(1982). Introspection, empathy and the semi-circle of mental health. *Int. J. Psycho-Anal.*, 63:395–407.

Levenson, E. (1972). *The Fallacy of Understanding*. New York: Basic Books.

————(1981). Facts or fantasies: the nature of psychoanalytic data. *Contemp. Psychoanal.*, 17:486–500.

————(1983). *The Ambiguity of Change*. New York: Basic Books.

Lipton, S. (1977). The advantages of Freud's technique as shown in his analysis of the Rat Man. *Int. J. Psycho-Anal.*, 58:255–274.

————(1983). A critique of so-called standard psychoanalytic technique. *Contemp. Psychoanal.*, 19:35–45.

Masson, J. (1984). *Assault on Truth*. New York: Farrar, Strauss and Giroux.

McLaughlin, J. (1981). Transference, psychic reality and countertransference. *Psychoanal. Q.*, 50:639–664.

————(1982). Issues stimulated by the 32nd Congress. *Int. J. Psycho-Anal.*, 63:229–240.

Mitchell, S. (1979). Twilight of the gods. *Contemp. Psychoanal.*, 15:170–89.

Racker, H. (1968). *Transference and Countertransference*. New York: International Universities Press.

Sandler, J. (1976). Countertransference and role responsiveness. *Int. Rev. Psycho-Anal.*, 3: 3–47.

————(1983). Reflections on some relations between psychoanalytic concepts and psychoanalytic practice.. *Int. J. Psycho-Anal.*, 64:35–4.

Schafer, R. (1983). *The Analytic Attitude*. New York: Basic Books.

————(1965). *Collected Papers on Schizophrenia and Related Subjects*. New York: International Universities Press.

Searles, H. (1979). *Collected Papers on Countertransference*. New York: International Universities Press.

Singer, E. (1977). The fiction of analytic anonymity. In: *The Human Dimension in Psychoanalytic Practice*, ed. K. Frank. New York: Grune & Stratton.

Spence, D. (1982). *Narrative Truth and Historical Truth*. New York: W. W. Norton.

Sullivan, H. (1953). *The Interpersonal Theory of Psychiatry*. New York: W. W. Norton.

Tauber, E., & Green, M. (1959). *Prelogical Experience*. New York: Basic Books.

Thompson, C. (1950). *Psychoanalysis: Evolution and Development*. New York: Hermitage House.

Viderman, S. (1979). The analytic space: meaning and problems.

Psychoanal. Q., 48:257–291.

Winnicott, D. (1958). *Through Pediatrics to Psychoanalysis.* London: Hogarth Press.

———— (1965). *The Maturational Process and the Facilitating Environment.* New York: International Universities Press.

Wolstein, B. (1964). *Transference.* New York: Grune & Stratton.

———— (1975). Countertransference: the psychoanalyst's shared experience and inquiry with his patient. *J. Am. Acad. Psychoanal. Dyn. Psychiatr.*, 3:77–9.

Prologue to Chapter 3:
REFLECTIONS ON MATURE LOVE AND COUNTERTRANSFERENCE

Psychoanalytic theories more influenced by the Interpersonal tradition are inclined both to view and to engage with their chronologically adult patients as adults, in spite of whatever immaturities or baby self-states they may possess. Critics have referred to this position as "adultomorphic". On the other hand, the perception, in the analytic encounter, that any given patient is more a baby than an adult creates what I and my close friend and colleague, Dr. Paul Kessel, believe is an excessive hierarchy between analyst and patient, the analyst invariably self-perceived as *the* adult in the relationship. In such a hierarchical dyadic structure it may be easier for analysts to feel kindly toward the "baby" in the room, in spite of personal qualities that might otherwise be unpleasant or difficult to live with.

The classical Freudian model has traditionally emphasized the universal presence of archaic sexual and aggressive drives and as long as these are viewed as belonging to the drive-dominated baby in the room, patients' sexuality and aggression may be less ugly or uncomfortable than these affective states otherwise might. The deficiency models, characterized by the middle school of Object Relations and traditional Self-Psychology, tend to understand patients often through what has been developmentally lacking, largely in the dimensions of nurture and of empathic adult objects with whom to either identify or internalize. Confronted by potentially distressing aggression or sexuality, for instance, an analyst might detoxify the anxiety created by these feelings by conceiving them as expressed by the baby in the room. Babies, by and large, are easier to love and to forgive, and most important for this chapter, more difficult to experience as objects of sexual or romantic desire.

Viewing patients as fellow adults—a psychoanalytic situation wherein both parties have agency, are both capable of giving and receiving and invariably influence one another, can create a more stressful environment for analysts. Countertransference anger and aggression cannot readily be tempered by emotionally stepping back with the rationale that this *baby* is neither fully responsible nor powerful as an adult combatant might be. Analysts' sexual desire and romantic feelings toward adult patients can be especially threatening because of the ever-present danger of boundary violations. Though it is entirely normal to feel such feelings toward another adult, analysts commonly feel that there is less risk of acting-out such desire when evoking what I would consider the self-protective position of conceptualizing a patient as less of an adult than they actually are. In contrast, Kessel and I believe the opposite. That is, to the extent that mutual sexual and romantic interest needs to be denied or dimmed by an analysts' illusion that they are not dealing with an attractive adult patient, such self-deception is more likely to lead to sexual boundary violations. And aside from this most extreme ethical crime, analysts' defensively hierarchical blindness to patients' romantically appealing personal qualities can readily be an assault to a given patient's strength—the ability to get another person to "fall in love".

Lest the reader be concerned that I am promoting analysts openly self-disclosing such feelings as a matter of course, I am not. I do ascribe to an analytic asymmetry wherein patients are asked to say whatever they are thinking or feeling and analysts are encouraged to be restrained and discrete, though the issue of self-disclosure is for another and future chapter. Most importantly, however, there is no asymmetry when it comes to feelings and analysts may be as prone to sexual and romantic feelings as their patients. To in any way to deny the existence of such feelings runs the decided risk of condescendingly reducing a patient to less than he or she might be.

Chapter 3

REFLECTIONS ON MATURE LOVE
AND COUNTERTRANSFERENCE*

The title of this paper includes three concepts noted for their varying and ambiguous definitions and vastness of scope: "love," "maturity," and "countertransference." Love" is probably the most confusing of the three and certainly the most difficult to research and grasp, regardless of one's philosophy of science. Freud wrote:

> Matters concerned with love cannot be measured by the same standards as other things: it is as though they were written on a page by themselves which would not take any other script. (1915, p. 378).

"Countertransference" takes a close second to love in terms of lack of definitional clarity and variety of clinical interpretations. Further, it is an emotionally loaded clinical concept. When love and countertransference are combined and the concept of "maturity" is added, one ends up with a topic with little room for certitude, clarity and finality.

Nevertheless, in spite of such cumbersome concepts, each with a ponderous literature behind it (psychoanalytic or otherwise), we shall attempt to state a single thesis and discussion. Our thesis is that psychoanalysts frequently experience feelings of mature, adult-to-adult love for their patients in ways which enhance the analytic work. Further, there is not necessarily anything improper about this in terms of furthering the analysis, technique, or morality. We believe that such feelings are sometimes transient; sometimes they endure over the course of an analysis and for years beyond. Furthermore, this is not a rare occurrence with only special or unusual patients or special or unusual analysts. Searles (1965, pp. 536–543) emphasizes such reactions in what he calls the phase of full or preambivalent symbiosis when working with seriously disturbed patients. Moreover (pp. 284–303) he links such analysts' reactions to particular dynamics of the patient. In contrast to Searles, we are not confining ourselves to a particular phase of the work nor to meeting particular dynamics.

---

*Hirsch, I. & Kessel, P. (1988). Reflections on mature love and countertransference. *Free Associations*. 12:60–83.

Before pursuing this thesis further, note that we stated *"not neces-sarily"* anything wrong and that we are referring to *the experience of feelings* and not to the expression of such feelings, either verbally or in other ways which go against the analytic grain. Such loving feelings may well lead to trouble, including the abandonment of the patient as an analysand. In fact, the impetus to write this paper came, in part, from our noticing that psychoanalysts sometimes speak of their patients as parents speak of their children or—in muted ways—as lovers speak of their loved ones. We have noticed that such positive attitudes may reflect an abandonment—via a distorted overevaluation—of the patient. This is usually made in a self-serving way in an attempt to bolster or maintain the analyst's self-esteem. Also, the attempt to cure with benevolence, compassion and kindness so that the analyst can feel good about curing his or her patient results in colluding with the patient to maintain the status quo in what Fromm calls a "gentleman's agreement" between patient and analyst: neither of the two really wants to be shaken up by a fundamentally new experience; they are satisfied with small "improvements" and are unconsciously grateful to each other for not bringing into the open the unconscious "collusion" . . . (1970, p. 3).

Shainberg (1977) describes this as a mutual effort at deception so as not to disturb each other's archaic world-view. Serving oneself in the analytic situation, in this way, and failing to see the patient for who he or she is, is the antithesis of the mature love to which we are referring. Parenthetically, we believe that this kind of non-genuine, blind love—blind in the sense of failing to see and confront the patient's unlovable characteristics—is all too prevalent and harmful. It has not received the same publicity as sexual acting out because it is less dramatic and less obviously harmful. It has sometimes been mistaken for concern, kindness and respect.

To repeat our thesis in a somewhat different way: in genuine engaged psychoanalytic work the analyst may commonly experience loving feelings for the patient and use these feelings in ways that foster the analysis. This thesis is based on the following important assumptions:

(A) In accordance with interpersonal psychoanalytic theory as well as the British object-relations theoretical framework, interpersonal relationships are given priority over drives in the understanding of the basic building blocks of human development and of the analytic interaction. That is, relationships, not drives, are the prime movers of people. Given this perspective, loving feelings need not be a manifestation of aim-inhibited drives which are sexual in origin, nor must loving feelings culminate in "excitement" (May, 1986). Loving feelings may often be a reaction to contemporary aspects of the patient's character and behavior. Such feelings need not necessarily be primarily rooted in neurotic historical dynamics and transferential problems. Further, loving feelings can be accounted for in a variety of ways because there is a variety of analytic relationships. Neither transference nor countertransference need be wedded to a single metapsychology or reduced to farther reaches of the mind than relationships.

(B) If such feelings are linked to mature attitudes and not primarily to self-gratifying and narcissistic ones, they cannot be acted upon without the patient's welfare and the welfare of the psychoanalytic mission being maintained. This calls for an elaboration. We are referring to an attitude and affect. Both can be discussed differentially, although they are intertwined. The affect is well described by Schafer (1983, p. 58) as ". . . appreciation . . . a spectrum . . . that range[s] from the analyst being mildly admiring to "experiencing wonder that may border on awe." Schafer is careful to point out—and we agree—that such feelings can be defensive and not necessarily a manifestation of what we refer to as mature love. Rollo May (1975, p. 116) defines love as ". . . a delight in the presence of the other person and an affirming of his value and development as much as one's own." This definition (of In the psychoanalytic situation, where the ultimate aim is autonomy, as opposed to the romantic situation, where the ultimate aim is union (Durré, 1980), such "delight"—or Schafer's more subdued "appreciation" is used in a productive analytic manner. This is not a matter of sublimation of erotic drives. In the "relational model" (Greenberg and Mitchell, 1983) such positive feelings need not necessarily be considered drive derivatives. Instead, such feelings may be considered an appropriate response within the analytic relationship.

Two authors, Yalom (1980) and Freidman (1985), summarize how love enters a psychoanalytic relationship. These authors do not write exclusively about psychoanalysis but they address how the therapist's love may be non-neurotic, non-drive-derivative, potentially therapeutic, and even necessary. Both Yalom and Freidman write from an existential framework; they thereby integrate many therapeutic positions. Both address and integrate the work of Fromm, Buber, May and Maslow, all of whom have written extensively on love and its implications for psychotherapy and/or psychoanalysis. All the above authors write about mature love and coincide in their view of it. All of them make the central point that mature love is an attitude; a way of relating to the world and people in it. There have been different ways of describing this attitude. Perhaps the best description is Schachtel's (1966) concept of "allocentric attitude." Schachtel limits himself to describing this cognitive-perceptual-affective stance *vis-a-vis* another and does not discuss in any detail how it comes into play in the analytic situation. Witenberg (1977) and Stern (1986) relate the allocentric attitude to psychoanalysis. Singer (1970) also does so implicitly. The following quotation from Schachtel summarizes the meaning of the allocentric attitude:

> This attitude is one of profound interest in the subject, and complete openness and receptivity towards it. A full turning towards the object which makes possible the direct encounter with it and not merely a quick registration of its familiar features according to ready labels. The essential qualities of the interest in, the turning towards, the object are its *totality* and *affirmativeness*. The totality of interest refers both to the object in which the perceiver is interested and to the act of the interest. The interest concerns the *whole object,* not merely a *entire being,* his whole personality, i.e., fully, not just with part of himself. The active interest is total and it concerns the totality of its object. Indeed, one is the function of the other. If one turns to the object with only part of his total being, e.g., with a certain appetite (hunger, sex), or to use it for some specific purpose, then one is interested only in certain aspects of the object and not concerned with the total being of the object. On this hinges the often observed fact that the object, the world, reveals itself to man only according to the degree and quality of the interest he takes in it. (1966, pp. 220–221).

Scahchtel's notion of allocentric attitude is similar to Maslow's (1962) "B-love" (love for the being of another person). With this kind of loving attitude others are related to not as sources of supply (as is the case in "D-love" or "deficiency love") but rather as complex, unique, whole beings. Maslow describes such mature love as an aesthetic experience. He says (p 43): "The truest, most penetrating perception of the other is made possible by B-love." He goes on to describe it as similar to the growth-fostering effects of confirmation (Buber, 1957a, 1957b, 1958, Jourard,1968). Maslow is not referring to psychoanalysis, but he well could be. Fromm's notion of mature love is described as an active concern for the life and growth of another. It is reflected in an ability to be responsive to the other and to let oneself see and know the other as fully as possible.

Fromm's book *The Art of Loving* (1956) provides a rich and detailed description of mature love altogether consistent with Schachtel, Maslow, Buber, Rollo May and others working from the relational model (Greenberg and Mitchell, 1983). Fromm does not write about such love in the psychoanalytic situation but his description of mature love is the psychoanalytic attitude to which we are referring, with one exception:

He emphasizes the attitude and activity of mature love, but not the affect. He leaves out the "delight" (May, 1975) and makes it appear as a moralistic chore. He emphasizes the *work of* achieving the discipline of mature love through concentration, patience, and supreme concern for the mastery of the art of love. He emphasizes how mature love is an activity requiring the productive use of one's powers so as to achieve a state of active concern. Probably psychoanalysts of all persuasions would agree with the operation of this sort of love on the part of the analyst. Our thesis is that such mature love can include all that Fromm describes as an attitude and activity, even a learned discipline, but that it includes loving feelings as well: the kind of loving feelings one may have outside the professional analytic relationship. Because such feelings are intertwined with an "allocentric attitude" (Schachtel, 1966), "B-love" (Maslow, 1962), an "I–thou" relationship (Buber, 1958) or "psychotherapeutic eros" (Sequin,1965) and because such feelings are not driven by sexual instincts, the authentic feeling of love that the analyst may have for the patient (Sequin, 1965; Hirsch, 1982, 1983) is acted upon in the service of genuine engagement (Ehrenberg, 1982), growth and autonomy. Indeed, in an analytic relationship, sexual involvement is by definition an unloving act in that it is self-serving and devoid of respect and concern. As Fromm (1956) emphasizes, mature love is an activity as well as an attitude. When Singer (1970, 1977) for example, writes of confrontation he is attempting to describe how the attitude is translated into activity. He speaks of the analyst's confrontations as a way of conveying that he or she cares enough to say frankly what he or she sees. It is a way of being there in the present (of being fully with the patient).

Kohut (1984) describes a different approach to analytic activity from Singer's. Kohut considers his efforts towards empathetic relatedness as close to love. It is difficult to maintain prolonged empathic involvement without strong positive attachment to the other person. To know is to love. Kohut's empathy is often displayed by silence or knowing when not to intervene. As with the majority of analysts, understanding is conveyed with few words. To Singer (1970, 1977) and perhaps to Boyer and

Giovacchini (1980), who feel less protective towards the patient, love is conveyed by the activity of observing painful things at the risk of provoking rage, hurt or scorn. Whether knowing or understanding is conveyed conservatively and quietly or by a more confrontational approach, the patient's experience of being deeply known can be a form of love given to him or her by the analyst.

Another assumption that underlies our thesis needs to be made explicit. Thus far we have relied on two assumptions: (a) relationship, not (sexual) drives, is primary, and loving feelings can be accounted for in a variety of ways, depending on the nature of the relationship; and (b) if loving feelings are linked to a mature attitude in the relationship they foster psychoanalytic gain and are not likely to be destructive to the analysis or to the patient. The third assumption is that the analyst, in the course of his or her "professional work" (Winnicott, 1960), is, ". . . much more simply human than otherwise . . ." (Sullivan, 1953) and may experience a wide variety of feelings, including loving feelings, which may be put to good use in the analysis. This third assumption is a statement about a way of viewing countertransference. The British object-relations analysts are generally credited with developing this view. Kohon summarizes this view as follows:

> The object-relations view is that the psychoanalytic situation is always created and developed from the specific and unique interaction between the patient and the analyst. The analyst is never an "outsider"; he is part and parcel of the transference situation. In fact one could argue that the transference is as much a function of the countertransference as the countertransference is a result of the transference. (1986, p. 53)

While the British object-relations theorists were developing this point of view, the American interpersonalists (Thompson, Crowley, and Tauber, 1952) were developing a very similar perspective on countertransference. Both the British school—particularly the British "Middle" or "Independent" Group and the American interpersonal school work from a relational model of psychoanalysis, not a drive model (Greenberg and Mitchell, 1983). Thus, the first assumption about the relationship is usually tied to the third assumption about the acceptance, and possible productive use, of countertransference. In very recent times, even some classical analysts who maintain the drive model at the same time embrace countertransference as a vital component of psychoanalysis (e.g., McLaughlin, 1981, Jacobs, 1986).

Largely due to certain unfortunate developments in the predominant classical school, however, countertransference has historically been associated with feelings which the analyst should not have. It has been generally believed among classicists that strong affects, particularly loving feelings, necessarily result in an interference with analytic neutrality and objectivity. Because loving feelings have been viewed as derivatives of sexual drives, the notion of countertransference love has been akin to breaking the incest taboo. This is particularly so because the classical analytic patient has been viewed as an Oedipal patient in whom transference neurosis has meant Oedipal issues and countertransference has been necessarily neurotic, Oedipally generated, and in grave danger of being acted out. Some analysts still view countertransference as referring only to the analyst's problems (either as a response to the patient's transference or, more globally, as due to the analyst's neurosis), which interfere with treatment. At an increasingly accelerated pace, however, analysts from a variety of persuasions have accepted the position usually first attributed to Heimann (1950, p. 81), that countertransference is an "instrument of research into the patient's unconscious," and the term has more and more come to refer to the totality of the analyst's feelings towards the patient. Hermann (1950), however, confined her description of countertransference to feelings—we believe that attitudes and activities can be included as well. Although we accept Heimann's premise about the productive use of countertransference, a premise which runs through the British school and the American interpersonal school and is current even among analysts of a more classical persuasion, we take issue with her notion that the countertransference feelings *always* reflect the patient's unconscious life. This way of viewing countertransference precludes the analyst's responsibility for his or her feelings and does not sufficiently consider the psychology of the analyst as the source of such feelings. It is in a sense another variation of the blank-screen model, which artificially intensifies "analytic tilt" (Greenacre, 1954) and the sort of inequality in the analytic relationship that could be subtly degrading to the patient. Certain views of "projective identification" (a concept with multiple meanings) have grown out of this clinical attitude.

When it comes to loving feelings in the countertransference, we agree in a sense with Winnicott (1947) who, while writing about the analyst's hate, presented the thesis that countertransference can be objective (realistic) or subjective (neurotic). We agree with him in that we believe that the analyst's loving feelings may be "objective" in that they are appropriate responses to· who the patient is. We disagree with Winnicott, however, in that we adhere to the totalistic view that loving feelings (or any feelings) are an irreducible intertwining of objective and subjective and of analyst and patient. Such feelings may largely have to do with who the patient is, coupled with the kind of loving attitude and activity described by Maslow, Rollo May, Buber, Fromm, and others. Likewise the attitudinal component of such love is never pure. That is, mature love is mixed with immature characteristics. As Schachtel (1966) points out, the allocentric attitude is not devoid of autocentric attitudes (see also Stern, 1986). The analytic situation lends itself to the analyst's experiencing loving feelings towards the patient, for both "objective" and "subjective" reasons: that is, because the patient's psychology and the analyst's psychology meet to generate an "experiential-field" (Wolstein, 1975b). This creates something new and beyond either participant: what Buber (1957b) calls the "in between." As Schafer points out, three different sets of factors enter into the analyst's "appreciation" of the patient: "[the] analysand's life history of achievement under adversity, the analyst's affirmative interpretation of the manifestly negative, and the marvelous intricacy of actions performed mostly unconsciously and preconsciously" (1983, p. 65). Searles (1979, p. 83) similarly refers to an "aesthetic" appreciation of the patient's illness. Analysts meet people often and over a long period of time. The meetings are largely devoted to grappling with intimate personal issues. All too rarely does such a meeting occur outside an analytic relationship, and when it is, it is often typified by deception and manipulation. Although the analytic relationship is by no means immune to such ways of relating (see Shainberg, 1977; Hirsch, 1982, 1983), it is at least usually the ongoing conscious intent of the participants to avoid it and there is greater likelihood of disclosure, genuineness, and intimacy, at least in the long run, if not in any given session or phase of the work. The analyst is in a position to develop an aesthetic appreciation of the patient's illness, history and current life—the totality of the other.

When the analyst develops an aesthetic interest of this nature, he or she can become close to the patient yet simultaneously maintain a professional distance. The analyst in such a circumstance can readily invest attention in the patient and be in a position to control this investment. Because of the unique situation of professionalism combined with attention, aesthetic interest and striving towards genuine intimacy (see Ehrenberg, 1974), the analyst can get to know the patient in ways beyond his or her knowing of others outside analysis. Such knowledge of the other over time is conducive to mature loving feelings based on who the other is, as opposed to immature blind "love" based on one's own needs. As previously stated, however, mature love and immature love are inexorably mixed. It is a matter of emphasis. The "as opposed" above is not the correct way to put it—"combined with" is more in line with our conception.

Searles (1965, pp. 240, 284–303, 355–356, 368; 1979, pp. 53, 490–493) writes of loving feelings for his patients in a variety of places and a variety of ways. In certain respects he keeps a foot in both the relational paradigm and the drive paradigm. In one paper (1965, pp. 284–303) he elucidates how such loving feelings are "objective" and "subjective" at the same time—that is, a function of patient and analyst. Although not making direct references to such concepts or writers, he shows how Maslow's "B-love" cannot be devoid of "D-love"; how an allocentric attitude includes autocentric elements: in short, how mature love and immature love intertwined. In this particular article, Searles argues that, "In the course of a successful psychoanalysis, the analyst goes through a phase of reacting to, and eventually relinquishing, the patient as his Oedipal love-object" (p. 284). He cites four intermingled and inseparable sources of what he refers to as the "therapist's Oedipal-love responses to the patient." Although we do not agree that Oedipal dynamics need be the source of such feelings, nor that such feelings need occur in a particular phase of the work, we nevertheless agree with the nature of the sources cited by Searles. These are as follows:

(A) The analyst's feeling-response to the patient's transference.
(B) The analyst's transference to the patient.
(C) The appeal which the improving patient makes to the analyst's narcissism that is, the Pygmalion in the analyst, who "tends to fall in love with this beautifully developing patient, regarded at this narcissistic level as his own creation, just as Pygmalion fell in love with a beautiful statue of Galatea which he had sculptured" (p. 300).
(D) "The nearer the patient comes to the termination of his analysis, the more he becomes *per se,* a likable, admirable, and basically speaking, lovable human being from whom the analyst will soon be separated" (p. 300).

Searles goes on to say that this circumstance stirs up feelings of painfully frustrated love comparable to that in the Oedipal phase of development. It is possible that, at least in some circumstances, loving feelings in the analyst can exist without stirring up frustrated love, specifically tied to an Oedipal phase of development. That is, we believe that the "likable," "admirable," "lovable" qualities Searles mentions can largely account for the analyst's loving feelings. Of course, the analyst's history must of necessity be involved. We prefer to leave it an open issue as to what in his or her history is stirred up, giving more weight to the reality of the patient and somewhat less to whatever is stirred up. Searles writes that,

> in the course of my work with every one of my patients who has progressed to, or very far towards, a thoroughgoing analytic cure, I have experienced romantic and erotic desires to marry and fantasies of being married to the patient. (p. 284).

From our point of view, the loving feelings—the mature loving feelings to which we are referring—coupled with the attitudinal components elucidated earlier, do not necessarily include such strong romantic and erotic components. We believe that Searles's allegiance to Freudian Oedipal dynamics accounts for his erotic and romantic emphasis. We can see, however, that in a particular analytic dyad such feelings and fantasies may exist and, when linked to a mature loving analytic attitude, will not be acted out in any harmful way. The romantic relationship and the therapeutic relationship are distinguished by the difference in intentions and expectations of both participants (Durré, 1980). Further, the professional-intimate loving relationship is potentially much more under control than the romantic loving relationship. Nevertheless, as Durré documents, romantic and sexual acting out does occur. In fact, a number of extremely prominent analysts have married their patients (see Durré, 1980, p. 243). Although Searles's mention of romantic and erotic fantasies (even with patients of the same sex) are often not the form of the mature loving feelings to which we are referring—we do agree with his statement that, ". . . it is by no means uncommon, I think, for the therapist to regard the patient, now and again, as being the dearest person in his life" (1965, p. 240). Searles (1965, p. 522) also mentions another element that contributes to the analyst's loving feelings. If an analyst sees a patient over the years, these years are full of events that bring joys and sorrows to the analyst. In a sense, the patient is "with" the analyst while the analyst is going through major emotional experiences. The patient becomes linked to the analyst's emotional history and is therefore emotionally part of the analyst's life.

Greenson (1974) and Loewald (1980), like Searles, also write specifically about the analyst's love. Contrasting their more conservative classical position about love with Searles's more radical writing helps to point out a major difference in analytic conceptions of countertransference concerning love, and of countertransference and the analytic relation ship in general. Greenson acknowledges that during the course of psychoanalytic treatment, every psychoanalyst experiences many shades and degrees of love, hate, and indifference towards each of his patients. This range of feeling is necessary for doing psychoanalytic therapy (1974, p. 259). However, he sees such feelings as distortions of the analyst, which he ranges among the analyst's transference reactions. He goes on to express his belief that such distortions can be useful if the analyst can grasp what it is about the patient's material which triggered them. Greenson assumed that the patient's material triggered the distortions and never considers the possibility that some actual qualities of the patient could help bring about genuine and primarily non-neurotic feelings on the part of the analyst. He writes that the analyst should like his patient, but not in an intense way, and that genuine non distorted analytic loving is manifested by concern in the form of neutrality.

Loewald (1980, p. 229) writes about the analyst's love in much the same way but leans towards a relational position. He says that an analytic growth-fostering attitude, ". . . requires an objectivity and neutrality the essence of which is love and respect for the individual and for the individual's development." This involves keeping a focus on the unique emerging core of the patient's self and objects while interpreting transferences and defenses. In order to focus on this core, the analyst must penetrate the patient's transference distortions and avoid imposing a view of who the patient should become, or molding the patient in his or her own image. This activity is much like Schachtel's allocentric attitude. Loewald gives weight to the new experience that will emerge from this analytic stance and believes that it interacts with interpretation to produce the therapeutic action of psychoanalysis. The analyst's "love" is the medium without which correct interpretation is ineffective. Interpretation is the mutative factor, but the setting needs an ambience in which interpretation can be received (see also Greenson, 1967; Stone, 1961). Recently, Pine (1985) has referred to these atmospheric features as the silent or non interpretative factors. He goes a little further than Loewald and other earlier classical writers in giving some mutative properties in and of themselves to qualities such as empathy, confirmation, allowing for identifications and being safer than the original family. Interpretation is still the primary but not the exclusive contribution to analytic change.

For Searles (1965), on the other hand, the "technique" of psychotherapy or psychoanalysis involves a deep feeling involvement in which both participants get caught up. For a more contemporary discussion of analytic change, in line with Searles's "technique" but free of Searles's being "caught up" in a segment of Freudian metapsychology, we believe there is a great deal of merit in the writing of Levenson (1972, 1983). Relational-model theorists such as Levenson tend to attribute more curative power to the analytic relationship than to interpretation *per se*. There are many different points of view regarding which kind of analytic participation is most mutative, but all agree that relationship is at least as important an element as interpretation in eventual change.

Members of what is broadly known as the British object-relations school, e.g. Balint (1952, 1968), Winnicott (1958, 1965, 1974), Khan (1958, 1974), Guntrip (1968, 1971) focus primarily on parent-child love configurations. Psychopathology is viewed as a deficiency disease and patients are seen as adult-children who were deprived of effective parenting. Part of the analytic aim is to provide an environment where the patient is allowed to abandon his or her normal measures of protection and regress to the preverbal period when the troubles first began. Winnicott's conception of a "holding environment," with the analyst portrayed as a "good enough mother', captures the spirit of this group of analysts. They provide a non interpretative warm maternal atmosphere. Words are insignificant since, as Balint makes clear, preverbal problems cannot be significantly aided with words. Once the patient has regressed to a thoroughly dependent state, the analyst provides a parenting-like experience which aims to be better in quality than the original. The analyst is given more license than in most analytic models to provide maternal gratification. Winnicott claims that the analyst does nothing more than what a good mother does with her child. He and Khan do not explicitly speak of the analyst loving the patient, but Balint and Guntrip come very close to this. Balint specifically discusses a primary love which the patient is lacking and looking towards the analyst to provide. One does not get the impression that erotic love is of any moment here. The patient, as a defenseless, regressed child, is in his or her most needy and vulnerable state and the response which the analyst provides can be viewed as, among other things, parent-to-child love.

Guntrip's giving of mature love, however, also bears similarity to the notion of mature love arrived at by Fromm, Buber, Maslow and May. He writes of the necessity for the analyst's capacity to respect and be concerned about the other person's reality in himself and apart from oneself, and to find true satisfaction in helping the other person to find and be his own properly fulfilled nature. (1968, p. 351). Clearly we agree with Guntrip's ideas about the analytic attitude of mature love, and also with his and the British Independent Group's emphasis on countertransference in general. However, we give credence to Weiner's statement that "trying to supply the love missed by a patient as a small child is comparable to supplying an adult pituitary dwarf with growth hormone" (1980, p. 131). This is not to say that a "psychological adult dwarf cannot grow. Growth is seen as a function of expansion of the self through the psychoanalytic inquiry as viewed by Levenson (1972), Ehrenberg (1974), Wolstein (1975a, 1975b), Gill (1982) and Hoffman (1983). From this conception of analysis and growth, the analyst's mature love as an attitude and activity is necessary, and there is room for loving affect on his or her part.

Surprisingly, the object-relations school has encountered little criticism from mainstream classical analysts. Essentially they have referred to the type of analysis described above as geared towards "pre-Oedipal" patients and not the classical, "Oedipal-level" patient. But an examination of the literature clearly indicates that all the object-relations analyst's patients (neurotic and pre-Oedipal) are worked with in the same manner, which suggests that this division is more political than substantive. It is ironic that Ferenczi, the precursor of object-relations theory, is one of the analysts most scorned and vilified by the Freudian mainstream. It was Ferenczi who, in his waning years, proffered the love cure: the naive assumption that since deficiency is the cause of psychological problems, replacement love is the only thing that will compensate. Unfortunately, Ferenczi died before he was able to integrate this into something more sophisticated and psychoanalytic. The object-relations theorists who followed him, Balint most directly and explicitly, took as their mission the integration of compensatory love and analytic technique.

Ferenczi's experiments led, in orthodox circles, almost to a phobia about mentioning anything about the analyst's love, and this remains today. Ferenczi's descendants managed to circumvent this by artificially and inaccurately dividing the patient population, calling most of their patients pre-Oedipal and allowing the orthodox analyst to believe that the two groups are working with different populations. In classical analytic think-ing, sexuality is a primary expression of love and the focus of feelings of love. The more supportive parent-to-child love engaged in by the object-relations group is not seen as incestuous but as overzealously nurturant.

The interpersonal model is primarily adult-to-adult. Some have criti-cized it as "adultomorphic." In a way it is closer to the classical group in that words are viewed as central. Regardless of how immature a patient is or how far back the patient's problems date, clarifications, observa-tions, confrontations and interpretations with words are still viewed as meaningful. The language used to describe the analytic relationship reflects the view of the patient as peer adult; terms like, "intimacy', "mutual influence," "co-participation," "shared experience," and "authenticity" are examples. The patient is not seen exclusively as an injured child, as with the object-relations group, but as an initiator as well, capable of making at least some choices about giving and receiving (Singer; 1970; Wolstein, 1974, 1975a; Levenson, 1983; Hirsch, 1981, 1983; Mitchell, 1984). The analytic ideal is a relationship in which each party is open to the observations of the other. The prototypical interper-sonal analyst tries to create an atmosphere where the patient is as free to observe the analyst as the analyst is to observe the patient. The analyst does not necessarily confirm or disconfirm these observations or in any way openly disclose facts or personal matters, but implicitly acknowl-edges that his or her unconscious is visible to the patient, as is the patient's to the analyst. The patient gains self-esteem, in part, by recog-nizing that his or her observations are potentially moving, impactful and respected and that he or she is capable of giving as well as receiving. The relationship is conceptualized more as dialogic (Buber, 1957a, 1957b, 1958) than as an administration of one or another technical procedures.

Many interpersonalists have a strong existential strain. For this group, openness of dialogue and clarification of experience can be ends in themselves. Explanations are less significant than descriptions; the "what" is more important than the "why" and the surface is as relevant as what lies beneath it. The analyst, in helping the patient to clarify experi-ence, is implicitly telling the patient that he or she knows first-hand about such experience (Singer, 1977). Self-disclosure is not usually practiced, yet anonymity is viewed as unlikely. The analytic experience, to some degree, is a mutual monitoring (Wolstein, 1975b) of what is transpiring between analyst and patient, with less concern for issues of timing than in other orientations. It is assumed that the tenor of the analytic relationship has historical and current parallels and that these relational parallels are explored. The new relationship evolves out of an exploration of a reliving of the old relationship, with the added feature that the process is mutually monitored. In addition to whatever love is felt explicitly by the analyst, feelings of love are channeled into the aim of establishing a co-participant and an intimate adult-to-adult relationship. Ehrenberg's (1974) notion of the "intimate edge" addresses the principle of the analyst staying with the most salient emotional features of the relationship at any given moment in the analysis. This ideal of the open attention to the. immediate experience between two people with a minimization of interpersonal hierarchy approximates one ideal of mature adult love.

The growing trend towards the study of both participants in the analytic field evolves out of Sullivan's (1953) concept of participant-observation. The observer cannot be separated from the observed. Prominent classical analysts (Spence, 1982; Schafer, 1983; Gill, 1982), like McLaughlin (1981), Tower (1956) and Bird (1972) before them, are writing about the degree to which the analyst influences and participates in the analytic process by dint of theory and values as well as actual behavior and feelings. They view transference as a creation of both participants and not emanating only from inside the patient's psyche. Perhaps the most interesting development from this merging of interpersonal, liberal-classical and object-relational trends is delineated by Hoffman (1983). He refers to a group of analysts whom he distinguishes as radical critics of the blank-screen paradigm, analysts of the "social paradigm" or the new group of "participant-observers." Hoffman names Levenson, Searles, Racker, Sandler and Gill. This group and others view the analyst above all as a subjective participant who openly invites a patient to clarify and react to the nature of this participation. There are two features of this group which make them most relevant to the study of analytic love. The first is that they view the analyst as engaged in a feeling process towards or in response to the patient at all times. That is, the analyst is always feeling something. The second is that they see the analyst as unwittingly reliving, with the patient, a reasonable facsimile of the patient's early significant relationships. This is not done premeditatively but is a natural outgrowth of the analyst's immersion in the patient's world.

Racker (1968), a Kleinian from Argentina, is most closely identified with the notion that the analyst is always experiencing strong feelings and is never neutral or objective. He does not speak of the analyst's personality *per se* but of the analyst as influenced by the patient. He refers to responsiveness and to the talionic principle: we tend to respond in kind to feelings addressed to us. Thus, anger breeds counter-anger, schizoid withdrawal and rejection evoke withdrawal in return, and love promotes manic delight and a return of love. According to Racker's point of view love is a common, everyday feeling on the analyst's part. It is not necessarily enduring, but it is frequently present. It comes from the blissful feeling of being loved and value, and the glow is felt and returned to those who generate it. Love is always part of the interchange, just as anger, hate, abandonment, etc. are. It has no special place in contrast to other feelings and certainly no associated taboos. It is not verbally disclosed by the analyst any more than hate, lust, boredom, etc., are normally disclosed. The analyst undoubtedly sees it and responds to it and the analyst does not deny it, any more than he or she denies the patient's other observations. In fact, Racker sees lack of awareness of any feeling as the greatest analytic danger. To be unaware is to be "drowned" in the countertransference, and acting out at such points is much more likely. Awareness of love and other feelings assists the analyst in understanding the meaning of the interchange and always provides useful data. Racker has written of the analyst's fighting for the truth and understanding what is feared and hated, as a special form of love. Thus he refers to the mature loving attitude we have described, coupled with emotional responsiveness. However, Racker's understanding of these matters, unlike our own, is derived from a Kleinian perspective. For Racker the analyst is not the initiator of loving affect but is always a respondent.

Searles, in contrast, sees the analyst as fully a person in the analytic dyad, one who cannot help but bring his or her uniqueness into the exchange. The analyst is not simply a respondent but is often the initiator, for better or for worse. When he talks of Oedipal love he is one of the few who state that the parents' sexual love for the child precedes the child's sexual interest in the parent. He is different from Racker in that he sees the analyst as also likely to initiate feelings of love or lust. There is nothing inherent in either role which makes one party always the initiator and the other always the respondent. Gill (1983, 1984) also speaks of the analyst as initiator. He notes that the analyst is often quite unaware of what he or she is conveying and that these responses have strong impact on the patient. Gill, like Searles, Hoffman, Levenson and Wolstein, relies on the patient to convey to him what he, the analyst, is not yet aware of. Again, the analyst does not self-disclose, confirm, or disconfirm but respects the perceptions as likely or plausible. Gill has not yet written specifically about analytic love, but from all indications would include this as a very plausible experience for the analyst to be undergoing at any given moment.

Levenson (1972 [transformation]), Sandler (1976 [role responsiveness]) and Searles (1965 [therapeutic symbiosis]) all speak of the inevitability of the analyst's repeating with the patient clear parallels to the patient's past and current relationships. Gill and Hoffman agree, and see this as the central part of every analysis. Some of the ways in which any given analyst engages with the patient reflect the unique personal properties of that analyst, while others reflect patterns strongly pulled for "by the patient. In repeating the core interactional patterns and making these verbally explicit whenever possible, as they occur, the analyst experiences the feelings of the key early figures in the patient's life. In almost every instance, patients have felt some love in their early life. Those who function at the highest levels and do the best in life have probably felt most love, Many patients, albeit with some problems, have been fortunate enough to receive very considerable love. The more love a patient has felt, the more the loving patterns will be repeated in the patient's current life and in the analytic dyad. All other things being equal, very loved people are easier to love. Deprived people are often so angry that love usually comes harder. They tend to fight love or drive it away. If one believes that early patterns are relived in the analytic dyad it is impossible not to acknowledge that loving, early patterns are among the prominent repetitions. It makes little sense to argue that only problem areas will be repeated. Although Racker has spoken of talionic love and Levenson (1975) of intimacy, Searles has written most poignantly about the repetition of what has earlier been defined as love. It is a logical extension of this so-called radical observing-participant group to begin to focus on the unwitting replay of positive early relational patterns as well as negative and ambivalent ones. Freud's paper on "Observations on Transference-Love" (1915) is asymmetrical in that he is focused on the patient's love for the analyst. As May (1986, p. 168) points out, "Freud's view of love in the analytic chamber has a curious asymmetry . . . Freud's consideration of transference love gives very short shrift to countertransference love.' Winnicott's paper, "Hate in the countertransference" (1947) is an important precursor to a series of papers in the 1950s that began a recognition of the "psychic symmetry" (Wolstein, 1975b) that calls for a coequalframe of reference in line with the humanistic psychoanalytic point of view.[1] As Wolstein points out, such a point of view is, ". . . not merely a preference but reflects the unity underlying all psychic processes" (p. 77). From this perspective the "in between" (Buber, 1957b) or the "experiential field" (Wolstein, 1975b) becomes a focus of study and it becomes impossible to isolate out "objective countertransference" (Winnicott, 1947), from "subjective countertransference" or, for that matter, transference per se. Perspectivism replaces absolutism and "countertransference love," neither objective nor necessarily neurotic, becomes relevant and worthy of consideration, not condemnation (Freud, 1915) on moralistic, technical, or any other grounds. Such countertransferential feelings are rooted in the relationship between the analyst and the patient, they are not necessarily derived from "aim-inhibited instincts" in the form of an infantile neurosis with Oedipal dynamics; nor must they include "excitement" (May, Robert, 1986). Such feelings are often a reaction to contemporary and realistic aspects of the patient. The analyst's loving feelings can be accounted for in a variety of ways because there are a variety of analytical relationships.[2]

The following quote from Angyal, free from metapsychological ties, expresses the attitudinal and affective intertwined components of mature love in the countertransference:

> Unless the therapist deliberately remains aloof there will be a natural development of feeling as in any other situation of prolonged acquaintance. As he learns to know and understand his patient he also learns to like him, and the more this feeling approximates devotion, the more help he will be able to give (1965, p. 27).

---

[1] The humanistic psychoanalytic point of view is not synonymous with interpersonal psychoanalysis, although interpersonal psychoanalysis may be at the same time humanistic. 'Humanistic' refers to the belief that all people must grapple with the same basic issues and that the fundamental issues are existential, not instinctual. Humanism further postulates that people can expand and individuate and that such development is the goal of psychoanalysis. The analyst can develop as well as the patient. Finally, humanism as used in this paper implies that people have the potential for development, regardless of how severe their problems may be, and that the difference between psychoanalyst and patient can best be seen as differences in ways of coping with similar issues in living.

[2] "Such countertransferential feelings," as mentioned in this paragraph, refers to any and all feelings in the analyst. The nature of the feelings depends on who the particular analyst is, who the particular patient is and what happens between them when they meet. Nothing is excluded from what these feelings may be, including sexual excitement and mature love as discussed in this paper. In the course of an analysis, both may occur. By definition (in terms of this paper), they do not occur simultaneously.

REFERENCES

Angyal, A. (1965). Neurosis and Treatment. A Holistic Theory. New York: John Wiley.

Balint, M. (1952). Primary Love and Psychoanalytic Technique. Tavistock.

——— (1968). *The Basic Fault*. Tavistock.

Bergmann, M. (1985). Transference love and love in real life, *Inter-national Journal of Psychoanalytic Psychotherapy* 11:27–45.

Bird, B. (1972). Notes on transference: universal phenomenon and hardest part of analysis, *Journal of the American Psychoanalytic Association* 20:267–301.

Boyer, B. and Giovacchini, P. (1980). Psychoanalytic Treatment of Schizophrenic, Borderline and Characterological Disorders. New York: Jason Aronson.

Buber, M. (1957a). Distance and relation, *Psychiatry* 20:97–104.

——— (1957b). Elements of the interhuman, *Psychiatry* 20:105–113.

——— (1958*). I–Thou*. New York: Scribner's.

Crowley, R. (1952). Human reactions of analysts to patients, *Samiska* 6:212–219.

Durre, L. (1980). Comparing romantic and therapeutic relationships, in K. Pope, ed. *On Love and Loving*. Jossey-Bass.

Ehrenberg, D. (1974). The intimate edge in therapeutic relatedness, *Contemporary Psychoanalysis* 10:423–437.

——— (1982). Psychoanalytic engagement, *Contemporary Psychoanalysis* 18:535–555.

Epstein, L. and Feiner, A. (1979). *Countertransference*. New York: Jason Aronson.

Feiner, A. (1977). Countertransference and the anxiety of influence, *Contemporary Psychoanalysis* 13:1–15.

Freidman, M. (1985). *The Healing Dialogue in Psychotherapy*. New York: Jason Aronson..

Freud, S. (1915). Further recommendations on the technique of psycho-analysis: observations on transference-love, in James Strachey, ed. *Standard Edition* 12:159.

Fromm, E. (1956). *The Art of Loving*. New York: Harper & Row.

——— (1964). *The Heart of Man*. New York: Harper & Row.

——— (1970). *The Crisis of Psychoanalysis*. New York: Holt, Rinehart & Winston.

Gill, M. (1982). *The Analysis of Transference*, vol. 1. New York: International Universities Press.

——— (1983). The interpersonal paradigm and the degree of the therapist's involvement, *Contemporary Psychoanalysis* 19:200–237.

——— (1984). Psychoanalysis and psychotherapy: a revision, *Inter-national. Review of Psycho-Analysis* 11:161–179.

Greenacre, P. (1954). The role of transference: practical considerations in relation to psychoanalytic therapy. *Journal of the American*

Psychoanalytic Association 2:671–684.

Greenberg, J. & Mitchell, S. (1983). *Object Relations in Psychoanalytic Theory.* Cambridge, MA: Harvard University Press.

Greenson, R. (1967). *The Technique and Practice of Psychoanalysis.* New York: International Universities Press.

—— (1974). Loving, hating, and indifference toward the patient, *International. Review of Psycho-Analysis* 1:259–266.

Guntrip, H. (1968). Schizoid Phenomena, Object Relations and The Self. New York: International Universities Press.

—— (1971). Psychoanalytic Theory, Therapy and The Self. New York: Basic Books.

Heimann, P. (1950). On countertransference, *International Journal of Psycho-Analysis* 31:81–84.

Hirsch, I. (1981). Authoritarian aspects of the psychoanalytic relationship, *Review of Existential Psychology and Psychiatry* 17:105–133.

—— (1982). Aspects of pseudointimacy in the psychotherapy relationship, in M. Fisher and G. Striker, eds, *Intimacy.* New York: Plenum.

—— (1983). Analytic intimacy and the restoration of nurturance, *American Journal of Psychoanalysis.* 10:359–371.

—— (1987). Varying modes of analytic participation, *Journal of the American* Academy of Psychoanalysis 15:205–222.

Hoffman, I. (1983). The patient as interpreter of the analyst's experience, *Contemporary Psychoanalysis* 19:389–422.

Jacobs, T. (1986). On countertransference enactments, *Journal of the American Psychoanalytic Association* 34:289–307.

Jourard, S. (1968). Disclosing Man To Himself. Princeton, NJ: Van Nostrand.

Kernberg, O. (1976). Object Relations Theory and Clinical Psycho-analysis. New York: Jason Aronson.

Khan, M.M.R. (1958). Introduction to D.W. Winnicott, in Through Pediatrics to Psychiatry. Hogarth.

—— (1974). *The Privacy of The Self.* New York: International Uni-versities Press.

Kohon, G. (1986). Countertransference: An independent view, in G. *Kohon, ed. The British School of Psychoanalysis: The Independent Tradition.* New Haven, CT: Yale University Press.

Kohut, H. (1984). *How Does Analysis Cure?* Chicago: University of Chicago Press.

Levenson, E. (1972). *The Fallacy of Understanding.* New York: Basic Books.

—— (1975). Changing concepts of intimacy in psychoanalytic practice, *Contemporary Psychoanalysis* 10:359–369.

—— (1983). *The Ambiguity of Change.* New York: Basic Books.

Loewald, H: (1980). The therapeutic action of psychoanalysis, in *Papers on Psychoanalysis.* New Haven, CT: Yale University Press.

McLaughlin, J. (1981). Transference, psychic reality and countertransference, *Psychoanalytic Quarterly.* 50:639–664.

Maslow, A. (1962). *Toward a Psychology of Being.* Princeton, NJ: Van Nostrand.

May, R. (1969). *Love and Will.* New York: W.W. Norton.

——— (1975). A Preface to Love, in A. Montague, ed. *The Practice of Love.* Englewood Cliffs, NJ: Prentice-Hall.

May, R. (1986). Love in the counter-transference: the uses of the therapist's excitement, *Psychoanalytic Psychotherapy* 2:167–181.

Mitchell, S. (1984). Object relations theories and the developmental tilt, *Contemporary Psychoanalysis* 20:473–499.

Pine, F. (1985). *Developmental Theory and Clinical Process.* New Haven, CT: Yale University Press.

Racker, H. (1968). *Transference and Countertransference.* New York: International Universities Press.

Rogers, C. (1961). *On Becoming a Person.* Boston, MA: Houghton Mifflin.

Sandler, J. (1976). Countertransference and role responsiveness, *International Review of Psycho-Analysis* 3:43–47.

Schachtel, E. (1966). *Metamorphosis.* New York: Da Capo.

Schafer, R. (1983). *The Analytic Attitude.* New York: Basic Books.

Searles, H. (1965). *Collected Papers on Schizophrenia and Related Subjects.* New York: International Universities Press.

——— (1979). *Countertransference and Related Subjects.* New York: International Universities Press.

Sequin, C. (1965). *Love and Psychotherapy.* New York: Libra.

Shainberg, D. (1977). Transforming transitions in patients and therapists, in K. Frank, ed. *The Human Dimension in Psychoanalytic Practice.* New York: Grune & Stratton.

Singer, E. (1970). *Key Concepts in Psychotherapy;* New York: Basic Books.

——— (1977). The myth of analytic anonymity. in K. Frank, ed. In: *The Human Dimension in Psychoanalytic Practice.* New York: Grune & Stratton.

Spence, D. (1982). *Narrative Truth and Historical Truth.* New York: W.W. Norton.

Stern, D. (1986). Unformulated experience and countertransference, Paper presented as part of the panel: Contemporary Interpersonal Approaches to Countertransference, sponsored by The Manhattan Institute for Psychoanalysis, New York. New York: 5 December.

Stone, L. (1961). *The Psychoanalytic Situation.* New York: International Universities Press.

Sullivan, H.S. (1953). *The Interpersonal Theory of Psychiatry.* New York: W.W. Norton.

Tauber, E. (1952). Observations on counter-transference phenomena, *Samiska* 6:220–228.

Thompson, C. (1952). Counter-transference, *Samiska* 5:205–211.

Tower, L. (1956). Countertransference,. *Journal of the American Psychoanalytic Association* 4:224–255.

Weiner, M. (1980). Healthy and pathological love—psychodynamic views, in K. Pope, ed. *On Love and Loving.* Jossey-Bass.

Winnicott, D.W. (1947). Hate in the countertransference, *International. Journal of Psycho-Analysis* 30:69–75.

——— (1958). *Through Pediatrics to Psychoanalysis. Hogarth.*

——— (1960). *Counter-transference, British Journal Medical Psychology* 33:17–21.

——— (1965). *The Maturational Process and the Facilitating Environment.* New York: International Universities Press.

——— (1974). *Playing and Reality.* New York: Penguin. Harmonds-worth: Penguin, 1980.

Witenberg, E. (1977). The inner game of psychoanalysis, *Contemporary Psychoanalysis* 13:387–398.

Wolstein, B. (1974). Individuality and identity, *Contemporary Psychoanalysis* 10:1–14.

——— (1975a). Toward a conception of unique individuality, *Contemporary Psychoanalysis* 11:146–160.

——— (1975b). Countertransference: The psychoanalyst's shared experience and inquiry with his patient, *Journal of the American Academy of Psychoanalysis* 3:77–89.

Yalom, I. (1980). *Existential Psychotherapy.* New York: Basic Books.

Prologue to Chapter 4:
THE UBIQUITY AND RELATIVITY OF NARCISSISM

Narcissism has a special significance in the analytic literature, for this quality, diagnosed as such, was long the determinant of whether or not a patient was capable of being analyzed. That is, for the majority of analysts in the USA, dominated by the Freudian hegemony that existed until the 1980s, one needed to have been diagnosed as "neurotic" in order to be seen as sufficiently mature enough to undergo an analysis. And, sufficient maturity was defined developmentally—having reached an Oedipal level of development. For the majority of clinicians, this precluded a significant proportion of the potential patient population, who, it was determined, did not have sufficient capacity to engage or relate to another to the extent that they could form a transference to an analyst. This narcissistic-neurotic binary, as all binaries, reflected the confidence that many analysts had in their ability diagnose and to predict with much confidence, who was and who was not capable of forming a semblance of a mature or attached relationship with another. There was little gray area, little sense that there were degrees of relating and that this might fall on a continuum. The certainties implied in diagnostic thinking reflected a medical rather than a humanistic orientation to psychoanalysis. It perpetuated the illusion that psychoanalysis was a science instead of a hermeneutic discipline.

In this chapter I argue for viewing narcissism as a personal quality that is shared in varying degrees by anyone human. As well, like with cholesterol, there is good narcissism and bad narcissism. That is, narcissism can be life enhancing or it can detract from optimal living. The term itself tells us very little, for each clinician needs to understand the unique form of narcissism that lies in every person who seeks analytic therapy, and each clinicians reading will inevitably be subjective. For example, narcissism as often thought of in it's purist form is characterized by vanity, an inflated sense of self, an absence of empathy, grandiosity and very little if any concern for others. This however, is an extreme and if such an individual sought out an analyst, these would be the very qualities that an analyst should attempt to address. In my view, self-absorption is the defining feature of anything worthy of being called narcissistic. And, we are all self-absorbed to one degree or another. Though all might not agree, being depressed is by definition to be self-absorbed, as is of course the ubiquitous quality of obsessive thinking and rumination.

Diagnostic thinking of any sort masks the subtleties and the nuance that all people share, though it defensively reduces the anxiety of uncertainty that must dominate the psyche of any analyst who is honest with himself. Analysts are well advised to learn from novelists who are able to describe people in a way that brings them to life, a sharp contrast with the effort to reduce anxiety by *shrinking* people into discrete categories.

Chapter 4

THE UBIQUITY AND RELATIVITY OF NARCISSISM*

Life is simplest and the world most easily negotiable when ambiguity is at a minimum. Even the Talmudist who spends his life in the study of the most complicated and unanswerable questions does so with an absolute belief in God and in his own calling as a scholar. The psychoanalyst too is plagued with the profoundly difficult task of understanding human functioning in general, making sense out of particular individuals and providing an interaction that will lead to change of enduring personal characteristics. In confrontation with such responsibilities where certainty about what one is doing is not generally achievable, many different solutions are available. One way to accommodate is to adopt a dogma, to proceed as if the very clarity and definite knowledge that is absent is indeed present (Becker 1983). Most individuals in the psychoanalytic profession, however, are personally beyond such a rigid solution. Nonetheless, it is not uncommon for a point of view to be arrived at, which are modifications of dogma. These are usually sophisticated and intelligent enough to escape detection as overly fixed and satisfy the desire for a reasonable amount of certainty. One example of this is to view psychoanalysis as a science as opposed to a hermeneutic enterprise (Holt 1976). Actually, operating in this field is impossible without guiding theoretical ideas, and by definition, each of us is limited to some degree by our articulated or unarticulated positions. Another solution to this problem is to be aware of our theoretical positions as ways in which we make sense out of unknowable psychoanalytic data and to view these, not as truths, but as our own personal structuring points. The work of Levenson (1972), Spence (1982), and Schafer (1983) have aided the analytic community to think in more modest terms about some widely accepted formulations. It is now, for example, considered less radical to suggest a wider variety of ways to conceptualize psychoanalytic data,

*Hirsch, I (1993). The ubiquity and relativity of narcissism. In: J. Fiscalini & A. Grey (Eds.), *Narcissism and the Interpersonal Self.* New York: Columbia University Press. pp. 293–317.

and the profession seems to be moving toward a greater pluralism (Cooper 1987).

One of the bastions of psychoanalytic absolutism has been the notion of diagnosis and the type of treatment, analytic or otherwise, that corresponds to a particular diagnosis. Though this is not universally accepted, the adaptation of the medical model to analytic work is still pervasive, and diagnostic considerations are the focal point for a considerable body of psychoanalytic literature. The aim of using diagnostic categories is usually a worthy one since it allows a constellation of characteristics to be identified and provides a shorthand way of letting others know one's observations and one's experiences in treatment. The risk is, of course, that the categories and models of treatment get reified and uniqueness and nuance are overlooked. The psychotherapist's response may be to the group norm or diagnosis and not to the unique individual. One can work with diagnostic categories without these categories becoming viewed as absolute, fixed entities, if indeed, the diagnosis is not viewed as such, but instead, as a personal characteristic of the patient. It can be used descriptively, more as an adjective than as a noun. I do not intend here to discuss the general question of diagnosis per se but will restrict my remarks to the key characteristic of narcissism.

Narcissism is pivotal because essential distinctions about personal development are often dependent upon whether the patient is deemed "narcissistic" or at a higher level of psychological integration. Historically, patients have been divided into analyzable vs. unanalyzable, based, to a degree, on the extent of narcissistic involvement. Those individuals who were perceived as essentially narcissistic were considered too immature or developmentally arrested to benefit from psychoanalysis. Psychoanalytic technique was thought to be too austere and depriving as well as too verbal for the more contact-hungry narcissistic patient. Further, it was believed that such individuals could not form a transference to the analyst since they were not sufficiently personally related to do so. Narcissism was and still is a broad category and could range from those who function well in life to blatant schizophrenia. It often seemed that anyone toward whom the analyst could not relate was deemed narcissistic and unanalyzable. Until recently the solution was simple; well-functioning to schizophrenic patients diagnosed as narcissistic were not seen by most analysts in analytic treatment, or if they were, were not diagnosed as such. They were relegated to supportive or other nonanalytic forms of therapy, and the population of patients was divided into neurotics who were analyzable and narcissists who were not. The efforts of American analysts (e.g., Sullivan, 1953; Fromm-Reichmann, 1959; Searles, 1965) and British analysts (e.g., Balint, 1968) to adapt psychoanalytic treatment to these categories of patients were largely ignored by the American mainstream analytic community.

Precipitated by the work of Kohut (1971), a representative of the American psychoanalytic majority of Classical analysts narcissism began to become of great interest to many American analysts in the 1970s. Kohut and those influenced by him became a breakaway school of their own (Self psychology) and have been very prolific in communicating their analytic perspective. At least initially one of the characteristics of their viewpoint was to dichotomize all analytic work into a neurotic-narcissistic (nonpsychotic) division. They proposed traditional, Classical analytic procedure as the appropriate treatment for the first category and a much modified and really quite different analytic stance for the narcissistic category of patient. Without going into considerable detail and therefore not doing justice to their method, the Self psychologists tried to provide sufficient analytic gratification for a population who would not remain in treatment if subject to the silent and depriving atmosphere of the standard American Classical technique. Their aim was to help strengthen the patients' "lack of self" or thwarted development by being available as a selfobject. This object sufficiently admires and is offered for identification in order to encourage arrested development to complete its natural evolution. The analyst tries to assist the patients in their defensive grandiosity and omnipotence, both as a way to maintain them in therapy and to keep their tenuous sense of self afloat long enough for them to get back on their natural (prewired) developmental course. After sufficient strengthening, the analyst might then be in a position to conduct a traditional, Classical, drive-defense conflict analysis. Some Classical analysts have been critical of Kohut's methods as simply another version of supportive therapy and of their reported results as nothing more than transference cures (Rothstein, 1980).

Kohut's point of view is actually in considerable harmony with that of the British Object Relations school (e.g., Winnicott, 1965; Guntrip, 1968), who up until the 1970s had very little influence upon American psychoanalysis. The interest stimulated by Kohut led to a strong surge of interest in the British Object Relations school and their own literature in psychoanalytic work with severely disturbed patients. Though British school patients were not specifically called narcissistic, those described in the literature often possess qualities associated with some of the less well-functioning narcissistic patients described by Self psychologists. Also, although the terminology used to describe the patient population is different, the British analysts have also been inclined to divide the patient population into two broad categories and provide considerable gratification to those who are not seen as neurotic and treated by traditional Classical methodology. The term *developmental arrest* (see Stolorow and Lachmann,1980) came to characterize the broad narcissistic population, and it appeared as if two distinct modes of treatment, according to diagnosis, were solidified. Matters became somewhat complicated when Kohut (1984) in his later work moved toward a broadening of the way he worked with narcissistic patients to include all (except psychotic) patients. That is, the line of development he originally viewed as present only in narcissistic patients had become, in his eyes, the basis of all psychopathology, narcissistic or otherwise. Once again, close examination of the major British Object Relations theorists leads to a similar conclusion; that is, what was originally viewed as diagnosis and treatment for a specific segment of patients was both the way of understanding and treating virtually all patients. As Greenberg and Mitchell (1983) have discussed, new theories of human development and of therapy are advanced by initially introducing the concepts through an atypical population. It could be said that what had begun as a firmly prodiagnostic orientation developed into a more unified way of viewing people in treatment. Both Self psychology and the British Object Relations school began to view narcissism for one and regressed positions for the other, as present to some degree in all people and the locus of psychopathology in general. The patients used as case examples for each group were sometimes well functioning and sometimes not, but their narcissistic (Self psychology) or schizoid (British school) characteristics were always the focal point of the analysis. This nondichotomous method of analytic treatment made diagnosis in its medical sense relatively useless. There is, however, some profound irony here. Despite Kohut's advance and numerous case examples from both schools, the thrust of the literature in the field lags behind and still speaks of two different lines of development and treatment—neurotic on the one hand and development arrest on the other. Further, even within these two schools, the literature stills pays lip service to diagnosis and prescribed treatment.

Similarities between Self psychology and Object Relations (as exemplified by Winnicott and Guntrip) theories of development and of therapy are numerous. Both view psychopathology, narcissistic or otherwise, as a function of developmental deficiencies—essentially, a deficiency disease. Both view the role of the analyst as one who compensates for these deficiencies by providing nutrients that were absent in the analysand's early years. The selfobject and the "holding environment" or "good enough mother" are designed to upgrade the patient's feeling of narcissistic adequacy or strength. The therapist-provided ingredients of unconditional positive regard, admiration, and encouragement of identification are designed both to strengthen the analysand's sense of self and facilitate a new beginning of natural growth of the self. The analyst assesses what the patient needs and objectively tries to provide it, within the confines of a professional relationship. The role of the patient can be described as somewhat passive and receptive. The analyst is the good parent who, in a sense, rescues the patient and reawakens the dormant growth potential. Like the Classical analyst who adopts a blank screen position, this model calls for objectivity and the analyst's sober judgment of what the patient needs before providing it. The analyst operates from outside the patient-therapist system and if functioning effectively, does not become caught up in the system, as say, in the participant observation model (Hirsch, 1987). Essentially, the analyst decides in advance what is the *best* relationship to provide for the patient and believes that this can be done without repeating with the patient some of the "bad" early experiences. Fairbairn (see Greenberg and Mitchell,1983), by the way, is an exception to this point of view. The Self psychology model and the normative Object Relations model thus adhere to diagnostic thinking. A clear method of treatment is prescribed according to the assessment of the problem. Judged from case examples provided by Kohut, Winnicott, and Guntrip, the problem is inevitably related to deficiency. The model is a reparative one and the role of the analyst is clear; within the confines of the therapy relationship the analyst must be a better parent than the originals.The two models do differ in a variety of ways that are not being addressed here, but their fundamental theories of therapy are concordant.

Perhaps the school of thought that least emphasizes diagnosis and clear prescriptions of therapy is the Interpersonal school. Sullivan's famous statement, ''We are all more simply human than otherwise," captures much about an analytic perspective that is non dichotomous in its views of human development and treatment of problems in living. Though Sullivan did speak of entities and some Interpersonalists still do, only minimal literature exists about specific diagnostic lines, and it is the exception when distinctions are drawn based upon quantity of narcissism. Searles (1965, 1979), perhaps more clearly than anyone in the literature, has drawn similarities between psychotic and neurotic development and functioning and has advocated that modes of treatment not be divided along diagnostic lines. He believes that all people possess similar personal qualities to varying degrees, and that narcissism and regressive qualities are quite present in the best functioning individuals. For the prototypical Interpersonal analyst, psychoanalysis is not a clearly specified technique, prearranged according to the diagnosis of the patient. It can be called more an approach than a technique, and the aim is to help the analysands see themselves and others as clearly as possible. Inquiry is geared toward that aim and is altered, not on the basis of diagnosis but on the basis of the unique dyadic relationships that develop between each patient-analyst pair (see Wolstein, 1974). Though Sullivan himself viewed the analyst as an expert, the trend in the contemporary literature, highlighted by Levenson (1972, 1983), views the analyst as anything but objective. Participant-observation or "observing participation" has come to mean that the analyst naturally becomes enmeshed in the patient's system and repeats with the patient the early "bad" integrations. Active inquiry and focus on the transference-countertransference interaction help both parties see this repetition, and are an aid in working toward forging new interpersonal and intrapsychic configurations.

Individual psychopathology, narcissistic or otherwise, is learned adaptive integrations of early interpersonal experience, and is imminently visible in the transference as well as in the examination of the patient's extratransference relationships. What is inside the patient is visible in interaction with others, and the world is arranged to coordinate with and repeat familiar interpersonal configurations. Individuals are viewed as architects of their own current world, and the patient is seen as active more than passive. Notions of "will" and existential thinking are strongly reflected. Examination of past and present configurations and drawing parallels between them help provide the analysand with the clarity necessary to function with less confusion or mystification (Levenson, 1983). Considerable effort is directed toward assisting the patient to see how past difficulties are perpetuated. Some Interpersonal analysts will work largely within the transference to reach these aims, and others will focus on relationships outside the transference. Those who work more within the transference are less divergent with mainstream psychoanalysis. Gill (1983, 1984), for example, has recently gone a considerable way to integrate the

Interpersonal school with the rest of the American psychoanalytic tradition, using the analysis of transference as the bridging link. Though the focus on transference divides Interpersonal analysts from one another, virtually all agree that analytic treatment ought to be based on unique dyadic interactions and not on fixed techniques of treatment for clear diagnostic categories of patients.

Another distinguishing characteristic in Interpersonal thinking is that it is a two-person and not a one-person psychology. Sullivan's (1953) conception of participant-observation in contrast with the blank-screen model of psychoanalysis is probably his most powerful contribution to psychoanalytic therapy. More recent literature (e.g., Greenberg and Mitchell, 1983) has successfully flushed out and articulated some profound differences in philosophy that draw distinctions between the Interpersonal model and those models that view the analyst as operating from outside the system. The participant observer is no longer the expert that Sullivan originally posited. The analyst is an unwitting player in the analysand's field. Starting out as an observer, the analyst becomes drawn in as a participant. Once In the system, examination of countertransference leads to clarification and a potential modification of the patient's repetitive patterns. In the two-person psychology model the analyst always speaks from his or her own perspective. This also contrasts with the Self psychologists' emphasis on the empathic position where the analyst disregards his own perception and speaks from an assessment of what is the patient's point of view. In this latter model the patient is viewed as too fragile to hear the other and the analysts subvert otherness in favor of efforts toward pure empathy. In the two-person psychology, the object of study is not the patient alone but the patient in interaction with the analyst or with others. This contrasts with a purely intrapsychic orientation, as well as with a pure empathic orientation, where the effort is to isolate the unconscious of the patient as a pure source of data, free of both the analyst's participation and point of view. These references should be examined for a thorough discussion of this important issue, though for the purpose here, note that objectivity and absolute certainty are never possible as long as the observer is part of what is observed. It can never even be known whether or not empathic attunement reflects the psyche of the patient or whether analysts are really reading themselves. From this two-person perspective it becomes difficult to talk of the patient in total separateness from the participating analyst. The analyst engages both as a trained professional and as a unique individual with his or her personal countertransference as well as countertransference evoked by any given patient. From this philosophical position it is hard to think of knowing the patient with certainty, or of distinct entities such as the patient's pure narcissism. It is equally incongruous to speak of prescribed methods of treatment for objectively determined clinical entities. If anything could be diagnosed it would be the relationship and not the analysand in vacuo. Much of the lack of acceptance of the Interpersonal point of view from within the psychoanalytic community can be attributed to anxiety provoked by the inherent relativism and lack of clear structure.

Whatever one's perspective, the treatment of patients with strong narcissistic characteristics is difficult (see Bromberg, 1983) and maybe more difficult when the analyst does not choose to adopt a prearranged method of treatment. Though a standard technical procedure may reduce anxiety, it can lead, as noted earlier, to excessive stricture and blurring of life's relativities. A two-person psychology (Bromberg, 1989; Ghent, 1989; Aron, 1990), by definition, makes the analyst a *real* object and not simply a pure transference or fantasy object. From standard Classical technique as well as with Kohut's and most British school writers' technique, the analyst is outside the system and is not a real object. The focus is upon the empathy that the patient *needs* from the objective analyst. Kohut's selfobject is not a real object; it is preordained that the analyst provide empathy, mirroring and identification to the patient in order to stimulate the latter's growth. Though some disagree, I think that this is similarly true for the supplier of the "holding environment" or "the good enough mother." Empathy is part of a technique that the analyst gives to the patient, whether or not the analyst actually feels this empathy (Blechner, 1988; Levenson, 1989). In contrast, in the Interpersonal approach, growth occurs in dyadic interchange and struggle, with the analyst as a real object. The analyst as second party has an actual effect on the patient with whom he or she participates. As noted earlier, the analyst becomes enmeshed in the analysand's world and uses the observing function to work out of it. Though the analytic aim is for the analysand to be able to fully utilize all potentials, he or she is always viewed in interaction with either real or past objects that have been internalized, real current individuals in the analysand's life, or in relationship the coparticipant analyst. The Interpersonal perspective is essentially a field theory. The analyst does not know in advance what will be done with the patient (Greenberg, 1981). The analyst tries to clarify the quality of the relationship that has spontaneously evolved between a full participant and an observing participant.

The patient fits neither the Classical model of the intrapsychic self-stimulated unconscious fantasizer nor the Self psychologists' or Object Relations' baby in developmental arrest in need of analytic nutrition (Mitchell,1988).

The pure quality of narcissism is most widely known (see Lasch, 1979) to be characterized by vanity, exhibitionism, arrogance, grandiosity, and self absorption. The other person tends to be used to make the narcissist feel good, and well-being depends upon receiving a continuously adequate quantity of positive regard. The other is not usually viewed as a whole person and is generally used as a supplier of nutrients—a self-object, to use a technical term. The basis for this is an absence of a sense of inner strength or substance, an emptiness that leaves one vulnerable to annihilation. The narcissistic individual does not tend to feel a clear and meaningful sense of self at the center or core. How others view this individual is likely to be taken as a reading of the self. This is why the prototypical narcissist so desperately searches for positive regard. If such a person is not admired, the result may very well be flight or a deep depression based on confrontation with feelings of nothingness. This extreme or pure narcissist is also inclined to avoid feeling dependent at all costs. Dependency is often profound but is not consciously experienced as such, for the feeling is strongly feared. Other people are important for the provisions they supply and thus are fragmented as individuals. To be dependent or to feel conscious love for a whole other person is to risk annihilation. The devastating effects of dependency on others are often what has led to a narcissistic withdrawal in the first place.

Bach (1977) and others have written about the difficulty for an analyst as well as for anyone else in the life of an extreme narcissist, to be subject to the stimulus deprivation of not being heard, experienced, or even registered as a fellow human being. In attempting to analyze individuals with strong narcissistic characteristics the analyst is often subject to feelings of utter uselessness. A common inclination for an analyst is to withdraw into personal narcissism as a way of self-nourishing. Another typical reaction is anger, and it is always a possibility that this can be used to retaliate for the patient's attack on the analyst's very relevance or significance. It is understandable why individuals with strong narcissistic traits have always caused a dilemma for psychoanalysts. As noted earlier, such patients were traditionally turned away because they were believed to be insufficiently capable of personal relatedness. A rejection of the patient's request for psychotherapy may be a form of retaliation (Hirsch,

1984). Another legitimized form of countertransference acting-out may be efforts toward harsh confrontations with reality. Though the analyst may be right on target, the analytic response may be based more on anger than on the desire to clarify. The sensitive patient may decipher this and flee from the relationship. Bromberg (1983) and Mitchell (1986) both convey that no new techniques are required to deal with strong narcissistic characteristics, though they caution the analyst to be aware of the angry wish to aggressively strip away illusions.

Writers who reflect Interpersonal psychoanalytic thought have not readily addressed the problem of narcissism because of their general disinclination to think in terms of clear diagnostic entities. Though both Bromberg and Mitchell isolate narcissism as a category, inherent in their thinking is a non dichotomous outlook on personal characteristics. They are describing individuals with very dominant narcissistic characteristics, virtually, the ultimate narcissist. Nonetheless, they do not support a distinct or prescribed method of treatment, and they view narcissism primarily as a way of relating to others and on a continuum. Though both authors convey that there is no need for a new or different form of psychoanalysis for such individuals, they do believe that in such work it is crucial to stay very attuned to the analysand's desire for affirmation. Fromm (1964), one of the seminal thinkers of the Interpersonal school, wrote extensively about narcissism, not so much as an entity, but, again, as a way of relating to others. His thinking and his willingness to work with narcissistic individuals reflected a clear advance over categorical and diagnostic points of view. His psychoanalytic emphasis was on delineating narcissistic qualities as they appeared in relation to others and, sometimes, in the transference. He probably placed too much effort on confrontation and was inclined to disregard the patient's wish to be affirmed. It is likely that he fared best with highly functioning analysands who were able to achieve narcissistic supplies from other sources in their lives. He nonetheless provided a valuable early model for those inclined to think in terms of two-person psychology and to eschew a more technique-oriented model of psychoanalysis. In addition, he referred to narcissism as a part of most individuals, in contrast to thinking in terms of clear entities. His point of view about the pervasiveness of narcissistic characteristics was advanced by Singer (1970). Fromm, Sullivan, and Singer set a tone for viewing characteristics like narcissism as elements on a continuum in virtually everyone.

Barnett (1971, 1983) has been instrumental in further expanding the discussion of narcissism in its pure form to a more pervasive, everyday characteristic found in all individuals. Barnett refers to narcissism as a part of almost all character pathology and an intricate element in the two broadest neurotic character types, the hysterical and the obsessive personality. He is not referring to distinct and clear diagnostic categories but is describing ways of being with others that reflect learned, internalized patterns of adaptation, that is, what can be called, character styles. Narcissism here is somewhat different from that discussed by Bromberg (1983), who addressed narcissism from an Interpersonal perspective as narcissism is defined closer to its more pure form. Barnett speaks of narcissism largely as self-absorption or personal inaccessibility. It is narcissism as a characteristic, not as a distinct and clear character type. Any way in which the person/patient self-protectively hides within himself or herself qualifies as a narcissistic characteristic. Characteristics such as grandiosity and extreme vanity are not necessarily present but are viewed as other (perhaps more extreme) versions of this central narcissistic characteristic of self-absorption. Barnett notes that all forms of narcissism are related to some sense of inner emptiness and impoverished self-esteem. Again, he is not absolute in his definition and therefore does not speak of a total internal vacuum. This may be the case with extreme forms of narcissism, but for him as well as most Interpersonalists, everything is on a continuum. Qualities often not considered part of a narcissistic constellation, such as obsessive rumination or preoccupation, depression, and the dramatic emotionality associated with hysterical qualities, are, for Barnett, examples of varying degrees of narcissistic unavailability. It is a way of defining most psychopathology according to the degree of relatedness of the individual in tandem with the effectiveness of functioning in other realms. That is, to cite common examples, if one is preoccupied with achievement and starkly lacking in concern for others or in intimate relatedness, that individual may function *very* effectively in work and marginally, at best, in love. Or if one is depressed as opposed to sad, therefore ruminative, dwelling on the past, feeling *sorry* for oneself, and exhibiting only minimal concern for those in one's life, that too could qualify as a strong narcissistic involvement. Again, if one is preoccupied with how one looks or on the impact that one makes and the desire for others to express strong interest in oneself, that individual may, nonetheless, function rather well in life. However, it is likely that the individual is impaired with respect to what is consistently available for others.

From the perspective exemplified by Barnett's writing, narcissistic characteristics do not come from only one etiological source. From examination of the Self psychology and much of the Object Relations literature, it appears that narcissism, like all other serious problems in living, evolves from deprivation or deficiency. Barnett points out that since narcissism is an aspect of most psychopathology, the development of those characteristics is inherently multiply determined. Many individuals who possess strong narcissistic traits come from families in which one or another parent was overinvolved, in contrast to depriving. In a family constellation where a parent infantalizes, overprotects, or overly admires the child, there may readily develop an overblown sense of self-importance and grandiosity. This may not be fully tested in the world) and therefore, the substance of their inflated feelings does not go beyond the doorstep of the home. In such instances the analysand may lead a private life of grandiose self-indulgence but not fully venture out to risk this fragile armor with the outside world. In other cases, perhaps where the parent is more encouraging of separation, the specialness and grandiosity may help catapult the patient to remarkable success in life. This achievement may be in work and not in love but can conceivably be in both. The individual who was given an inflated sense of importance and not selfishly kept locked at home by the family may be quite adept at getting others to be sources of admiration. As many configurations are possible here as there are unique parent-child combinations. What is of significance is the expansion of the characteristic of narcissism outside the slim range of a particular etiology and a one-dimensional, diagnostic scheme. The notion of unique dyads between patient and analyst follows from the viewpoint that developmental lines are pluralistic and themselves products of unique interactions that do not follow prescribed patterns.

It follows that Barnett does not offer new and clear methods of therapy for what he describes but makes us more sensitive to the prevailing narcissistic features at the core of many problems in living. In a sense, narcissism for him is like schizoid phenomena are for the British Object Relations analyst. Individuals retreat, more or less to protect themselves from their vulnerable core of insufficiency. This does not imply "arrested development" or a "lack of self" as it does in some other psychoanalytic models. From this perspective there is no such thing as a *non self*. The individual is always viewed as having a self that comes from both identification with significant others and whatever independent development may exist from there. At worst, the self is tenuous and not very separate from early internalizations, but it is never a *non self*. Psychoanalytic treatment, therefore, can never be a "replacement therapy" (Hirsch, 1983; Mitchell, 1988) and is always an analysis of character. The Interpersonal model of analysis is less a developmental model than an enrichment model (see Levenson, 1983). The analytic aim is more an enrichment of the present than a reparation of past insufficiencies. At the very beginning of the development of Interpersonal psychoanalysis, Thompson (1950) posited that the current problems of our patients have to do with how they relive and repeat their past deprivations, not the past deprivations themselves. The individual is seen as unconsciously but actively shaping his or her life to conform to the past. The analysand is not viewed as the passive victim of the past. In the analysis of character it is crucial for the analyst to address the analysand's withdrawal as it occurs in the here and now of the transference. The emphasis is more descriptive than interpretive. A central aim is to help patients be clear and to understand the "what" of their experience and not necessarily the "why" (Levenson,1983). Analysts use their own experience to help clarify to patients the esthetics of their interaction. By so doing, analysts provide the enrichment of clarity of the self as well as an experience that is not a repetition of past interpersonal integrations, i.e., a new experience (Gill, 1982; Fiscalini, 1988).

Bromberg (1983) expresses concern that extremely narcissistic patients are incapable of hearing and taking in the analyst and thus may not benefit from some of the verbal aspects of analytic work. Particularly, he fears that transference observations may be viewed as expressions of the analyst's narcissism and may lead to termination of treatment. He suggests a gradient between the use of the verbal and nonverbal admiring function of the analyst. This is a complicated issue, since in normal analytic interchange, dependent on how the analyst feels about any particular patient, there is always some gradient from admiration to dislike that is communicated. Unclear to me is whether or not mirroring (admiration) can be provided if the analyst does not genuinely feel this toward the patient. That this can really be part of a technique is uncertain. To be sure, the patient is better off if the analyst can find something to spontaneously like or admire. Since the analyst's feelings are inevitably unconsciously communicated, I believe the best that can be done is to try to get to the bottom of the dislike for some patients so that such feelings are not acted out (Epstein & Feiner, 1979). A development of affection toward, and an active interest in the analysand may lead to feelings of intimacy that in turn supply the necessary quantity of empathy (Ehrenberg, 1974; Hirsch,

1983). It may be that patients of all sorts drop out of treatment more often when they sense a lack of being liked or respected. Of course, it is inherent in contemporary two-person analytic procedure to carefully investigate all facets of the analytic interaction. Certainly, individuals who are more paranoid or narcissistic are more sensitive to like and dislike, and it is crucial to help them convey these observations to the analyst.

Gill's (1982) reemphasis of the significance of working in the transference merits note here and is offered in some contrast to those who recommend avoidance of transference dialogue with narcissistic patients. I say transference "dialogue" to distinguish from transference interpretation. In fact, if Gill is any example, most transference dialogue refers to observations of the patient by the analyst or invitations by the analyst to the patient to make observations about the analyst's participation. In working with patients who are highly sensitive to the analyst's subtle attitudes, it is especially significant that they be encouraged to articulate their perceptions about the analysts involvement. This not only helps alert the analyst to affect that is out of awareness but also may counter patients' tendency to act out their response to insufficient attunement and related injury and anger. If, for example, narcissistic patients do not feel admired or feel actively disliked and say nothing about it, they may very well be inclined to terminate the analysis. If, however, analysands are repeatedly encouraged to be vocal about such perceptions, reactions to the analyst become much more a part of the analytic data and are less likely to lead to the flight or stagnation that silence will often precipitate. My experience, therefore, is contrary to those who find more fragile or narcissistically vulnerable patients unwilling to work in the transference. Like Gill (1982) and Searles (1979), I find that when I do *not* work in the transference with such patients, they are more likely *to* terminate or remain unchanged. In fact, in line with Searles (1979) and Fromm-Reichmann (1959), I believe that the more severely disturbed the patient, the more crucial it is to emphasize transference experience.

Case Examples

Mr. L is an economics professor and business consultant in his late forties. He has never been married and was raised in a lower middle class Italian section of Brooklyn. His early ambition/sparked by his mother's desires, was to be a priest, and he attended Catholic school through college and got as far as the first year of seminary. He has four sisters, all married housewives with children, and though he is in contact with each of them, Mr. L is not close to any. Until his middle college years, he shared a bedroom with two of his sisters. Mr. L's father was a barber and earned a better-than-middle-class income, but the family never moved from the ghetto-like neighborhood where they still reside in a two-bedroom, tenement apartment. The patient has always suspected that his father was a small-time operative within the criminal world, and that his income did not entirely come from his shop. His father was and is a "macho/gruff", highly critical, and sarcastic man whose greatest pleasure is making others the butt of his jokes and his scorn. He is even this way with his grandchildren. His attitude toward his only son was taunting and mocking. Though he sent him to strict Catholic schools, his father himself was not religious, and he belittled his son for being a serious student, religious, unathletic, and awkward with girls. The father was quite strong and athletic and never shared this with Mr. L, who clearly belonged to his mother, for whom he was the apple of her eye. The patient's father was and still is extremely dependent upon his wife but does everything possible to disguise this. Mr. L's mother was also not especially religious but desperately wanted her only son to become a priest. She doted over him in every way from buying all his clothes through college to supplying him with *Playboy* magazine to satisfy his unrequited adolescent lust. The patient, through college, was a good boy in every way. He entirely obeyed his mother, kept away from girls despite being preoccupied with them, and was an outstanding student.

During his first year of seminary Mr. L "cracked-up," could not think or learn anymore, and had to drop out of school Though he had to couch this change as an illness, in retrospect, this saved his life, for it gave him an excuse to leave home, travel, and do a variety of things he had always felt too disloyal to do. For a couple of years he "recuperated" by traveling around the country and Europe, both living and working in some places and having sexual experiences for the first time. When he returned to New York he started graduate school in his favorite academic area in college (economics) and earned his doctorate. He got a good faculty position because of some early publications, and his specific interest within economics made him desirable as a consultant to investment companies. He therefore has always earned a good living, but since he received tenure, has stopped publishing and tends not to pursue more potentially lucrative consulting positions, preferring to stay with older ties. He still ruminates that his true calling was the priesthood and that he is a failure for not being able to stay in the seminary.

This is so despite a very lukewarm religious involvement. When he began therapy he claimed that he had never recovered from his "emotional breakdown" in the seminary and that he should have become a priest. This clearly helps him maintain a strong tie to his family.

Mr. L has led an active romantic life and in recent years has had a number of one-year to three-year relationships with women who were very nurturant, and who prized him as a potential husband. He has not been able to bear the idea of marriage and family, viewing it as stultifying and deadening, and when it comes to that level of commitment, he has always fled. When he began analysis with me he referred to his women as "fungible." They are all interchangeable, and he could get on well with any of them for a period, but to make a longer commitment was to lose the one great pleasure in life - sex. His stated aim was to have as active a sex life as possible, and he knew from experience that as soon as any relationship became too serious his sexual desire markedly waned.

He began analysis with me roughly three years ago after having had two other "analysts" who had retired. He had seen one for thirteen years and the other for ten, each once per week. He referred to them as analysts because they were quiet and nondirective, but he actually did not know if they were trained as such. I checked and found out that they were not. He sought further psychotherapy because he could not stop ruminating about his being a failure for not becoming a priest and he could not throw his whole self into his work. He ostensibly wanted to write in areas in which he had unique and extensive knowledge and wished to expand his consulting work to make it more interesting but had done neither for quite some time. He had no overt wish to change his pattern with women, to marry, or to have children. He desired a string of affairs with attractive women for as long as his sexual interests remained at high pitch. He was discontent, however, with a paucity of close male friendships.

Work with Mr. L has been unstintingly punishing. He has strongly identified with his father's brutal mocking, and there has hardly been a session when he has not condemned psychoanalysis in general, my particular incompetence, my failure to be helpful, my platitudes, my personal bankruptcy, etc. He unceasingly describes not being helped in his previous twenty-three years with his two other therapists and asserts how absurd he was to stay with them for so long and now to continue with me. He claims that he knows of no other alternative to deal with his constant unhappiness about not choosing the one calling where he really could do some good in this world, the priesthood. It sounds by now like an absurd obsession, but he holds to it.

It is obvious that Mr. L is profoundly tied to his family of origin, has identified with his father's sadistic way of relating to others, and is inextricably bound by dependency and guilt to his mother. He gives himself fully to no other women and does not allow himself to enjoy the profession he chose for himself based on his own intrinsic interests. Everything is a compromise; he has some involvement in love, some in work, and some in his analysis but most repeatedly demeans and diminishes each of the spheres. Women are interchangeable, work of no real value, and his analyst essentially a fraud. As with each of his women and the old firms for whom he still consults, he is as markedly dependent upon me as he was toward his two previous therapists. Yet, on a conscious level, he experiences no personal tie, connection, or affection whatever. I, like his women, am fungible. He is aware that if he gives himself more emotionally in any context, he will be as controlled and dominated as he was by his mother. He fears he will lose himself and his identification with his pseudo-strong father. He turns weakness into strength and is always on the offensive with me. He criticizes me for such insights being worthless and for not leading to change. His ties are either guilt or dependency based, and he hates himself for his dependency and hates me for his being dependent upon me, though he does not acknowledge the dependency as personal.

Though Mr. L lacks the extreme vanity and exhibitionistic characteristics of the prototype of a pure narcissist, his degree of self-involvement and his difficulty in making positive personal ties point to a decidedly narcissistic investment. One of the ways in which I have differed from his two previous therapists is in my considerable focus on transference experience. He rarely was overtly critical toward his two other therapists. I believe that something in their relationship to him helped him separate somewhat from his family and to make ambivalent involvement in love and in work. The process was very slow, particularly because it was once a week an, in part, because of the lack of immediacy present in transference work. Though Mr. L, based on his object ties, could easily be called narcissistic, my method of engaging him bares no essential difference from that with other patients who have made stronger personal ties in life or are less self-absorbed. I make no special effort to bolster his fragile self-esteem or to provide the warm paternal engagement he so sorely lacked as a child. As much as this was the case with his father, he was *too* admired by his mother. Sometimes narcissism comes from parental over involvement, the communication to the child of being too special or precious. His mother's involvement, as selfish as it was, has led him to feel rather confident with women and to expect to be the object both of their attraction and their eternal love. He does not feel compelled to give much in return. Indeed, he has been very able to achieve this with women who tend to find him quite appealing. In fact, I find him quite interesting and appealing in many ways and, despite his obsessional qualities, am rarely bored. Mr. L is very sensitive to any moments of withdrawal and will often accurately point out when my attention is flagging. Nonetheless, despite his self-absorption and consistently punishing ways, my involvement is almost always at a high pitch. This response may reflect my own unwitting maternal gratification toward him.

Much of what I consciously attempt to do with the patient is to draw parallels with me to his current and past relationships with other people and with his work. I am inclined to do this more or less with most of my patients regardless of how much narcissism is apparent. Mr. L often does accuse me of trying to make myself too central and reminds me unendingly that I am not important, that he feels nothing toward me, and that I could die tomorrow without his shedding a tear. If this were not also true for many others in his life, his women usually included, it would be difficult to bear, for he is very vocal about this. I convey to him that he fears my being too important and thereby dominating and castrating like his mother, and he agrees but says, "so what." I point out that he is dependent on me as he is on his women and colleagues and hates me for this, and to that he says, "so cure me of this; it's only been twenty-six years." When he softens up at moments and then soon attacks again I note the sequence and how similar he is to his father with respect to softening-up and loving, and he attacks even more, reminding me once again how pathetic I am to use a word like *love* to describe his feeling toward me, a fee-for-service employee.

Though Mr. L does not acknowledge it, in the three years there has been progress. On an external level, he has found new companies that utilize his rather unique strengths, and the work has been more exciting and lucrative. He is still not publishing but has given a few oral papers that were very well received. Parenthetically, he has always been a highly rated teacher and liked by students, though he tries everything possible to get out of working with them on doctoral theses. The patient has had two experiences with women that he acknowledges as love. He is currently in a total obsessive quandary about whether to marry a woman who is threatening to leave if he does not. He claims not to be able to tell whether or not he really loves somebody or whether it is dependency and fear of losing that person. Though I think this is so, he is indeed showing more loving interaction than he has in prior times. He has recently said that he wishes to have at least one child of his own and no longer expresses the wish to spend the rest of his life in pursuit of numerous sexual experiences. Sometimes he says that in wanting a child he has succumbed to my values and it is not truly his. He also conveys that sex is not so central to him because of his desire for other forms of love and that this is a tragic loss for lust rather than a gain for intimacy. It is indeed possible that the patient has identified with what he views as my tame, sober, and asexual family life, and that the therapeutic "movement" is a function of these identifications. My faith in repeated transference invitations leads me to think that this mitigates against such strong transference cure and that he is actually shifting from his attachment to the past and from his protective, narcissistic self-absorption and selfishness, to a new, albeit still quite ambivalent, stronger degree of engagement. It seems likely that his external changes reflect internal movement as well.

M is nineteen years old and began analysis when he dropped out of college less than one year ago. He is an only child and lives with his mother, who is of the "New Age" and works in a bookstore specializing in holistic medicine and nutrition. She comes from a wealthy family and is supported by a trust fund and by alimony from her two former husbands, the first of whom is M's father. M's father is a New York City physician who himself has been in analysis for issues related to passivity and depression.

The patient's parents were divorced when he was ten, and his mother moved with him and her new husband to Vermont. They lived a sort of wealthy hippie life, and M went to a good but very unstructured middle and high school. He had very little contact with his father, who was thwarted by M's apparent minimal interest in his phone calls and visits. M simply says that his stepfather was okay and he liked his friends, and that he just felt no real interest in his father and avoided him as much as possible. He viewed his father as being too "right wing," and by this he means in favor of more rules, expectancies, structure, and standards. It is likely that M's father did not pursue his rejecting son with special fervor and was all too easily defeated. M reports being happy in Vermont and in the unstructured school, where little was demanded and where his creativity was nourished. His one complaint was related to being shy with girls. They seemed to like him, but he was always very awkward. His mother and stepfather divorced toward the end of high school, and when he started college at a good mid western school, they moved back to New York City. However, he immediately missed the relaxed and laissez-faire atmosphere of Vermont, and had great difficulty with the academic demands of this university.

He hung around school and befriended the more radical, drug-oriented crowd, but when exams or papers were due, he retreated. He also developed a problem with his potency and could not perform fully with a young woman at school. He clearly was not meeting scholastic requirements, and left school on a leave of absence and began analysis at his father's urging soon afterward.

M recognizes that he is bright (his SAT scores were very high), and yet has little ambition to even read or follow politics, both of which had been of strong interest at other times. He spends much of his time in bed watching TV or movies, staying up to the early morning, and sleeping much of the day. He has had few personal contacts since most of his friends are from Vermont. He is worried that his impotence will always prevent him from having girlfriends, and now, even when he masturbates, he fails to achieve full erection. He always experiences some vague sense of depression and pessimism about his life. He feels pressured by his father to get a job and/or take courses in preparation for returning to school full-time, but has resisted this pressure and continues to try to avoid his father as much as possible. He went to a urologist to try to determine if his impotence was physical but failed to go back for the conclusive tests, thus resting with the vague idea that he has a physical disability. His mother has directly conveyed to him that she is lonely and likes having him around. He often watches TV in her bed, sometimes with her there also. On some occasions they will sleep together in the same bed. Mother does not encourage him to take courses or to work, and has made it indirectly clear that she opposes his analytic work with me. M fairly often misses sessions because he is sleepy, or has a cold, or just does not feel like coming, and his mother will call for him at times and make excuses. On one rainy day she forbade him to come and called to tell me that he was sick

M relates to me much the way he does to his father. He views me as trying to wrestle him out of a passive, unstressful life in bed with his mother, and is disappointed that I lack the accepting manner of the faculty at his high school. He is very bright and can be articulate, but he is often quiet and ethereal. He has some remarkable gaps in everyday knowledge such as not clearly knowing the sequence of the names of the month of the year. When he first came to me, he also did not brush his teeth or shower very often, not recognizing that this was unusual. When I expressed surprise, he began to brush his teeth and bathe more regularly. He readily acknowledges the is living in his own world much of the time, and that he holds back from telling me much of what is on his mind. When M started treatment he smoked marijuana daily but has since reduced this considerably. Nonetheless, he has a tired, stoned, disinterested manner much of the time. Periodically he will seem excited by something we address, but more often than not this will be followed by a missed session. He is never overtly angry with me but does not consciously convey attachment or affection. When with me, he states or otherwise conveys that he would rather be back in bed or in Vermont. He does not ever speak of missing any of his friends in Vermont but longs for the atmosphere of acceptance and no demands. He actively does not express in words affectionate feelings for his mother either.

Certainly M can be seen as having strong narcissistic characteristics. He is profoundly self-absorbed and unrelated and again, though not particularly vain or exhibitionistic, does view himself as very much the center of the world. He too suffers from extreme maternal over involvement, albeit also of a selfish maternal position. He expects people to come to him and has never had to reach out. He has also been injured by a father who has not had enough to do with him, and whose depression and withdrawal he is in identification with. His poor personal hygiene and lack of awareness of some everyday facts of life contribute to suggesting that he could, with continued withdrawal and loyalty to his mother's desires, become frankly schizophrenic. Indeed, I believe without successful intervention he could one day wind up hospitalized. The extreme degree of narcissistic pathology, however, does not lead me to distinct modifications from normal technique. Though M has a poorly defined autonomous self, I make no conscious attempt at mirroring or becoming a selfobject. I do find him quite interesting and with great potential, and perhaps this is the unconscious mirroring that I convey. Though he lacks a sturdy masculine identification, I make no conscious effort to have him identify with me. If he does, as with brushing his teeth and bathing, I examine it with him rather than silently encourage treatment as an identification process (Singer, 1965). I have dealt with transference material from the outset, conveying to him his apparent lack of interest in me, his view of me as "right wing" like his father, his desire to get me to rescue him from his mother as his father has never done, what he may be conveying to me by missing sessions, etc., I have not provided the mirroring, unchallenging atmosphere that other analysts might. His narcissism is transference material that I actively point out and do not willingly try to gratify. I also try to identify when I fall into trying to mobilize him like his father or when I am enjoying his engagement with me like his mother. At times I fit into both patterns of interaction and *try* to address how the patient pulls me in and repeats with me his maternal and paternal integrations. I convey in words that I see aspects of will and of choice in his narcissistic withdrawal.

Aside from a few behavioral changes, a stronger recognition of the incestuous relationship he shares with his mother, and other broadened awareness, there is no clear change in his basic pattern of living to this point. The analysis is still young, and I believe that active interest and inquiry into his way of engaging in the here and now, as well as outside, has allowed a relevant connection to begin developing. To view him as suffering from a deficiency disorder would run the risk of repeating maternal overindulgence. It seems more productive to me to see him as actively identifying with his passive, depressed father and as fulfilling his mother's incestuous wishes at the price of his own autonomy. My multiple roles within this system need not be restricted to gratifications or prior notions of compensatory selfobject ties. I do not think that he must be treated as fragile, nor would it be useful to adopt a position that would, in effect, throw cold water in his face to arouse him from his mother's bed. Trying to stay between these two extremes is often difficult, and his transference perceptions are useful in keeping me balanced.

I have fundamentally attempted to convey three things. One, narcissism, rather than a specific diagnosis, is a characteristic on a continuum. Second, it is a rather ubiquitous characteristic, to some degree or another, in individuals who might normally not be thought of as such. Finally, despite considerable current literature devoted to changes in analytic technique to accommodate extremely narcissistic individuals, it is not usually necessary to veer from one's normal analytic procedure, provided that one pays close attention to the immediacy of the transference. I therefore disagree with those who have found individuals with strong narcissistic characters to be unavailable for the verbal aspect of analytic work and for work in the transference and in need of special technical innovations.

In these two case examples, both analysands can be seen as possessing considerable narcissistic involvement. They are markedly self-absorbed and, at best, strikingly ambivalent in their relationships, when they have relationships at all. They share a history of overinvolved mothers who both inflated their importance and interfered with their developing autonomy and inner strength. They view themselves as special geniuses and, paradoxically, as weak and insubstantial at the core. They both have fathers with whom they identify considerably and who receded in contrast to their wives, leaving their sons with identifications with weakness and unrelatedness. They are both terrified of manifest attachment, love, and dependency, yet are profoundly dependent. Though these two individuals do not share all the characteristics of the *pure* narcissist discussed as a prototype in the literature, they have a number of such characteristics. It is possible that one can categorize them as having developmental deficits, particularly M, but no such formulation is necessary in order to work with them in an analytic frame.

In my participant observer or observing participant model, my aim is to actively inquire and to express curiosity and interest about the world of the analysand. The inclination is more toward questions and observations than it is toward interpretation. The latter implies more "knowing" than is often the case. In this role of inquirer and observer, I gradually and unwittingly become enmeshed as the weak father, the sarcastic father, the overly interested mother, my special and precious relationship with them, etc. When I am aware of the nature of the interaction, it is usually immediately addressed. There is no effort to protect or nourish these individuals or to serve them in some compensatory manner. I always invite their transference observations of me and do not hold back my own observations about their characteristics as they appear in the transference. I do not offer myself as an object for identification, by virtue of inquiring into whatever effort I see on their part to identify with me. I do not believe that I '"hold" these individuals in a selfobject transference or always try to see things from their perspective. My own perspective in this two-person psychology is often clearly differentiated from the analysand's perspective. I do not view myself as especially cautious, though my aim is not to strip them of all their narcissistic illusions. In essence, though Mr. L and Mr. M may possess more narcissistic characteristics than the norm, I view this quality on a continuum, and as requiring no special technique to address.

Finally, it may be evident from the description of these two analysands that I am considerably interested in them, and that my engagement with them possesses more vitality than might be so with some other patients. They did serve as subjects for this essay. It can be said that work has proceeded with some success because of my interest, and that my analytic perspective has little to do with anything. In that case I would be little but a good enough mother or a selfobject despite my best efforts otherwise. Perhaps all patients, narcissistic or otherwise, change for the better based on the transference cure of love and admiration. I raise this possibility to underscore that the nonverbally expressed interest and involvement with the patient is always an issue, and difficult to factor out of one's theory of therapeutic action (Fiscalini, 1988). It is, therefore, necessary to proceed as an analyst in a way that best suits each analyst's theory and person, with the humble recognition that one can never be certain what confluence of interactions leads to the effects of the analytic enterprise.

REFERENCES

Aron, L. (1990). One-person and two-person psychologies and the method of psychoanalysis. *Psychoanalytic Psychology* 7:475–85.

Bach, S. (1977. On the narcissistic state of consciousness. *International Journal of Psychoanalysis* 58:209–233.

Balint, M. (1968). *The Basic Fault.* London: Tavistock.

Barnett, J. (1971). Narcissism and dependency in the obsessional-hysteric marriage. *Family Process* 10:75–83.

——— (1983). Narcissism and dependency in the organization of personality. Unpublished paper presented at The Manhattan Institute for Psychoanalysis, New York, NY.

Becker, E. (1983). *The Denial of Death.* New York: Free Press.

Blechner, M. (1988). Differentiating empathy from therapeutic action. *Contemporary Psychoanalysis* 24:301–310.

Bromberg, P. (1983). The mirror and the mask: On narcissism and psychoanalytic growth. *Contemporary Psychoanalysis* 19:359–387.

——— (1989). Interpersonal psychoanalysis and self psychology: A clinical comparison. In D. Dietrick & S. Dietrick, eds., *Self Psychology: Comparisons and Contrasts.* Hillsdale, NJ: Analytic Press.

Cooper, A. (1987). Changes in psychoanalytic ideas: Transference interpretation. *Journal of the American Psychoanalytic Association* 35:78–98.

Ehrenberg, D. (1974). The intimate .edge in therapeutic relatedness. *Contemporary Psychoanalysis* 10:423–437.

Epstein, L. & Feiner, eds. (1979). *Countertransference.* New York: Jason Aronson.

Fiscalini, J. (1988). Curative experience in the psychoanalytic relationship. *Contemporary Psychoanalysis* 24:125–142.

Fromm, E. (1964). *The Heart of Man.* New York: Harper & Row.

Fromm-Reichmann, F. (1959). *Psychoanalysis and Psychotherapy: Selected*

Papers, D. Bullard, ed. Chicago: University of Chicago Press.

Ghent, E. (1989). Credo: The dialectics of one-person and two-person psychologies. *Contemporary Psychoanalysis* 25:169–211.

Gill, M. (1982). *The Analysis of Transference,* vol. 1. New York: International Univerersities Press.

—— (1983). The interpersonal paradigm and the degree of the therapist's involvement. *Contemporary Psychoanalysis* 19: 200-237.

—— (1984). Psychoanalysis and psychotherapy, revision. *International Review of Psycho-Analysis* 11:161–179.

Greenberg, J. (1981). Prescription or description: The therapeutic action of psychoanalysis. *Contemporary Psychoanalysis* 17:239–257.

Greenberg, J. and Mitchell, S. (1983). *Object Relations in Psychoanalytic Theory.* Cambridge, Mass.: Harvard University Press.

Guntrip, H. (1968). *Schizoid Phenomena, Object Relations and the Self* New York: International Universities Press.

Hirsch, I. (1983). Analytic intimacy and the restoration of nurturance. *American Journal of Psychoanalysis* 43:324–343.

—— (1984). Toward a more subjective view of analyzability. *American Journal of Psychoanalysis* 44:169–182.

—— (1987). Varying modes of analytic participation. *Journal of the American Academy of Psychoanalysis* 15:205–222.

Holt, R. (1976). Drive or wish? A reconsideration of the psychoanalytic theory of motivation. In M. Gill & D. Holzman, eds., *Psychological Issues.* Monograph 35. New York: International Universities Press.

Kohut, H. (1971. *The Analysis of the Self* New York: International Universities Press.

—— (1984). *How Does Analysis Cure?* Chicago: University of Chicago Press.

Lasch, C. (1979). *The Culture of Narcissism.* New York: Norton.

Levenson, E. (1972. *The Fallacy of Understanding.* New York: Basic Books.

—— (1983. *The Ambiguity of Change.* New York: Basic Books.

—— (1989. Whatever happened to the cat? Interpersonal perspectives on the self. *Contemporary Psychoanalysis* 25:537–553.

Mitchell, S. (1986). The wings of Icarus: Illusion and the problem of narcissism. *Contemporary Psychoanalysis* 22:107–132.

—— (1988). *Relational Concepts in Psychoanalysis.* Cambridge, Mass.: Harvard University Press.

Rothstein, A. (1980). *The Narcissistic Pursuit of Perfection.* New York: International Universities Press.

Schafer, R. (1983). *The Analytic Attitude.* New York: Basic Books.

Searles, H. (1965). *Collected Papers on Schizophrenia and Related Subjects.* New York: International Universities Press.

—— (1979). *Countertransference and Related Subjects.* New York: International Universities Press.

Singer, E. (1965). Identity vs. identification: A thorny psychological issue. *Review of Existential Psychological Psychoanalysis* 2:160-75.

———— (1970). *Key Concepts in Psychotherapy.* New York: Basic Books.

Spence, D. (1982). *Narrative Truth and Historical Truth.* New York: Norton.

Stolorow, R. & Lachmann, F. (1980. *Psychoanalysis of Developmental Arrests.* New York: International Universities Press.

Sullivan, H.S. (1953). *The Interpersonal Theory of Psychiatry.* New York: Norton.

Thompson, C. (1950). *Psychoanalysis: Evolution and Development.* New York: Hermitage House.

Winnicott, D. (1965). *The Maturational Process and the Facilitating Environment.* New York: International Universities Press.

Wolstein, B. (1974). 'I' process and "me" patterns. Contemporary Psychoanalysis 11:146–160.

Prologue to Chapter 5:
INTERPERSONAL PERSPECTIVE: THE ANALYST'S
PARTICIPANT-OBSERVATION WITH THE SPECIAL PATIENT

There is no writing more pleasurable for me than when I write psycho-analytically about my favorite interests: novels, movies, TV series and sports. Indeed, most writing I do requires a disciplined push to shut myself in a room for hours, fueled by impending deadlines, while reluctantly abandoning indulging in those very interests noted above. "Portnoy's Complaint", was and still remains the most enjoyable novel I ever read. When invited by the book editor in which this chapter appears, I was thrilled. I read this book as soon as it was published, having known of Phillip Roth from his first published book, a compilation of short stories.

Roth, about five years my senior, comes from a background simi-lar to my own and I resonated strongly with his satirical skewering of our shared universe. I was 28 and single when I read "Portnoy", and if I felt an identification with Roth and his characters in his first book, this was now intensified. His preoccupation with sexual conquest of beautiful women, his having been idealized and Oedipally indulged by his mother and his cynical take on superficial Jewish religious observance, some-times felt like he was writing about me. What really sealed this identifi-cation was his paralleled love for the Brooklyn Dodgers, a profound love that remains with me to this day. Even more—Roth's idealization of the Dodger center fielder, Duke Snider, and Roth's dream of playing that position himself, was and I must say still is at age 78, an enduring fan-tasy and dream of my own. To this day I have never identified with a fictional character more than Roth's character and I assume, aspects of Roth himself at a similar age.

It is no wonder that I relished the opportunity to not only write about Portnoy, but to take revenge on his Freudian stereotype analyst, Dr. Spielvogel. As noted in other of my chapters, I too at a young age (28) consulted with a classical Freudian analyst far less experienced than Spielvogel, and was rejected for analysis because of his diagnosis of me as excessively narcissistic and therefore unsuitable as a psychoanalytic patient. After becoming an analyst myself and reflecting on that awful experience, I concluded, narcissistic or not, that my prospective analyst both hated me and was probably somewhat envious of the single life I was leading at the time. To the more senior, Spielvogel's credit, he accepted Portnoy as a patient, though his hatred and envy of his patient was indeed enacted, albeit differently.

I believe that Spielvogel used the Freudian value of reserve and relative silence to sadistically deprive Portnoy. He let Portnoy go on for a full year, multiple times weekly, in his narcissistically entertaining, often hilarious "shtick", without so much as saying one word. When he finally spoke, he totally obliterated his patient by his sadistically pithy, "Now we shall begin." One can translate this comment to read, you have not succeeded in entertaining me, I admire you not at all and you have wasted your time with your narcissistic year-long rant. In totally negating Portnoy, Spielvogel dealt with his envy for his very interesting and much younger patient by claiming a total Oedipal victory, conveying to his patient that the latter is "a nobody." Of course I recognize Spielvogel as a Freudian stereotype, though I assume that Roth must have felt some of what I criticize, in his own real life analysis. In the chapter that follows, I elaborate the theme of the centrality of analysts' subjective feelings toward patients, as well as contrast what I, as an Interpersonally identified analyst, might have done in contrast to this Freudian stereotype.

Chapter 5

INTERPERSONAL PERSPECTIVE:
THE ANALYST'S PARTICIPANT-OBSERVATION
WITH THE SPECIAL PATIENT*

It feels fitting to me that I write this chapter. Though I have always read a great deal of fiction, some of it qualitatively better than *Portnoy,* this still remains the most thoroughly enjoyable novel I have ever read. I first read *Portnoy's Complaint* in 1969, after it was published. Philip Roth is five years older than I but our lives at the time had very much in common. Indeed, our life history also had a number of points in parallel He articulated my personal experience better than anyone had done to that point and did so with hilarious humor. His wit is this book equals that of the two most profound comics of my generation, Lenny Bruce and Woody Allen. Roth touched on many personal truths for me and helped me laugh at myself. That is a wonderful combination of experiences and I am indebted to him for it. I reread *Portnoy* some twenty-three years later in preparation for writing this chapter. Though my own life has changed significantly, I believe I laughed just as much. The experience could not have possibly been as profound the second time around and was distant from some of the issues of relatively young adulthood or very prolonged adolescence, but the psychological wisdom is still formidable.

I would like to share an anecdote. Shortly after reading *Portnoy,* I was having a quiet dinner at a luncheonette on the Upper East Side of Manhattan, a block or two from my own office. Five yards down the counter was Philip Roth and I stared throughout the meal. I knew intuitively that he was on his way to see his analyst, for the district is the home of many practitioners. Extremely curious to see who was this Spielvogel, I followed Roth to a townhouse that indeed was a psychiatrist's office. The name on the doorbell was German or Austrian and indeed had two parts to it, like Spiel and Vogel. I had never heard of this analyst nor did he especially appeal to me from the way he was presented in the novel (I am a very different sort of analyst than the prototypical Freudian blank screen, Spielvogel), but the experience left me feeling even more a part of Roth and his exposition.

Hirsch, I. (1994). Interpersonal perspective: The analyst's participant-observation with the special patient. In: P. Buirski, Ed. *Contemporary Schools of Analytic Therapy.* Northfield, NJ: Jason Aronson, pp. 107–137.

I begin this chapter with a summary of he interpersonal approach to psychoanalysis, and then examine the personality of Alexander Portnoy and discuss how I would work with Portnoy in contrast with how Dr. Spielvogel did.

INTERPERSONAL PSYCHOANALYSIS

Harry Stack Sullivan was the American "psychoanalytic pioneer" who helped shift the emphasis from drive discharge to interpersonal relations as the basic building block of human personality. He is not unique, in that most deviation from this basic classical Freudian position has rotated around that same issue. As more early psychoanalytic correspondence gets published, it is clear that Sandor Ferenczi in particular is a major forerunner of both interpersonal theory and the British object relations school. However, it is evident that Carl Jung, Alfred Adler, and Otto Rank also broke with Freud on the fundamental question of the primacy of sexual and aggressive drives and drive derivations. In contemporary times, relational or non drive psychoanalysis may be overtaking classical Freudian psychoanalysis as the dominant point of view. The term *relational* is an umbrella concept, under which a number of somewhat different psychoanalytic perspectives exist. Interpersonal psychoanalysis, object relations theory, and self psychology are the three dominant subthemes. These positions are different from one another in a variety of important respects. However, each pays minimal attention to drives and emphasizes historical and current relationships with others, and the internalization of those relational configurations, as the key to understanding why people are the way they are.

Interpersonal psychoanalysis, for many, is connected with Sullivan and has probably been the most criticized and/or ignored of the contemporary developments in psychoanalysis. For one, Sullivan's theory represents the only significant psychoanalytic orientation that was not initiated by an analyst who was originally trained as a classical Freudian analyst. This lack of credentials has always hurt his credibility as well as that of the interpersonal school in total. In addition, many have believed that his theory of human development gave short shrift to the intrapsychic world of the individual and that Sullivan's only interest was in the observable relations between people. Some have read him as being positivistic, a variation of American behavioral psychology. These criticisms have some basis, although others have found clear reference to an internalized self in his writing (e.g., his concept of personification). If indeed there is an internalization of one's history of interpersonal relations and expectancies that are dominated by these intrapsychic configurations, the basic psychoanalytic notion of unconscious motivation must be part of the picture. Sullivan was reluctant to focus on speculation about what was inside. He. believed that this has led to reification of posited structures and this in turn had led to theory dominating over observation. He was more comfortable with what could be seen between people and believed that this vantage point minimized an overly abstract and theoretical approach to understanding people.

Regardless of whether or not Sullivan himself sufficiently emphasized the inner world of the individual, unconscious process, and the analysis of transference, it is clear that some of his early colleagues did and that most contemporary interpersonal analysts do so. Clara Thompson, Sullivan's closest colleague, more than anyone else, made the effort to integrate Sullivan into mainstream psychoanalysis. She was classically trained in the United States and much of her writing is an effort to place Sullivan in a historical perspective and adjust his sometimes arcane concepts to more traditional thinking Her work cannot at all be interpreted as antithetical to notions of unconscious motivation. She wrote significant pieces on the concepts of transference and countertransference, comparing the classical and interpersonal meanings of these key concepts. She facilitated the evolution of interpersonal psychoanalysis, which, like all points of view, has changed over years. The writing of the leading interpersonal thinkers such as Edgar Levenson and Benjamin Wolstein, as well as the relational theorist Stephen Mitchell, can clearly be seen as extensions of Clara Thompson's elaboration of Sullivan. Unfortunately, many analysts still associate interpersonal psychoanalysis only with Sullivan and have never read the interpersonal literature beyond his basic writing. It is not unusual to see "new" ideas developed in the field that are almost exact replicas of interpersonal writing, without attribution to that literature. Interpersonal analysts often live with the feeling that the wheel is constantly being rediscovered (see Hirsch 1985).

In addition to a development theory that stresses relationships over drive discharge, interpersonal thinkers developed a theory of therapy that focuses upon the analyst as part of the analytic process. The participant-observation model is a sharp contrast to the blank-screen model. According to the former model, despite every effort toward neutrality and objectivity, the observer cannot help but become part of what is being observed. Just as the laboratory scientist effects the results of the experiment, based on personal bias (often unconscious), the analyst always unwittingly influences the psychoanalytic data of the patient. In the classical Freudian model of Spielvogel, the patient's biologically based drive patterns of libido and aggression are seen to spring forth as givens, quite independent of the analyst's participation. Similarly, child development is primarily a function of a prewired set of drive-related phenomena, with parental participation as a secondary factor. Biology and drives are more significant than psychology and relations with others. The interpersonal developmental model, like the psychoanalytic model, is one of mutual participation.

Freud's seduction theory is an excellent example. Freud originally believed that parental seduction was the cause of child and adult psychopathology as well as childhood sexuality. He then shifted his theory in the early part of the century and because of the shift, psychoanalysis developed along more biological and intrapsychic, as opposed to interpersonal, lines. If Freud had stayed with a modified or metaphorical version of the seduction theory, he would likely have continued to view childhood sexuality not as a biological given but as related to parental seductive feelings or interactions with the child. The interpersonal analyst sees the interaction with the significant others as the initiating factor. This interaction becomes internalized and woven into the fabric of developing personality. Freud viewed instinctual forces within the child as the basis for sexual (and aggressive) feelings toward the parents and toward others. The child as seething cauldron allows for relative innocence on the part of the parents and the analyst.

In the classical analytic situation, the patient's attribution of sexual or aggressive feelings to the analyst is inevitably interpreted as a distortion or a projection. The blank-screen analyst believes that he or she is not a participant but is only an observer. The patient is almost always viewed as inaccurate in attributions and everything reverts to the biologically based drives and their locus within the patient. The analyst does not have to ask if he or she is either initiating or otherwise participating in the patient's experience of the situation. From a classical Freudian perspective, countertransference participation is an error to be corrected. From an interpersonal point of view, countertransference enactment is unavoidable. It is a given that must be used to further the cause of the analysis.

Interpersonal psychoanalysis is in harmony with Freud's abandoned seduction theory. In the psychoanalytic situation, the patient and the analyst unconsciously influence each other. The analysts' participation is unwitting. Participant observation is not a prescription of what to do but a description of what inevitably occurs (Greenberg, 1991) when any two people get together. One of the primary activities of the analytic inquiry is to clarify the nature of that unconscious interaction (Levensen, 1991). The analysis of transference refers not only to what the patient brings to the analytic situation but to the participation of both parties (Gill 1982). The object of analytic inquiry is not the intrapsychic world of the patient *in vacuo* but the field of interaction between analyst and patient. The patient is the more dominant participator and the analyst the more recessive. The patient shapes the world, as all of us do, to conform to the past and to expectancies based on internalized past relationships (Mitchell 1988). This is the interpersonal version of the repetition compulsion. The analyst unwittingly becomes caught up in this system, since the observer cannot help but become part of the observed. To us, the analyst can never really be a screen and is destined to analyze from within the patient-analyst system (Singer 1970).

One can never simply assume that the patient is projecting or distorting. The patient's observations are always seen as at least plausible and reality is not the exclusive property of the would-be objective analyst. From this point of view, there is no objective reality. Interpersonal psychoanalysis has evolved to a perspectivistic or relativistic philosophical position (Hoffman 1983). Because both parties participate, patient and analyst are seen to each have perspectives on truth or reality. These shared psychic realities (Wolstein 1975) are viewed as a more appropriate line to clarity of experience than the more authoritative interpretation. The latter is, more often than not, a declaration made by an objective party to a subjective one. This is more in harmony with the model criticized by Heinrich Racker (1968), as a relationship between a well or objective analyst and a sick or distorting patient.

Spielvogel, the Freudian archetype, does not seem to view either countertransference experience or the relational field as primary areas of inquiry. The study of the productive use of countertransference experience (Epstein and Feiner 1979) was developed by analysts of the interpersonal orientation and the object relations school. Spielvogel believes that his silence successfully maintains his neutral blank screen and that his attitudes and feelings are not unconsciously conveyed to Portnoy nor influence Portnoy.

An interpersonal approach suggests quite the opposite. Just as parents' unspoken attitudes and feelings have profound effect, the analyst often participates without knowing it. From a contemporary interpersonal perspective, psychopathology is a function of rigid loyalty to one's family (Searles 1979). This often dissociated love and loyalty maintains ties to the past, which may be in stark contrast to new experience and new relational configurations. Conflict is ever present but there is no conflict between id and ego or superego. Conflict reflects guilt over leaving behind the ties that bind one to past figures and forging a life that is separate and different in quality. Very often, the more pathological the history, the more rigid and disabling are the loyalties.

In a participant-observation model, the analyst unwittingly but inevitably enters the patient's world and therefore has the opportunity to facilitate new experience and separation from internalized family configurations. Despite efforts at neutrality and objective analytic distance, the analyst becomes caught in the web of the patient's old configurations. The analyst unconsciously acts out with the patient repetitions of the old while consciously working toward new and richer experience. The study of countertransference experience allows the analyst to see how the past is being repeated within the transference-countertransference matrix. If the analyst is viewed as outside of the field, the real risk is that mutual repetition remains unrecognized and unanalyzed. The tendency to interpret the patient's comments about the analyst as transference distortions closes off avenues of self and interactional examination. From an interpersonal viewpoint, the patient moves forward when he or she is optimally aware of initiating old patterns or repetitions, within and outside of the transference. The analytic relationship must break the pattern of repetition on the one hand, but it cannot do so without first becoming caught up in the repetition, on the other hand. This is why the analysis is believed to take place from within the system and why awareness of countertransference enactments is so pivotal to the interpersonal analyst.

The interpersonal school, perhaps more than any other perspective, is antagonistic toward notions of diagnosis and of clear prescriptions of therapeutic technique related to diagnosis. Sullivan's most famous phrase, "We are all more simply human than otherwise," captures much about an analytic attitude that focuses more on unique individuality than on categories derived from a medical model of therapy. Though Sullivan did speak of diagnostic entities and some interpersonal analysts still do, there is only minimal literature in this area.

Harold Searles (1979), strongly influenced by Sullivan's analytic work with schizophrenic patients, perhaps more clearly than anyone else in the literature has drawn similarities between psychotic and neurotic lines of development and experience. He believes that all individuals possess similar personal qualities to varying degrees and that the madness seen in hospitalized schizophrenic patients is quite within all of us. Individual psychopathology reflects learned internalized interpersonal configurations and the patient's adaptation as well as adhesion to consistent familial experience. Regardless of the nature or degree of psychopathology, these patterns are visible in the transference and can be worked with in the transference. The patient is viewed as the architect of his or her world. Contemporary experience, the transference relationship included, is ultimately shaped to conform to the patient's past experience with and expectancies of others. Notions of will and existential thinking in general are strongly reflected in the interpersonal paradigm. The contemporary interpersonal analyst is likely to devote considerable effort to the patient-analyst relationship as a repetition of and perpetuation of earlier experience. As Searles has made very clear, all people strive to repeat their problematic history and therefore, metaphorically love their own pathology. On the other hand, people are viewed as striving toward self-actualization, and the tension between these two personal aims, regardless of diagnosis, is universal.

The question of diagnosis is significant here. Most analysts, if they were forced to make a diagnosis of Portnoy, would probably call him narcissistic. This is of particular importance because different analytic schools have very different ideas about how to work with narcissistic patients, or even whether or not narcissism is a clear diagnostic category in the first place. A very personal revelation is pertinent here. I earlier referred to perceived similarities between myself and Roth, particularly back at the time of publication of' *Portnoy's Complaint.* I had at the time recently finished my doctorate in psychology and was looking forward in two years to begin psychoanalytic training. I wished to begin my own personal analysis and consulted a rather traditional classical analyst for that purpose. After our interview he told me that he could not see me in analysis per se, since he viewed my problems as basically not neurotic but narcissistic. Without going into further detail, until I went for a second consultation elsewhere, I feared I had no future as an analyst myself. Of course, I feared· much more; essentially I saw a loveless life ahead of me.

Spielvogel, to his credit, is intent on analyzing Portnoy despite his narcissism. This issue is relevant because historically, psychoanalysts have viewed individuals who are considered narcissistic as not analyzable. This belief started with Freud and the concept of the transference neurosis. The neurotic individual was seen as sufficiently related to others to engage intensely in the transference, while the narcissistic person was seen as too affectively withdrawn to do this. Psychoanalysis developed along a two species line: diagnosed neurotics were analyzed and non neurotics or those with too much narcissistic involvement were not. Little distinction was made between the most extreme form of narcissistic involvement like psychotic depression or schizophrenia and milder forms of the narcissistic characteristic such as I or Portnoy displayed. Interpersonal analysts were the only group of analysts that did not develop a special technique to work with narcissistic patients and/or that excluded them from analytic consideration.

Object relations analysts in Great Britain and in South America have never excluded people as analytic patients based on diagnostic criteria, as have classical analysts, but the former have developed different techniques to work with non neurotic patients. This is similar in spirit to the American self-psychologists. As an orientation, self-psychology developed out of classical psychoanalysis with the express purpose of broadening technique to include work with non psychotic, narcissistic patients. For them, Portnoy would be a dream. Like the object relations analysts, the self-psychologists purport to adhere to classical techniques for neurotic patients and their own revised technique for narcissistic patients. Diagnosis is thus pivotal in their thinking.

In essence, both schools believe that narcissistic patients suffer from early deficiencies and before analysis of transference in the usual sense can take place, the analyst must make up for these early deficiencies by providing a nourishing, somewhat gratifying analyzing environment. Self-psychologists and object relations analysts speak somewhat differently about this but they agree that early deficiencies must be compensated by the analyst. Traditional classical analysts, by and large, write this off as supportive psychotherapy and maintain the analyzable versus non analyzable dichotomies. Interpersonal analysts, with their Sullivanian roots in working with schizophrenic patients, have not agreed with this distinction from the outset. There is no distinctive technique within interpersonal psychoanalysis that addresses clearly different modes of analysis with different diagnostic categories. Many contemporary analysts, following the lead of Searles (1979), Merton Gill (1982), and Edgar Levenson (1991), believe that acute attention to the transference-countertransference matrix allows for psychoanalysis to be applicable to a very broad range of patients. Clearly, Spielvogel was more of that mind in working traditionally with Portnoy than was the analyst with whom I originally consulted.

Narcissism, from an interpersonal perspective, indeed is a broad characteristic. The pure quality of narcissism is most widely known to be characterized by vanity, exhibitionism, arrogance, grandiosity, and self-absorption. The other person tends to be used to make the narcissist feel good, and well-being depends upon receiving a continuously adequate quantity of positive regard. The other is not usually viewed as whole person and is generally used as supplier of nutrients. The basis for this is an absence of a sense of inner strength or substance, an emptiness that leaves one vulnerable to annihilation. The extremely narcissistic individual does not generally feel a clear and meaningful sense of self at the core or center. How others view this individual is likely to be taken as a reading of the self. This is why the prototypical narcissist so desperately searches for positive regard. If admiration is not forthcoming, the result may very well be flight or deep depression based on confrontation with feelings of nothingness. Dependency is often profound but is not consciously experienced as such, for the feeling is much feared. Other people are important for the provision they supply and thus are fragmented as individuals. To be personally dependent or to feel conscious love for a whole other person is to risk annihilation.

As with all qualities, narcissism rarely exists in pure form and is always on a continuum. Everyone is narcissistic to some degree. If psychopathology is partially viewed as impairment of the ability to love, narcissism can be seen as an element in all problems in living. It is a way in which everyone protects him or herself from full presence with the other; it is a degree of personal inaccessibility. One of the more common, everyday forms of this is self-absorption. There are different modes of self-absorption. Among the more common are depression and dysphoric self- concern, ruminative or other ideational preoccupation, strong vanity and selfish pursuit of desires. These qualities exist on a continuum within people representing the highest to the lowest levels of psychological functioning. The interpersonal analyst tends to think of narcissism as descriptive of these personal qualities and not so much as a diagnostic entity. It characterizes ways people are with themselves and in their relational world. From this perspective, it is, therefore, possible to function quite outstandingly in one's work, as did our Portnoy, while at the same time being miserably unhappy and destructive to others in one's personal relationships.

In thinking of narcissism in this way, it is obvious that narcissistic characteristics cannot possibly emerge from one particular etiological source. From the perspective of many object relations and self-psychology theorists, narcissistic characteristics are exclusively a deficiency disease. The interpersonal analyst is more likely to think in relativistic terms. Narcissistic personality traits are not all-or-none qualities and are likely to be multiply determined. For example, many people who exhibit strong narcissistic qualities come from families in which one or another parent was overinvolved, in contrast to depriving. In a family constellation where a parent infantalizes or overprotects, or overly admires the child, there may readily develop an overblown sense of self-importance and grandiosity. This may leave the individual somewhat unprepared for all of the rigors of life. They may expect to be equally loved and admired everywhere and have little sense of reciprocity in relationships. When others are less loving or less tolerant than the family, feelings of emptiness, depression, and insubstantiality may become acute. From this developmental pattern, the self-absorbed or inflated individual clings to his or her internalized family constellation as a way of maintaining a sense of comfort as well as providing the family members with what they require.

Many people who achieve a great deal in life come from backgrounds where they were overly indulged. They were viewed, as was Freud himself, as the most special child in the family and the primary source of familial pride and esteem. In many respects this is a wonderful message to be brought up with, for this specialness is often carried forward into the world and reenacted with other people and with institutions. It can make for a charmed life, where one continues to have the knack of getting what one wants from the world. This quality leads to trouble when separation issues are not resolved or when little is expected in return by the family. Analysts can easily fall into countertransference love with a patient who was so special to his or her family. Some people are blessed with the ability to be most universally admired and respected. If this is not analyzed, as it often is not with some high-achieving patients, the analytic procedure is simply a repetition of the past. When the patient, despite being genuinely admired by the analyst, is sufficiently self-absorbed, it is more difficult for the analyst to feel this unambivalent countertransference love. Many have written of the analytic difficulty of coming face to face with patients who do not give or who do not reciprocate. Analysts can easily feel useless and deprived and talionically withdraw into personal depression as a way to self-nourish.

Another reciprocal reaction is anger and subtle forms of attack. This could take the form of excessive silence or harsh confrontation, depending on one's personal and/or theoretical bent. When functioning best, the interpersonal analyst maintains an evenly hovering attention to both transference and countertransference experience and is able to use the latter to enrich the analysis. The interpersonal analyst, because of the way the theory informs, is unable to have the luxury of existing outside of the intersubjective field.

PORTNOY THE PERSON

Alexander Portnoy is too special to his mother and some of this is based on her own selfish possessiveness of him. To his mother, Portnoy is perfection. He is beautiful and brilliant in the same way I imagine Freud was to his mother. In comparison with his depressed and struggling father, Mrs. Portnoy's son is a god. He seems to have won his mother, over his only male rival, hands down. He hardly needed to do anything beyond simply existing. He was so nourished by his mother that he almost could not help but become brilliant. He was fed with all the nutrients that make one live up to inherited potential for intelligence: attention, attunement, verbal engagement, and consistent outpourings of love.

The best moments of mother's life were Portnoy's preschool years. They stayed home together and talked all day. She never noticed the time go by as she did her household chores and talked with her precious son. Portnoy's sister, like father, is bland in every way, in comparison. For mother, her daughter is ancillary, while her son is her whole life.

Mother is ubiquitous. Portnoy cannot move without his mother being there. Even his first grade teacher, whom he adores, is reincarnated as mother in an elaborate romantic fantasy. Mother is a far more complete person than father. She appears stronger in health and in character, less depressed and more lively and intelligent. One has the impression that were it she working instead of plodding papa, the family would be more economically comfortable. A boy can feel wonderful about himself when so thoroughly loved by such an able and strong woman.

Portnoy carries this feeling forward in life; he can do no wrong in the eyes of women and in his professional achievements. His brilliance is thoroughly nurtured and he is the smartest and most verbally clever wherever he is. Women admire him as his mother adored him. He expects this and he repeats his centrality and his specialness in his academic and professional life and with women. This is consistent until his fateful encounter with the Israeli women who view his narcissism as effeminate self·indulgence.

Portnoy has little personal sense of reciprocation in male-female relatedness. Women exist for his satisfaction and pleasure, not as entities in and of themselves. They are present to satisfy, desire, and admire him, like mother. They can be faceless and interchangeable, like sister. He is markedly dependent on women but not on a particular woman. Any one will do as long as she can adore him and is exciting sexually. Women can be exciting by virtue of their physical appearance or by possessing certain attributes, particularly social status. His interest in women has little to do with their personal qualities.

The down side of mother for Portnoy is the selfish power she has over him and the guilt she evokes regarding thoughts of separation. While it is enormously enhancing to be so loved and admired, mother's intentions are not only in her son's interest. Mother Portnoy wishes to possess her son entirely. He is so far superior to her husband that her desire for him is boundless. She does not want him to lead a separate life and to truly love another woman. This is her narcissism, though it takes the disguised form of giving to her son. In excessive giving she is also taking possession. Separation from mother produces profound guilt in the protagonist. He has thoroughly internalized his mother and everything that would make him his own unique person produces con-siderable conflict.

Portnoy's life is a strugle betwenn being good for his mother and being bad as a way of shedding or gaining control over mother. He con-sistently struggles between being a good boy and a bad boy. Bad refers to independent strivings, which Portnoy needs to exaggerate in order to maintain some semblance of separateness. To be an overtly passive and dependent good boy is a death sentence. In his own life, his arch-good-ness is exemplified by his memory of helping his mother and her friends sort out their mah-jongg tiles. He is a boy so good that he loses his "boyness" and acts like a girl. He is a preschooler doing the house-hold chores with mother in her happiest moments. If he maintains his manifest goodness there are two logical consequences in his fantasy: suicide and homosexuality.

The ultimate good boy is his neighbor, Ronald. Ronald was so thoroughly dominated and castrated that when he committed suicide as an adolescent, he attached a note, pinned to his neatly pressed shirt, indicating that one of his mother's friends had called. The ultimate mama's boy nerd does the good-boy thing even as he finally tells his mother that he cannot take her any more. The only private place he can find away from mother is his death. Portnoy's homosexual fantasy has him living the life of a woman with his effeminate male lover on Fire Island. They cook and keep house just like mother. In this scenario, Portnoy is totally identified with his powerful mother. He is a woman, playing mah-jongg and cooking and gossiping just like mother and her friends.

If Portnoy is not bad and rebellious, he feels he cannot prevent one of the above configurations. His badness in adulthood takes the form of extreme efforts to take control of his mother through the sexual subjugation of women. His rebellion in adolescence is record breaking masturbation and sexual preoccupation. Even for an adolescent, Portnoy's masturbatory feats are impressive. His relationship with his omnipresent mother is eroticized. She is all over him. He masturbates profusely because he is overstimulated by her but also because it is his way of gaining control over his desire. He refers to his penis ("wong") as the only thing he could call his own. He takes it in hand to prevent his mother from taking it over entirely. Jerking off, as obsessive as it is for him, is largely an autonomous act. It both reflects living close to a sexy mom and not allowing mom to take charge of his sexual organ and his total self. Every time he masturbates or "fucks the family dinner," he is saying that he is both enmeshed in the family and stroking toward autonomy. If he stops for a moment, his sexuality and his personal center belongs entirely to mother.

It is the norm in the neighborhood for the mothers to refer to their sons as their lovers, and this is brazenly and openly done in front of their dull, pedestrian, constricted husbands. By making sure his penis never leaves the grip of his fist, he is also helping to preserve his father as someone whose penis may be available for mother. Portnoy is not competitive with father. If mother desired father's penis, Portnoy would be able to ease up flogging his own.

As he gets older, Portnoy's badness continues along the same lines. He maintains his autonomy by using women to stroke or suck upon his penis. These women must be different from mother. They cannot be Jewish, for one, and they have to possess something toward which he strives. They may come from a higher social class, a radically different culture, or simply be extraordinarily beautiful or sexy. Portnoy repeats his specialness with each one of his women but he also turns the tables on them. He uses these women far more than they use him. Unlike mother, these women never control and dominate him. Portnoy exploits his women, takes all he can get from them and then leaves. It is an analogue to adolescent masturbation; each conquest like each independent stroke leaves him feeling a notch more free of mother's grip.

Portnoy enters analysis for a few good reasons. He recognizes that he is unable to love and that he treats women cruelly. He is afraid that he will spend the rest of his life in flight from mother and in relentless pursuit of sexual conquest. In addition to this very central fear, he also suffers from considerable guilt. I believe that he is genuinely guilty about the way he treats women but he is also neurotically guilty over not giving mother what she wants. At age 33, mother desires another Portnoy in the form of a grandchild. The good boy Portnoy who is reliable and compulsive, and neat and clean, just like mother, is way overdue regarding this responsibility. He has done everything he was supposed to do in school and professionally to make mother proud, but in this realm he hurts her deeply. She views his serial pursuit of non-Jewish women as a rejection of herself. Indeed this is so but the good boy is in considerable conflict over continuing this. Portnoy finally begins analysis because he meets his "mother" in the form of two Israeli women with whom he is impotent. In going to Israel, Portnoy is attempting to return to mother and do what a good Jewish boy should do. However, the Israeli women he meets are too close to mother, either by virtue of being very Jewish or by being very strong. The sexual virtuoso cannot perform. Sexual performance has saved him both from suicide and from homosexuality and now he has lost his erection and his primary source of perceived strength and autonomy. He enters analysis, desperate to regain his potency in the form of being a special patient, just like he was mother's special boy. I also believe that he begins analysis for the two other and more constructive reasons I noted. By the time he is ready to start therapy I think that Portnoy recognizes his tortured battle with guilt as well as his repeated inability to truly give to another. If he were only commencing analysis to regain his potency under the admiring eye of his analyst-mother, he would indeed be more thoroughly narcissistic than I view him as being.

So much to say about mother and so comparatively little to say about father. It is tragic for all concerned that Portnoy's mother loves him so much more passionately than she does her husband. If only father were more positively prominent, mother might have left little Portnoy alone somewhat more. Father stands out mostly in the negative. He is pictured as hard-working but barely successful, and that because he does the "shit work" that nobody else will do. "Shit" dominates father's life. He is perennially constipated and, when not working, inevitably on the toilet. He is always discontented either about his bowels or his work and has very little, beyond a reliability and a good work ethic, to give to Portnoy. Portnoy never had to struggle to defeat father and win mother's love. Father was defeated originally by his far stronger and more capable wife and by her idea of a son, even before Portnoy was born. Portnoy is in the sunlight and his depressed father is in the shithouse, from the moment Portnoy is a light in his mother's eye.

The interpersonal analyst does not necessarily view the oedipal struggle as the central theme in human neurotic development. There are some families in which this prototype indeed does seem to have significance and others where only a stretch would make the data fit the theory. Interpersonal analysts have been critical of Freudian theory as too strong a theory, leading to situations where actual unique experience is violated in order for the data to fit the strong theory. In Portnoy's family, mother and son are a pair, as are father and daughter. In many respects, Portnoy is more identified with his competent and spirited mother than with his depressed, bland father. I do not see active rivalry in the Portnoy family, for the ground rules and territories are clearly mapped out. Sister and father are muted in the background or in the bathroom, and mother and son are on stage together.

It is important for Portnoy to be different from father and to compensate for his defeated self. He assumes a somewhat negative identification with father; striving to be opposite to him as much as possible. Portnoy is a climber; he wants to be first in his class, an important man in New York City and the darling of all the women. He wants women from the upper echelons of WASP culture. Father slaved for the upper class Protestants and Portnoy wants to be accepted into their world and to sexually degrade their daughters. In part, he is trying to transcend father and, in part, gain revenge for his father. If Portnoy is viewed as a nonentity by a woman, as he was by the second Israeli woman, he is deflated and feels just like his flatulent, toilet-bound father.

Portnoy does not relate well to men. His esteem comes from his perennially being first in his class and from the love of women. There is virtually nothing in the novel that describes male to male relatedness in any way. It does not seem as if he had truly close friends, although he was interesting enough and athletic enough not to have been an outsider in the world of boys and men. Nonetheless, I sense a subtle bond between Portnoy and father beyond the negative identification. I believe that Portnoy feels his father's depression and fadedness and appreciates his pluck in not bailing out all together. Father is a survivor and he moves along with minimal nutrition. He feeds himself and is steady and reliable. His stubborn strength, in this regard, is admired by Portnoy and bodes well for his own survival in the face of narcissistic loss. Portnoy also knows that he is loved by his father and has never doubted this. There is something very gentle in the man, for he never has retaliated for his son's early winning away of the love of his wife. Father is not a jealous father or a vindictive father. He genuinely wants the best for his son. Though there is not much open affection, I sense that Portnoy knows that he is not only admired by mother but loved and admired by father as well.

The negative side of all of this enmeshment, once again, is guilt. Portnoy is in conflict about separating from father as well as from mother. Father is a simple man and cannot comprehend Portnoy's complicated, contemporary ways. As long as Portnoy remains unfulfilled as a person, he maintains a strong relational tie to father. Portnoy is successful and admired but he is never free or happy. Rumination is his form of constipation. Portnoy cannot live relaxedly or find his own idiom. However much he achieves in contrast with father, he is tied to father on the toilet bowl of rumination and dysphoria. Thus, Portnoy's psychopathology is not only related to his incestuous ties to his mother but to his adhesion to father's dysphoria. In this most unfortunate way, Portnoy is profoundly identified with father. The two of them are always worried about something and never experience contentment for longer than a bowel movement or an orgasm.

It is interesting that Portnoy's metaphor for true fulfillment in life is playing out in center field, with wide open space between himself and everyone else. His affinity for center field, embodied by the heroic Brooklyn Dodger, Duke Snider, reflects Portnoy's potential resolution. For one, Portnoy's father did play softball with the men in the community and sports was one form of connection with father and freedom from mother. Sports was an area of achievement that mother had no part of or interest in. In playing baseball or softball, he was more like father than mother. He found an ideal father in the handsome Dodger center fielder, and for those moments he did not find it necessary to ruminate, achieve, or masturbate. He could relax in the privacy of center field with green grass all around and no human intrusion in proximity. This was his space; dad was idealized and mother could not get near him. If Portnoy could have this space as something integral and enduring in his life, frantic masturbation and compensatory sexual exhibitionism would be unnecessary.

It is likely that Portnoy will always be a man that needs some reasonable distance from people. Intimacy will probably always be difficult. On the other hand, he has incorporated enough love from both parents so it is possible he can be capable of non guilty love and be a man of great achievement in the work or creative realm. If Portnoy is able to control the distance and tempo of his relationships, as he is able to do out in center field, he may be in a position to let go of his penis and become a reciprocating or generous person, to some degree. This proximity issue will be a central one in the transference with any analyst, as will the question of the admiring versus the depriving stance of the analyst.

From my description of Portnoy as a person, it is probably clear that I do not see drives as central in human development. With all of his sexual obsession and activity, and all of the eroticism between Portnoy and his mother, it is easy to formulate a drive-based description of his development. This is most likely Spielvogel's point of view, judging from the blank-screen analytic stance that goes hand in hand with a one-person drive psychology. It is evident from my reading of the data that I do not view the protagonist's drives as initiating the family configuration. I am more inclined to see the significant others, mother and father, as the precipitating force in Portnoy's intensely sexualized relationships. Portnoy does not have excessive drives, but an excessive mother who both over stimulates him and controls him. Mother was the cause, if you will, of her son's incestuous feelings, sexual preoccupation, and defensive need for control and domination over women. His perversions were not part of his biology but a reaction to real, external experience with the primary woman in his life.

Similarly, I view Portnoy's narcissism as a function of his overblown centrality in the family, more so than libido turned inward or deficient loving. Portnoy was too loved or too special, albeit mother's love was selfish as much as it was generous. He was no more preoccupied with himself than was his mother with him. Thus, his narcissism, also, was based on real, external interpersonal experience that gradually became internalized.

I have made an effort to describe Portnoy and his development from an interpersonal perspective. However, other non drive or relational theorists may indeed understand Portnoy in a very similar way. That is, all relational points of view see human development as primarily a function of consistent, interpersonal experience. There is less likelihood than with Freudian theory to see individuals developing along clearly outlined lines or stages. Theory per se plays far less of a role in understanding the person, and the descriptions may sound more like that of a lay person than someone using a technical or scientific language. Many interpersonal analysts downplay developmental theory as part of an effort to avoid stereotyped, theory-based views of people, and this is true for some other relational perspectives as well. The interpersonal psychoanalytic theory of therapeutic action, however, is somewhat distinct from the other relational positions and quite different from Spielvogel's traditional blank screen.

PORTNOY IN ANALYSIS

Spielvogel, the Freudian blank screen, observed Portnoy for a long period of time before telling him that he had not yet begun. Why was he silent for so long and why did he finally and pithily tell Portnoy that all his output was essentially meaningless bullshit? Classical technique justified Spielvogel's silence. The patient is supposed to reveal himself, the transference to unwind. When the transference is solidly and clearly developed and the patient has been free from analytic intrusion, it may then be time to interpret. Spielvogel no doubt perceived Portnoy's exhibitionist narcissism from the initial session. He watched it repeat and repeat in the same form, while presuming to stay outside of the picture, as the blank screen dictates. I contend that Spielvogel was not outside of the picture at all, and that his silence helped him delude himself that he was. Spielvogel was watching a brilliant, manic, exhibitionistic display from a most witty and entertaining patient. I imagine that, indeed, the analyst enjoyed Portnoy sometimes, or maybe frequently. Spielvogel also observed someone who he felt was narcissistically talking to himself and not to the analyst. In other words, he felt that Portnoy was consistently masturbating in front of him and asking him to admire his beautiful strokes.

Based on Spielvogel's one comment, I believe that he eventually grew to hate Portnoy. His comment was like a retaliation: "You think you are so special but you have been saying nothing all of this time—wasting your own precious sperm." Spielvogel probably felt that Portnoy just wanted his awe and admiration. Self-psychological technique would lead to a recognition of this desire for admiration and a likely decision to provide it for the patient. Spielvogel probably did provide it, unwittingly, but at some point felt unreciprocated and himself deprived. He watched his own countertransference but did not monitor it carefully. If he did, he would probably not have so devastatingly retaliated when he finally said something to his patient. From my perspective, he had to be destructively furious at this selfish, grandiose patient of his. Why else would he so thoroughly have wiped out everything that Portnoy had conveyed? I think he was telling Portnoy that this bland old man will not be treated like his father or his sister and will not admire him like his mother. Spielvogel was. making the statement that he was more potent than his patient; he can castrate with one brief stroke. It was father's and sister's revenge for a life history of blandness and second-class existence. Spielvogel was not passive or sweet like father. He did not love his patient and he was not going down in defeat to this fascinating younger man. Spielvogel was the fierce rival Portnoy never experienced at home; he was the Germanic punitive agent in contrast with Portnoy's passive, *shtetl* Jew, inadequate father.

This blank-screen analyst is far from outside of the transference-countertransference matrix. He superficially acts like a neutral and objective observer but enacts his countertransference feelings with a fury. If Spielvogel did not conceive of himself as a blank screen, he would have recognized that his feelings were not being subsumed for the treatment but enacted or acted out within the analysis. This is inevitable and not problematic if recognized. Spielvogel's theory impedes his recognition of countertransference enactment and so it occurs anyway, under the guise of bona fide Freudian analysis, and reflects the absolute worst abuse of classical technique. Not all Freudian analysts are as smug as Spielvogel. Only an enraged analyst would be as severe as this one. Spielvogel had infinite opportunities to convey to Portnoy that the latter was exhibiting, competing, talking at and not to him, profoundly self-absorbed, using his intelligence to obscure his feelings, viewing the analyst as a bland nonentity father or an admiring mother or a cock-sucking girlfriend. If he had done any of this at any point, he might not have so stubbornly sat on his anger until it tersely exploded. Spielvogel was constipated on the toilet, like father. He was so angry at this special younger man's ability to defecate that he finally let go and drowned his patient in an exploding interpretation. He rubbed Portnoy's face in it.

The outdated traditional concept of resistance also lends credibility to Spielvogel's technique. He conceptualizes Portnoy as being in resistance by virtue of his narcissistic exhibitionist display. Since resistance has dominated, the analysis has not yet begun. What, however, is nonresistance, or the correct material? Should Portnoy have been more out of control, nonsensical, freely associative? Maybe so, in some ideal world, but this is not who this patient is as a person. Portnoy was being himself and showing himself in the playground of the analytic relationship. What more or better can a patient do but be himself? This manic, self-absorbed, over ideational man was indeed being those ways in the here-and-now of the transference. The concept of resistance implies that the patient is doing something wrong. It is an evaluative notion that is implicitly, if not explicitly, critical and judgmental.

Should Portnoy be somebody other than who he is? Would this make him a good patient instead of such a hostile, self-aggrandizing one? Invoking the notion of resistance is tantamount to telling someone to stop being who he is and to be more like what the analyst wants. It is one thing if the patient excessively misses sessions, comes late, does not pay bills, and so forth. These enactments threaten the basic structure of the relationship and physically impede analytic engagement. Portnoy is talking and pointedly conveying to his analyst one of the essences of who he is. Of course, he is not showing all of himself. Were he to do that, he would probably be finished with his analysis. He is vividly displaying his defensive character structure and therefore doing all that an analyst could ever want his patient to do. Unfortunately, Spielvogel sits on his feelings and develops a hatred for Portnoy via a prolonged, judgmental silence, followed by a devastating talionic blow.

Interpersonal analysts are not more prone to love their patients or less prone to feel destructively hateful than are Freudian analysts. They are not nicer, kinder, gentler, or more decent human beings. The advantage of the participant-observation model over the blank screen model lies in analysts' greater likelihood of awareness of both countertransference feelings and enactments, particularly the latter. Were I in Spielvogel's place, I never would have waited so long to speak. Quite in contrast, I probably would have verbally intervened very early, perhaps even in the initial session. As exemplified by Gill, I would have likely addressed the transference themes as they emerged. I hope that I would have pointed out to Portnoy that he was talking at me and not to me, that he was being exhibitionistic and looking for my admiration. I would have told him that his words and ideas and his brilliant mind often obscured his genuine feelings. When I was feeling admiring or awestruck by his brilliance or his incredible wit, I would have conveyed that he was trying to impress me or perhaps have me adore him as do his mother and his girlfriends. At times when I felt overwhelmed, competitively infuriated, bland in comparison to his sexual exploits, and so forth, I may have pointed out that he probably views me as similar to father or sister. I would likely address his disrespect for me and his powerful desire to be different than my depressed, constipated self. In short, my comments would be guided by my reflected upon countertransference feelings. They would not normally be disclosures of my feelings but a trans-position of my feelings and enactments into a description of what I believed was transpiring in the here and now. In addition, to the extent that the here and now countertransference field resembled historical patterns of interaction, the links of similarity in pattern would be made. My comments would be more descriptive than interpretive. They would likely address the "what" of the field rather than the "why." The analysis would consist of moving back and forth from the field of the here and now playground to history and to current life, lining up the consistent patterns of interaction.

From my perspective, there is no value in waiting as long as Spielvogel did to intervene. The transference themes emerge immediately and if analysis of transference is the *sine qua non* of the process, the best road to it is to address transference themes from the beginning. In addition to this being more economical in time, it is less mystifying. The silent analyst makes himself into someone more profound than he actually is. It gives too much power to the analyst, who, after such verbal deprivation, sounds like a genius when he says anything. Spielvogel is Germanic, authoritarian, and judgmental, and his technique easily fits these personal characteristics. The interpersonal analytic philosophy is more democratic. It is a two-person psychology and not a relationship between a sick, distorting patient and a well, neutral, and objective analyst. Analytic commentary, from the beginning, more visibly portrays the analyst as visible and fallible. Comments are not premeditatively for this purpose or to have this effect but are an artifact of the method of working. This lends itself to a view of analyst as co-participant in contrast to expert or authority. The patient is more encouraged to comment on the nature of the content and form of the analysts' participation.

In the blank-screen method, the patient's commentaries tend to be more toward the analyst's depriving silence while the participant-observation method stimulates a wider range of observation on the patient's part. The freedom for the analyst to address the here and now themes from the beginning serves as a control for the buildup of feelings within the analyst. If Portnoy's anger, selfishness, disrespect, and so forth are pointed out early, it is less likely that these feelings will fester within the analyst, as they did with Spielvogel. Even within classical analytic circles, there has been a shift away from· the concept of transference neurosis. This is the concept that most validated long periods of silence in order to facilitate an ultimate transference crescendo. Most Freudian analysts currently believe that intense transference experience exists on and off throughout the entire analysis, in contrast with the one period of transference neurosis. From a more current perspective, the active pointing out of the transference themes from the early stages of analysis onward has many advantages over Spielvogel's archaic technique. This approach has always been characteristic of most contemporary inter-personal analysts.

Despite every effort at neutrality and objectivity as well as the intention to constructively use countertransference feelings, analytic enactment is inevitable. The analyst unwittingly plays out with the patient the fundamental patterns in the patient's interactional life and becomes enmeshed in the system. Analysis thus occurs from within the system.

Were I Portnoy's analyst, I would have viewed him as special from the beginning. His brilliance, wit, and professional accomplishments would likely have dazzled me. I am especially excited by humor, and I know that I would have laughed with Portnoy on many occasions. Portnoy led a life of being special—in his family, in academic and professional circles, and with women. He did everything he could to invoke this feeling in his analyst, and although I can only assume Spielvogel felt it at some time, I am certain I would have. I very possibly would have become lost in this specialness, looking forward to vastly entertaining as well as poignant session after session. Were I aware of Portnoy being so special to me, I would have commented on the issue of specialness. More than likely, however, I would have not articulated it to myself and simply enacted with him, some facsimile of all those who have been so admiring. He most likely would have loved my response (which would be in tone or form, not in conscious intent) and escalated his performance as he actually did with Spielvogel.

As Portnoy became more grossly manic and exhibitionistic, and his repertoire became more obviously a comic shtick, I might have woken up to having been part of a narcissistic experience. I would have felt deceived and tricked. What I thought was a genuine connection to me was really an unrelated show. I was nothing but an adoring mother, having fun during my workday, admiring my favorite patient. I did not exist as an entity except to service this dynamo patient with blow jobs. Or I may have recognized that I was a bland father or sister in comparison to this star. From this role, I could have felt like a competitive fool, a loser, sitting on the toilet while the hero is holding court on center stage or in center field. He was Duke Snider and I was a substitute player in the minor leagues. Degradation breeds the fury of the underclass. From both positions-the deceived mother or lover, and the loser father or sister, my awestruck admiration would likely have congealed to rage. I believe this was the revenge and hatred of Spielvogel.

I hope that I would have addressed the above themes as I was aware of experiencing them, and thus avoided massive talionic retaliation. Addressing these themes means using the feelings about which I am aware to point out what I see transpiring in the analytic field or playground; for example, "It seems to me that the only thing you value about me is admiring you as did your mother and your girlfriends" or "It appears that in your eyes, I am a dull, bland, and ineffective man, as was your father and your sister in contrast with you," or "If I am not excited to see you or don't find you very special, you feel as devastated as you did with your Israeli woman."

My efforts to directly address these themes from within the analytic dyad have two major purposes. The first reflects the emotional impact of the patient's awareness of transference issues in the immediate, and the second, the effort to form a new relational configuration. For all non classical analysts, insight is only part of what is mutative. The analytic relationship certainly does provide increased awareness; the more it takes place in the here and now, the better. This, however, is never enough. The analyst must also develop with the patient a relationship different in quality from what has been historically internalized. This new relationship is not prescribed in advance or consciously pursued as such. If so, it would be too artificial and inauthentic. To be valuable, the new relationship must occur naturally; an artifact almost of analytic inquiry, observation, interpretation, and so forth. In the process of trying to clarify experience, the analyst works out of the repetitions that are so compelling. When I became aware of how I was caught up in Portnoy's world, my use of countertransference would aid me in trying to emerge from my enmeshment. It is the analyst's effort to try to climb out of his embeddedness in the patient's world that ultimately leads to new and mutative experience.

What may have eventually emerged from my consistent monitoring of transference themes, as I saw them develop from the very beginning? I believe that Portnoy's "cure" would lie in my ability to work out of my awestruck, admiring response, my depressed and deflated response, and my angry and retaliatory response. Were I able to do all of this in the context of my analytic inquiry and observation, Portnoy's characteristic way of being in the world may have shifted and this movement internalized. The cured Portnoy ideally would be less self-involved and more related, less guilty about his achievements or assets, and more able to tolerate his depressed or inadequate aspects. Portnoy, I suspect, will always be somewhat narcissistic, overly ideational, and emotionally distant. He and I may have become teammates, as long as I respected his position in center field where he could be a bit of a hero and maintain a comfortable distance from me. With all of my interest in the here and now transference, I would have to be cautious not to smother the man, and to leave him enough grass to roam alone.

There are no brilliant analysts and no interpretation is a breakthrough. The process is long and difficult and it is quite clear that no particular analytic technique has proven to be superior over any other. Every analyst must do what personally makes most sense and this of course has much to do with every analyst's transference identification with his or her own analyst. Spielvogel may recover from his destructive hatred; one awful comment does not spoil an analysis. I would have loved Portnoy as I loved Roth's book, and I would have hated Portnoy as did the first analyst I consulted hate me. I would have loved to work with Portnoy, since in love or hate he is so talented and in so many ways quite special. I undoubtedly would be intimidated by his being so special and so much more brilliant and witty than myself. The key for his successful analysis with me would be to learn to live with my experience of inferiority to him and to not be either a simple admiring fool or a vengeful tyrant.

REFERENCES

Epstein, L., and Feiner, A. (1979). *Countertransference.* New York: Jason Aronson.

Gill, M. (1982). *The Analysis of Transference.* Vol. 1. New York: International Universities Press.

Greenberg,]. (1991). *Oedipus and Beyond.* Cambridge, MA: Harvard University Press.

Hirsch, I. (1985). The rediscovery of the advantages of the participant-observation model. *Psychoanalysis and Contemporary Thought* 8:441–459.

Hoffman, I. (1983). The patient as interpreter of the analyst experience. *Contemporary Psychoanalysis* 19:389–422.

Levenson, E. (1991). *The Purloined Self.* New York: Contemporary Psychoanalytic Books.

Mitchell, S. (1988). *Relational Concepts in Psychoanalysis.* Cambridge, MA: Harvard University Press.

Racker, H. (1968). *Transference and Countertransference.* New York: International Universities Press.

Searles, H. (1979). *Countertransference and Related Subjects.* New York: International Universities Press.

Singer, E. (1970). *Key Concepts in Psychotherapy.* New York: Basic Books.

Wolstein, B. (1975). Countertransference: the psychoanalyst's shared experience and inquiry with his patient. *Journal of the American Academy of Psychoanalysis* 3:77–89.

Prologue to Chapter 6:
CHANGING CONCEPTIONS OF UNCONSCIOUS

In the context of a supervisory consultation, Dr. Judith Roth and I found ourselves struggling to understand what was motivating her patient to consistently engage in ways that did not seem in her best interest. We both reflexively began looking for what mental contents had been repressed, though neither of us identified with the traditional Freudian idea that the unconscious consisted largely of unacceptable and endogenously based drive states and the compromises that regulated these. We became aware that the classical Freudian literature had, so to speak, cornered the market in efforts to comprehend both what existed in the unconscious and how this influenced how people engaged in the world of other people. That is, when searching the psychoanalytic literature for specific references to unconscious motivation, there was little to find in either the Interpersonal writing or the broad spectrum of Relational literature. The article that follows represents our effort to write about the unconscious and unconscious motivation in a way that reflected more contemporary trends in our field. In this vein we tried to flesh-out what unconscious refers to from the perspective of the Middle School of Object Relations and it's partner, Self-Psychology and the Interpersonal tradition that reflected our own psychoanalytic identification, and compare and contrast these with classical Freudian conceptualizing.

In comparison with repressed drive states trying to find gratification in a discouraging universe, what we referred to as the developmental arrest models seemed to think of the unconscious as a true self, living in a world too unfacilitating to safely emerge. This true self is seen as endogenous or pre relational, and it represents the buried potential that exists to some degree or another in all of us. In contrast with the archeological search for repressed and unacceptable sexual and aggressive desires, inevitably making themselves known in the transference and explicated by analysts' interpretations, this model views the analyst as providing an environment good enough to facilitate developmental potentials that had been theretofore arrested. In contrast with the facilitating analyst, patients' original caretakers, usually parents, were seen as not providing a human environment that either encouraged or recognized their children's inherent true potential. The traditional Freudian emphasis on analysts' interpretations recedes in background, as the role of the analyst as a nurturing and empathic other, compensating for deficient parenting, emerges in foreground.

What is thought to lie within the unconscious from the Interpersonal perspective is fundamentally what Mitchell (1988) has called, internalized relational configurations. That is, without articulating or formulating (Stern, 1997) such experience, all humans identify with their significant others and the relational configurations that exist exogenously in the familial environment. People are thought of as both viewing the world and engaging with the world of others that reflect an embeddedness in the interpersonal world with which they developed. These patterned and powerfully repetitive familial and familiar ways of being, reflecting what might be thought of internal objects, both dominate our lives with others and as well, emerge in the transference. In the context of analysts' responsive countertransference, the analytic relationship becomes a mutually enacted repetition of unformulated familial experience, providing a widow to what has been internalized and the unconscious motivation to repeat what is most known and most cherished.

REFERENCES

Mitchell, S. (1988). *Relational Concepts in Psychoanalysis.* Cambridge, MA: Harvard University Press.

Stern, D.B. (1997). *Unformulated Experience.* Hillsdale NJ: The Analytic Press.

Chapter 6

CHANGING CONCEPTIONS OF UNCONSCIOUS*

Inherent in anything called psychoanalysis is some notion of unconscious process. This is perhaps Freud's greatest contribution to understanding people. We are all influenced by motivations that are out of
our awareness or are not yet formulated. As psychoanalytic theories
have become more pluralistic, we no longer have a uniform definition
of unconscious experience nor a consensus on its place in psychoanalytic treatment. Psychoanalysis has become more interpersonal and,
thus, what defines the therapeutic goals has shifted from the pursuit
of hidden truths to the creation of an authentic subjectivity that
develops within the relational matrix of the therapeutic dyad
(Wolstein, 1982); (Levenson, 1991); (Greenberg, 1991); (Mitchell,
1993). With this shift in emphasis, it has become unclear what we
mean when we talk about unconscious experience. Differing theoretical models all refer to some notion of unconscious, although
in most non classical models what this unconscious is has not been
made entirely explicit. For most analysts, dreams, slips of the tongue,
inadvertent actions, nonverbal expressions, and transference material
are some of the windows through which we glimpse unconscious
experience. But what is being glimpsed, and who is doing the
glimpsing? As the archeological view of the unconscious has changed
(Spence, 1982), so too has our understanding of how we come to
know unconscious experience and what we do with it in psychoanalytic treatment.

Changes in the conception of unconscious stem from shifts in psychoanalytic theorizing, though there still are often surprising overlaps among
disparate theories. This article will compare and contrast how unconscious
is conceived and dealt with in analytic treatment within the theoretical
traditions of classical psychoanalysis, the developmental-arrest model, and
interpersonal psychoanalysis. Our emphasis will be on the interpersonal
perspective, which, until recently, has not sufficiently defined the nature
of unconscious experience (Stern, 1994), despite the current emphasis

*Hirsch, I. and Roth, J. (1995). Changing conceptions of unconscious. *Contempo-
rary Psychoanalysis* 31:263–276.

on relational models in psychoanalytic theorizing (Greenberg & Mitchell, 1983).

The recent changes in the conception of unconscious will be discussed along three dimensions. The first dimension addresses what unconscious experience consists of, that is, the mental contents of unconscious. Specifically, the classical model, in which the unconscious is seen as containing drive derivatives and defenses against these drives, will be contrasted with the developmental-arrest model, in which unconscious consists of "true self" as inborn potentials. These two differing views will then be compared to the interpersonal perspective, in which unconscious experience primarily reflects internalized interpersonal relationships and identifications. The second dimension we will explore relates to how the unconscious is seen to emerge. The traditional view is an archeological method of detection, whereby hidden selves, fantasies, conflicts, or memories are uncovered in the form of historical truths, while the more recent, contructivist view holds that unconscious truth is relative and is discovered and created in the form of a narrative truth. The third dimension to be addressed is the analyst's position in relation to the patient and unconscious material. Here, a one-person psychology, in which the analyst stands outside the interactional field while objectively examining, interpreting, or nurturing the patient's unconscious, will be contrasted to a two-person psychology, in which the analyst is an observing-participant who unwittingly enacts with the patient's internalized relational conflicts. This analyzed two-person interaction becomes the setting for a subjective examination of unconscious and a narrative perspective of history.

The Classical Model

For Freud, and for many Freudians, the unconscious is a distinct entity consisting of repressed sexual and aggressive impulses and their derivatives. In Freud's topographical and structural models the unconscious is a dynamic force with its own distinct internal structures. The unconscious is a container of mental contents(Greenberg, 1991), that is pre-wired to mediate experience and exists prior to interpersonal experience. It is a "geography of hidden truths" (Fourcher, 1992 p. 323) consisting of wishes for instinctual gratification and conflicts around these that are kept out of awareness. The analyst, as an objective screen and a nonparticipating interpreter, uncovers the buried truths that the patient alone can rarely access. Repressed wishes are revealed as they emerge in transference, dreams, and patient's associations. If the analyst stays out of the way, unconscious material will spring forth from the patient's insides and will be visible in distortions of perception or as projections. Once resistance is analyzed, unconscious material is interpreted to the patient at the point of urgency in the transference. Interpretation takes the form of genetic insight that is seen as mutative (Strachey, 1934). Freed from the clutches of repression and equipped with insight, the patient is in a better position to renounce archaic drive states and go on with the business of mature living. Here the analytic process is, ultimately, the study of the internal world of one individual - the patient, although the analyst may use his or her own unconscious process to shed light on the patient. It is important to note that some later Freudians have broadened Freud's view of what is unconscious to include object representations and their associated affects (Sandler & Sandler, 1987); (Greenberg, 1991).

Freud's archeological view of the unconscious has affected the way psychoanalysts, regardless of their persuasion, think about unconscious experience. Interestingly, many analysts who subscribe to theories that are not drive-based nonetheless associate unconscious with drive derivatives. Curtis (1994) suggests that this is because non-Freudian views of unconscious content have yet to be spelled out. Further, many hold a view of unconscious as a reified repository of "hidden truths" (Spence, 1982) that almost has a physical corollary. These truths are discovered primarily by the analyst, as opposed to being constructed by both the patient and the analyst (Fourcher, 1992). The analyst excavates and interprets, while the patient alone enacts and regresses. The analyst is seen as capable of standing outside of the intensity of the therapeutic dyad while interpreting unconscious material to the patient. The analyst's own subjectivity is not seen as either affecting what unconscious material emerges from the patient's inner world or the interpretation of that material. This view of the unconscious seems to be held even by many analysts who believe that what lies within is primarily determined by a life history of interpersonal experience.

The Developmental-Arrest Model

While the Freudian unconscious can be likened to a seething cauldron, a British developmental-arrest perspective defines the unconscious as one's true self that has been submerged or undeveloped. From this perspective, the unconscious consists of the patient's buried potential that has not emerged because of problems earlier in development; these have cre-ated deficits or defects that cannot be fixed without going back to that point in development at which the problem arose (Balint, 1968). From this developmental-arrest perspective, the analyst's task is to develop a therapeutic strategy that will nurture the hidden core of true self. The ana-lyst here is not so much an interpreter as a non intruding facilitator or a nurturer who can find the seeds of the patient's undeveloped true self, or thwarted self, and provide the optimal holding environment to awaken the potential that lies dormant. The patient's inborn "idiom" (Bollas,1987) is protected under layers of false self-development. The patient's true self is thought to have gone underground to avoid destruction at the hands of caretakers who could not tolerate the development of the growing child. The true self is endogenous to the patient; indeed, according to Bollas it is pre-experiential (Bollas, 1987). Through a process of induced regres-sion to the point of the "basic fault," the true self emerges in the original state and is further facilitated by the patient's use of the analyst (see Balint, 1968). This takes place in the safety of the analyst as good-enough mother (Winnicott, 1965). By definition, this analyst stands outside of the rela-tional mix (Hirsch, 1987); (Mitchell, 1988); (Levenson, 1991). This does not mean, however, that the analyst is inactive or abstinent. Rather, the analyst believes that growth and development of the inborn idiom can be nurtured in the patient without the analyst getting lost in the patient's rela-tional matrix. The analyst serves the facilitating function of the good object or the "used" object (Winnicott, 1965), and it is within this context of objective safety and analytic gratification that the true self emerges.

In the developmental-arrest paradigm, the analyst essentially diag-noses and prescribes the particular therapeutic environment that is per-ceived as needed by the patient (see Little, 1990). The patient is relative-ly naive, resting in the arms of a wiser, parentified therapist. The thera-pist's attunement, holding and containing functions, empathy, optimal distance, and willingness to be used are the primary catalysts for the patient's growth. The internalization of the analyst as the good object replaces the parental bad object, and the patient's unconscious (defined here as *true self* and *creativity*) can emerge. In a sense, new permissive internal objects replace old restrictive ones, and the "Sleeping Beauty" (Mitchell, 1988) as true self emerges. This therapeutic positioning is strategic and premediated and depends on the analyst's reading of what the patient needs. That is, the analyst is viewed as objectively able to determine what is best for the patient, to distinguish between the patient's wishes and the patient's needs, and to provide what is right or necessary. Parenthetically, this position is not held by all British object-relations analysts (see Kohon, 1986). Kohon views the analytic process as less systematic, and less parental. The analytic interaction is characterized more by mutual and unwitting participation, out of which develops a corrective experience. This object-relational perspective is in harmony with that of many analysts identified with the interpersonal approach.

While the traditional Freudian unconscious is excavated by a non-participating interpreter, the developmental-arrest unconscious is revitalized by a not fully participating facilitator (Hirsch, 1987), (Mitchell, 1993). In the later model, transference is conceived as the unconflicted need for basic attunement and nourishment. As in the classical model, transference exists solely within the patient. The analyst can somehow transcend his or her subjectivity to observe or facilitate the unconscious. What may be lost in both models is the analyst's own idiosyncratic participation and the transference-countertransference matrix in which the analyst fully and unwittingly participates (Racker, 1968); (Sandler, 1976); (Searles, 1979); (Wolstein, 1982); (Gill, 1983); (Hoffman, 1983); (Levenson, 1983); (Stern, 1983); (Hirsch, 1987); (Mitchell, 1988); (Greenberg, 1991); (Aron, 1992); (Ehrenberg, 1992). It is this unwitting participation that most distinguishes the interpersonal approach to psychoanalysis.

The Interpersonal Models

From a contemporary interpersonal perspective, unconscious experience is inherently interactive and ambiguous. Its contours are negotiated by both the analyst and the patient. Neither has claim on defining what is truly unconscious, and neither is without unconscious motivations. As such, both get enmeshed in the interpersonal enactments that ensue. With this interpersonal perspective, the content of the unconscious shifts from drive derivatives and inborn idioms to interpersonal experiences that are unarticulated. Further, the way in which the unconscious is believed to emerge and the analyst's stance vis-à-vis unconscious experience also shift: the unconscious is not excavated or nourished by an analyst who stands outside enactments, but is lived out, negotiated, and constructed within the transference-countertransference matrix.

It is Harry Stack Sullivan (1953) who lays the groundwork for this more fully participatory view of unconscious experience. His conception of participant-observation places the analyst within the field of analytic inquiry. For Sullivan, the analyst's observations and interpretations are themselves interactional. The patient's problems are born and maintained within an interactional context. Sullivan sets the stage for conceptualizing unconscious, not as a singular, objective entity residing inside the patient, but rather as an experience reflecting the patient's interpersonal history that can only be glimpsed through the analyst's subjective lens and participation. Sullivan does not carry his ideas out to their radical conclusion, however, in that he also sees the analyst as "expert in interpersonal relations," thus largely avoiding the examination of here-and-now enactments in the transference-countertransference matrix and placing the analyst as an observer of the patient's extra-transferential relationships (Hirsch, 1987);(Levenson, 1991). The role of the analyst is to know the patient as others do and to facilitate awareness of how the patient is viewed by others. The analyst is a consensual validator who makes the patient aware of who he or she *really is*. Further, the analyst is seen as being in a position to disconfirm historical expectancies, providing the patient with a new set of expectancies about people and, thus, avoid being the old and bad object (Hirsch, 1987); (Levenson, 1991). Sullivan believed that the analyst's stance, optimally, leads to a breakdown in rigid patterns of living that the patient has perpetuated. The analyst's engagement and openness to inquiry disconfirm the patient's unconscious fantasies that are based upon real historical experience.

The concept of personification is really Sullivan's claim to understanding unconscious as internalized interpersonal experience, though he preferred to focus his inquiry on what was manifest. Personifications are those aspects of experience of significant others, those "surviving imprints," which are held onto and continue to exert a very live presence, shaping current interactions with others (Sullivan, 1953). Personifications represent transformations of subjective experience of significant others in one's life. They are caricatures of experience with real people toward whom one feels loyalty and profound attachment (Fromm, 1964). New experience is both colored and shaped by this internalized earlier template. For Sullivan, unconscious reflects what individuals have internalized from a life history of interpersonal engagements and, hence, is solely interpersonal. Personifications refer to what later interpersonalists have called "internalized relational configurations" (Mitchell, 1988), what Fairbairn(1952) has termed "internal objects," and what Greenberg(1991) refers to in his discussion of unconscious representations.

For Sullivan, life revolves around the pursuit of security and the avoidance of new, uncomfortable experience. Interpersonal anxiety leads to inattention and dissociation. Children develop those aspects of themselves that have been met with approval by their parents and may dissociate those aspects that have been met with disapproval Thompson, 1950). Later, the self-system organizes around those ways of being and relating that are familiar and familial and rejects those that are new and the cause of discomfort for the caregivers. The patient seeks to maintain those experiences that maximize security. Modes of being and interacting that make the self or others too anxious go unnoticed. Inattention, then, is motivated by interpersonal anxiety and leads to both repression and lack of recognition (Stern, 1983). Whatever produces significant anxiety may be dissociated and may consequently lead to the development of a brittle sense of self. This notion is close in spirit to Winnicott's (1965) false self-integrations.

Like traditional classical theorists and developmental-arrest theorists, Sullivan believed that the analyst can remain largely outside of the transference-countertransference mix(Hirsch, 1987). The analyst is an expert in interpersonal relations who is able to participate without becoming lost inside the patient's internalized interpersonal matrix of experience. While most contemporary interpersonal analysts no longer view themselves as objective "experts," some do maintain that it is best to stay outside of the transference-countertransference matrix (Havens, 1976); (Witenberg, 1987). These interpersonalists tend to believe that they can avoid being the bad or old objects. They posit that the analyst is able to provide corrective experience without first becoming lost in repetition of pathogenic internalization. From this interpersonal perspective, unconscious experience is lived out in two-person dyads in the patient's *outside* life with others, while the analyst is able to sidestep his or her own enmeshments in the patient's internal world. The analyst is an expert observer of the patient's extra-transference experience, through which unconscious fantasy is revealed. This perspective contrasts with the more radical extension of the full meaning of participant-observation (or observing participation) in which the focus is on internal processes as they are lived out in the analytic interaction (Searles, 1979); (Gill, 1983); (Hoffman, 1983); (Levenson, 1983); (Stern, 1983); (Fiscalini, 1988); (Mitchell, 1988); (Hirsch, 1990); (Greenberg, 1991); (Ehrenberg, 1992).

In the classical psychoanalytic perspective, unconscious drive-related material is rejected from consciousness but is nevertheless registered and, in some way, symbolized. The patient's unconscious instinctual wishes and/or drive derivatives reveal themselves in a relatively recognizeable, formulated, and meaningful shape through uncontaminated tranferences that are projected onto an analyst, who is seen as a blank screen. While unconscious thought may be typified by primary process characteristics, as primitive, literal, and irrational, meaning can usually be deciphered. For Sullivan, however, unconscious experience includes the dissociated and unformulated, all of which is motivated by interpersonal anxiety. Dissociation narrows the range of potential experience and may lead to the inability to symbolize new incoming information (Stern, 1983). By keeping things unformulated, the patient can protect both himself and loved ones from anxiety. Unfortunately, this dynamic comes at a considerable cost, since anxiety also interferes with the acquisition of new knowledge and the ability to think imaginatively (Thompson, 1950). Material may also be unformulated because the patient cannot yet grasp its meaning and give it form (Stern, 1983). Psychoanalysis then becomes a process in which the interpersonal unformulated becomes articulated. By struggling to give voice to the unformulated, the patient and analyst imagine missing links in experience (Bromberg, 1993). This is, perhaps, the essence of working with dissociated experience. Self-other configurations that have been dissociated are lived out in two-person transference-countertransference enactments and are approximations of the patient's unformulated experience (Hirsch, 1994). In the classical perspective, there is an assumption that the analyst can know the "truth" of that which has been repressed and can both discover and articulate it by him or herself. Enactments are thought to be one-person enactments (the patient only) and exact replicas of early experience. From the above relational perspective, there is no way of fully knowing that the experience happened in the way it is now being lived out in the analytic matrix. Instead, the patient and analyst construct narratives (Spence, 1982) that are the best approximations of what has been unclear and unarticulated in the patient's history. Ultimately, therapeutic progress involves discovering old configurations that have been unacknowledged and creating new configurations that have never been experienced (Wolstein, 1982); (Stern, 1983).

Mitchell's (1988) relational-conflict model and conception of internalized relational configurations offer practical tools for conceptualizing unconscious experience as the product of a synthetic and interpersonal negotiation between patient and analyst that approximates the patient's internalized experience and reflects *both* their subjectivities. Building on interpersonal contributions, as well as those of Fairbairn, the relational-conflict perspective is a two-person psychology, wherein the patient's ways of being and relating are seen as developing within an interpersonal matrix that is set in motion in early childhood and continues to evolve over the course of a lifetime. This model is a full extension of Winnicott's (1965)assertion that there is no such thing as an infant but only infant-mother pairs. That is, people's lives are seen as inseparable from the interpersonal contexts in which they live. These relational contexts are carried within, in the form of configurations that reflect the history of one's interpersonal interactions with significant others, and they are replayed throughout life (see also Fairbairn, 1952); (Schachtel, 1959); (Fromm, 1964); (Singer, 1970); (Searles, 1979). The problems that bring patients to treatment are seen as resulting from rigid patterns of relating that truncate a more dimensional experience in living. Specifically, people's difficulties result from their adhesion to loved ones of the past with whom they are embedded and from whom they cannot separate (Fairbairn, 1952); (Schachtel, 1959); (Fromm, 1964); (Feiner & Levenson, 1968–1969); (Singer, 1970); (Searles, 1979); (Hirsch, 1992).

From this perspective, unconscious consists of a bewildering repertoire of internalized self-other configurations or personifications. Relational configurations refer to templates of ongoing interactional patterns that the patient has experienced in relation to key figures, which begin very early in life and are usually consistent throughout development. These configurations are usually unarticulated or dissociated (Hirsch, 1994) and lead to expectations that the present and future will be the same as the past. Thus, we anticipate and pursue what confirms our unarticulated templates of what the world is like and, in so doing, repeat the past and maintain personal equilibrium at the expense of engaging in new experience. Problems arise when current experience is rigid and does not adapt to new environments. The child who withdraws from an abusive parent may expect a teacher to be abusive as well, and so may withdraw, anticipating or even provoking abuse, and thereby become unavailable to potentially new, rich, and unexpected interaction.

Embedded in internalized interpersonal configurations are identifications with key figures and, as noted, an inclination to repeat. Parents, siblings, and significant others are internalized in order to preserve loving attachments to them and to maintain a stable sense of self (Searles, 1979). Paradoxically, the most persistent identifications may be those that reflect painful and troublesome qualities (Fairbairn, 1952). According to Fairbairn (1952) and Fromm (1964), one strives to preserve whatever fragments of connection there are to the primary caregiver and to maintain whatever was experienced as love. The less there is, the more tenacious the adhesion. Identifications become the inner blueprints that guide expectations of future experience, but they may interfere with the establishment of separation and the capacity to develop flexible and enriched ways of being. Repetition preserves the unarticulated loving bond by perpetuating what is familiar and familial and what has always defined one's basic sense of self (Feiner & Levenson, 1968–1969); (Singer, 1970); (Searles, 1979). The quest for familial love and safety and the fear of disruption of self motivate this desire to stay in place, and fuel the repetition compulsion (Russell, 1991). One's world is thus shaped to conform to past configurations; because of this, individuals actively become the authors of their own misery and, according to Searles, are devoted to their pathology. From this perspective, unconscious consists of the repetitious preservation of the beloved familiar interpersonal configurations and identifications.

Defining unconscious experience as the repertoire of one's unarticulated, internalized interpersonal configurations broadens what is meant by unconscious to include a wider variety of affective experience. The classical unconscious is primarily associated with drive derivatives. The interpersonal unconscious consists of repetitive configurations that are associated with a range of affects. These include sexual feelings and aggression, but may also reflect the gamut of affective experience. Often more salient than sex and aggression are feelings of loss, pain, and vulnerability, as well, of course, as yearnings that conflict with the wishes and demands of significant others. These feelings are frequently dissociated because they have been met with anxiety or disapproval from caretakers (Sullivan, 1953). This dissociation process limits the range, not only of affective experience, but of interpersonal activity. The capacity to feel what we have to feel, what Russell (1991) calls "affect competence," is inextricably linked to the richness, complexity, and flexibility of internalized interpersonal configurations. Enrichment of experience thus becomes the primary aim of psychoanalysis (Levenson, 1983).

The relational-conflict model defines unconscious experience as inherently interpersonal. The goal of analysis is not the discovery of buried truth, but rather the living-out and articulation of old internalized interpersonal patterns and the facilitation of new experience. Relational configurations are discovered and created by the analyst and patient together, as they both become immersed in the transference-countertransference field. It is through this immersion that unconscious is lived out and enacted in dyadic action. Patients "are their unconscious fantasies and live them with the analyst through the act of psychoanalysis" (Bromberg, 1989 p. 282). Analysis occurs post-enactment.

The analyst's participation in the patient's transference is unwitting (Gill, 1983); (Hirsch, 1992). Because the analyst is a participant, albeit an asymmetrical one (Aron, 1992), he or she is working from inside the system. Rather than interpret the patient's unconscious content, the analyst and patient both describe the lived-out enactments that reflect what has been internalized (Levenson, 1991). The patient is encouraged to articulate his or her perceptions of the analyst's participation (see Hoffman, 1983) and not to protect the analyst from anxiety. The patient's perceptions of the analyst, are as important as those that the analyst has of the patient (Wolstein, 1982); (Stern, 1992). The goal is to demystify the analyst in the transference and, thereby, to also demystify the family in the patient's internal world (Searles, 1979); (Levenson, 1991).

From what Hoffman has called a social-constructivist perspective (1991), (1992), the concept of the unconscious is a relative one (see also Stern, 1992). What the analyst knows about the patient's unconscious is inextricably bound to the analyst's own subjective lens and is inherently ambiguous. This is the logical extension of Sullivan's concept of participant-observation (Hirsch, 1985, 1990). The patient can never be fully grasped as an isolated individual, separate from the analyst's own subjectivity (Aron, 1992). In the classical and developmental-arrest models the unconscious is absolute. It is a distinct entity consisting of the fundamental truths of an individual's being that can be objectively perceived by a not fully participating and expert practitioner. Unconscious experience from a constructivist perspective differs radically; it is inherently subjective and co-created. Ultimately, what is discovered from this two-person interaction is not a singular truth or reconstructed memory, but rather a construction (Levenson, 1983), storyline (Schafer, 1983), or narrative (Spence, 1982) that makes sense to *both* the analyst and the patient. Stern (1992) notes that the analyst's individual qualities are important and that a different analyst in the same situation might discover different aspects of what is not conscious or not formulated by the patient. From this point of view, the analyst's unconscious experience cannot always be distinguished from that of the patient.

The relative unconscious can never be fully known, except as it is lived in the subjectivity of the here-and-now analytic relationship and corroborated by anecdotes of extra-transferential patterning. It is the living out of the unarticulated, internalized interpersonal configurations that renders them "visible," in the sense that the analyst and patient can arrive at a clarity that resonates with both of their experiences of the therapeutic relationship. Together, they negotiate a mutually constructed understanding of history that has been informed by their interactions. These understandings are not fixed in time and continue to be transformed over the course of the patient's life, even after the analysis is over (Mitchell, 1993). What is lost with this concept of unconscious is the illusion that the analyst is an archeologist discovering hidden truths about the naive patient while abstaining from intense affective engagement and enactment.

Conclusion and Summary

The unconscious from a two-person psychology perspective consists of internalized interpersonal configurations that have been unarticulated and that continue to exert control over the course of one's life. These configurations serve as templates that guide one's expectancies and interpretations of events but interfere with the ability to form new self-experiences and to develop new ways of being. This interpersonal unconscious becomes "known" as it is experienced by both the patient and the analyst in the here-and-now of the transference-countertransference matrix. Both participants are unable to step outside of their own subjectivity. Discovering the absolute unconscious is less important than the articulation of repetitive and internalized patterns of relating and the ultimate expansion of experience. This does not mean that the concept of unconscious is insignificant. On the contrary, unformulated and unarticulated interpersonal configurations are seen as the substance of unconscious. What has changed is what is done with this unconscious experience. The archeological pursuit of absolute truth and the illusion that the analyst can be a nonparticipating, objective interpreter, or an objective facilitator, dictates a positivistic analytic stance. The interpersonally informed analyst lives out unconscious experience—the unformulated and unarticulated internalized relational configurations as they are mutually enacted in the therapeutic field. It is through the repetition and articulation of these engagements that patients work their way out of safe but limiting patterns of experience. The analyst who acknowledges unwitting interaction must repeat the old and destructive internalized configurations before anything genuinely new can develop. Awareness of participation occurs post-enactment.

REFERENCES

Aron, L. (1992). Interpretation as expression of the analyst's subjectivity *Psychoanal Dial.* 2:475–507.

Balint, M. (1968). *The Basic Fault* London: Tavistock.

Bollas, C. (1987). *The Shadow of the Object: Psychoanalysis of the Unthought Known* New York: Columbia University Press.

Bromberg, P.M. (1989). Interpersonal psychoanalysis and self psychology: A clinical comparison In: *Self Psychology: Comparisons and Contrasts,* D.W. Detrick & S.P. Detrick (eds.). Hillsdale, NJ: The Analytic Press, pp. 275–291.

———— (1993). Shadow and substance: A relational perspective on clinical process. *Psychoanalytic Psychology* 10:147–168.

Curtis, R. (1994). Psychoanalysis at the Edge: the Emerging Model of Motivation and Mental Organizing Processes. Unpublished manuscript.

Ehrenberg, D.B. (1992). *The Intimate Edge* New York: W.W. Norton.

Fairbairn, W.R.D. (1952). *Psychoanalytic Studies of the Personality* London: Tavistock Publications.

Feiner, A.H., & Levenson, E.A. (1968–1969). The compassionate sacrifice: Exploration of a metaphor. *Psychoanalytic Review* 55:552–573.

Fiscalini, J. (1988). Conceptualizing the psychoanalytic process. *Contemp. Psychoanal.* 24:125–142

Fourcher, L.A. (1992 Interpreting the relative and absolute unconscious. *Psychoanal. Dial.* 2:317–329.

Fromm, E. (1964). *The Heart of Man* New York: Harper and Row.

Gill, M.M. (1983). The interpersonal paradigm and the degree of the therapist's involvement. *Contemp. Psychoanal.* 18:535–555.

Greenberg, J.R. (1991). *Oedipus and Beyond. Cambridge,* MA: Harvard University Press.

———— & Mitchell, S.A. (1983). Object relations in psychoanalytic theory Cambridge, MA: Harvard University Press.

Havens, L. (1976). *Participant-Observation.* New York: Jason Aronson.

Hirsch, I. (1985). The rediscovery of the advantages of the participant-observation model. *Psychoanalysis and Contemporary Thought* 8:441–459.

———— (1987). Varying modes of analytic participation. *Journal of the American Academy of Psychoanalysis* 15:205–222.

———— (1990). Countertransference and participant-observation. *The American Journal of Psychoanalysis* 50:275–284

———— (1992). An interpersonal perspective: The analyst's unwitting participation in the patient's change. *Psychoanalytic Psychology* 9:299–312.

———— (1994). Dissociation and the interpersonal self. *Contemporary Psychoanal.* 30:777–799.

Hoffman, I.Z. (1983). The patient as interpreter of the analyst's experience. *Contemp. Psychoanal.* 19:389–422.

———— (1991). Discussion: Toward a social-constructivist view of the choanalytic situation. *Psychoanal. Dial.* 1:74–105.

——— (1992). Some practical implications of a social-constructivist view of the psychoanalytic situation. *Psychoanal. Dial.* 2:287–304.

Kohon, G. (1986). *The British School of Psychoanalysis: the Independent Tradition.* London: Free Association Books.

Levenson, E.A. (1983). *The Ambiguity of Change.* New York: Basic Books.

——— (1991). *The Purloined Self.* New York: Contemp. Psychoanal. Books.

Little, M. (1990). *Psychotic Anxieties and Containment.* New York: Jason Aronson.

Mitchell, S.A. (1988). *Relational Concepts in Psychoanalysis.* Cambridge, MA: Harvard University Press.

——— (1993). *Hope and Dread in Psychoanalysis* New York: Basic Books.

Racker, H. (1968). *Transference and Countertransference.* New York: International Universities Press.

Russell, P.L. (1991). Trauma, repetition, and affect. Paper presented at Massachusetts Institute for Psychoanalysis Symposium April,1991.

Sandler, J. (1976). Countertransference and role responsiveness *Int. Rev. Psychoanal.* 3:43–47.

——— & Sandler, A. (1987). The past unconscious, the present unconscious and the vicissitudes of guilt. *Int. J. Psychoanal.* 64:413–425.

Schachtel, E. (1959). *Metamorphosis.* New York: Basic Books.

Schafer, R. (1983). *The Analytic Attitude* New York: Basic Books.

Searles, H.S. (1979). *Countertransference and Related Subjects.* New York: International Universities Press.

Singer, E. (1970). *Key Concepts in Psychotherapy.* New York: Basic Books.

Spence, D. (1982). *Narrative Truth and Historical Truth.* New York: W.W. Norton.

Stern, D.B. (1983). Unformulated experience. *Contemporary Psychoanalysis* 19:71–99.

——— (1992). Commentary on constructivism in clinical psychoanalysis. *Contemp. Psychoanal.* 28:331–363.

——— (1994). Conceptions of structure in interpersonal psychoanalysis. *Contemp. Psychoanal.* 30:255–300.

Strachey, J. (1934). The nature of the therapeutic action of psycho-analysis. *Int. J. Psychoanal.* 15:127–159.

Sullivan, H.S. (1953). *The Interpersonal Theory of Psychiatry.* New York: W.W. Norton.

Thompson, C. (1950). *Psychoanalysis: Evolution and Development.* New York: Hermitage House.

Winnicott, D.W. (1965). *The Maturational Processes and the Facilitating Environment.* New York: International Universities Press.

Witenberg, E. (1987). Clinical innovations and theoretical controversy. *Contemp. Psychoanal.* 23:183–198

Wolstein, B. (1982). The psychoanalytic theory of unconscious psychic experience *Contemp. Psychoanal.* 18:412–443.

Prologue to Chapter 7:
THE WIDENING OF THE CONCEPT OF DISSOCIATION

This chapter logically follows the previous one. In the part of the Relational universe that is most compatible with the Interpersonal tradition, dissociation has taken a central seat in the effort to understand unconscious process and unconscious motivation. This term, once associated exclusively with more severe psychological problems or profound trauma, now is used as descriptive of the widest range of unconscious experience. Certainly severe trauma can be dissociated and as well, so can extreme early experience that leads to disconnection to the external world. However, I argue that much of how each individual becomes who they are, is indeed dissociated, as is much of what motivates each of us to continue living in ways that are repetitively familiar and comfortable.

Stern's (1997) term, "unformulated experience," best captures what I refer to. That is, as alluded to in my prologue to the previous chapter and in that chapter, the normal building blocks of how people become who they are, are based largely on identifications with significant others and in the patterns of relatedness that exist in everyone's formative environment. Such experience is rarely formulated in words or consciously experienced. Indeed, this is distinguished from repression, this latter term implying that experience has been formulated in words and then forgotten. People don't consciously articulate that they are identifying with a particular adult or that they are internalized a relational pattern that is emblematic of their family. This just happens naturally and captures and reflects what lies in everyone's unconscious. The normal inclination to live in ways that are known but not articulated is the basis of unconscious motivation, i.e., we all are motivated to repeat what we have internalized.

Looking at the concept of dissociation in this way removes it from the domain of trauma only or from the disconnection from experience that characterizes the extreme dysfunction of losing contact with the world of others. The psychoanalytic process in its essence is the effort to understand dissociated or unformulated unconscious motivation and possibly to use this understanding to embrace new and unfamiliar experience. This wider and more contemporary way of thinking about dissociation places it as far more central than the concept of repression in psychoanalysis' continual quest to comprehend how people become who they are and how change might be possible.

REFERENCE

Stern, D B. (1997). *Unformulated Experience.* Hillsdale, NJ: The Analytic Press.

Chapter 7

THE WIDENING OF THE CONCEPT OF DISSOCIATION*

Although H. S. Sullivan (1953) gave more explanatory power to dissociation than repression, as a way to understand the human psyche, until recent years dissociation has not been a widely used conception. The classical psychoanalytic model had been so dominant and influential in the United States that even analysts from other perspectives tended to use Freudian language even when it was incompatible with their theory. Through the use of concepts that reflected a one-person psychology instead of the two-person psychology of participant-observation, Sullivan's interpersonal legacy was ignored even by many who were influenced by him. For instance, the term "resistance" was used to refer to resistance to memory rather than resistance to alternate forms of relatedness to the analyst in the transference. The key concept of *transference* often referred to the inner world of the patient only, without regard to the influence or interaction of the participating analyst. It took an innovative classical analyst (Gill, 1982) to relationalize the concept and to integrate interpersonal philosophy with interpersonal language. The seminal work of Greenberg and Mitchell (1983) made many analysts far more conscious of the philosophical and practical distinctions between drive and relational theories and helped lead the way to a sort of retooling of the theoretical lexicon. The concept of dissociation is now becoming far more prominent in the literature (e.g., Bromberg, 1994, 1996; Davies and Frawley, 1994; Hirsch, 1994) to address phenomena once ascribed to repression only.

Despite dissociation being a key ingredient in Sullivan's understanding of all the problems of living, until its recent revival it was associated with more serious psychological difficulty, early or preverbal pathology, and the extreme splitting often connected with psychic trauma. The questionable category of multiple personality disorder was perhaps the most widely used referent when speaking of dissociation.

Repression, on the other hand, was widely viewed as the more common and normal way that experience was rendered out of consciousness. Repressed material has been encoded in language and memory and is

---

*Hirsch, I. (1997). The widening of the concept of dissociation. *Journal of American Academy of Psychoanalysis* 25(4):603–615.

thought to be accessible, usually in disguised form, in psychoanalytic engagement. Repression is commonly thought to be associated with verbal, as opposed to preverbal experience, and with conflictual affect in contrast with annihilating or traumatic events. Repression usually refers to feeling states or drive states that reflect internal conflict and therefore must be compromised, disguised, distorted, or temporarily obliterated. The memory of these affective states is called up in analysis, normally in the form of parapraxes, dreams, and transference enactments. Indeed, these affective memories have been residing in latent space and the side of the patient that has been longing to get well feels liberated (albeit conflicted) by the ability to bring them into language. In part because the conflicts that provoked repression occurred during verbal years and were normally not related to annihilation anxiety, they have been associated with a relatively healthy psyche. Again until recent years, analyzability was seen as dependent on unconscious material being repressed and not dissociated (Hirsch, 1984, 1994). The former was emblematic of neurosis, whereas the latter was linked with more serious character pathology. The inability to veridically recover past experience and put it into words was thought to reflect disconnection from self, from historical self-other relatedness and consequently, from the potential to meaningfully and intimately engage with one's analyst transferentially.

Greenberg and Mitchell's (1983) impetus to distinguish relational theories from drive theories have aided the former to become more autonomous from the language of drives and from conceptions that are linked primarily to classical models of the mind. Sullivan's concept of dissociation has been rejuvenated and a growing literature refers to unconscious process, which may often be more reflective of dissociated phenomena than that which is repressed (Bromberg, 1994; Hirsch, 1994; Hirsch and Roth, 1995; Stern, 1994). It should be noted that there is no inherent contradiction between the two concepts, they are not mutually exclusive. If it is not already clear, however, I believe that the two concepts reflect a different emphasis about the intrapsychic world and how experience becomes internalized. Though drive-related internal conflict, according to classical analysts, is pretty much the only thing that leads to repression, there are a number of ways (including conflictual) that experience may be dissociated. Dissociation may reflect anything from normal and benign experience to the most serious psychic trauma. There are many reasons why experience may not be encoded in language and retrievable as such. Some experiences do reflect extreme circumstances such as trauma, whereas other explanations are more ordinary. No contemporary psychoanalytic writer has more clearly addressed this subject than Stern (1983, 1987, 1989, 1994, 1996), who has coined the term "unformulated experience," as a superordinate concept to dissociation.

According to Stern, there are many reasons that experience fails to become encoded in language and therefore accessible to retrieval. Some reasons are related to anxiety and conflict and others are not. For instance, in the course of a life there are many experiences that are not noticed because they are either not especially relevant or, on the other hand, are so familiar that the psyche just passes them by. These experiences fade or decay and there are no words available to refer to them. Such experience is nondefensive except in that one must be able to screen out material in order to avoid psychic overload. Further, such experience is not thought to be of central significance in the development of personality. For Stern, with much reference to Sullivan, the dissociation of "not-me" experience, in contrast, is key to the development of personality. *Not me* refers to experience that is too inconsistent with an existing sense of self. Through the process of selective inattention, incompatible experience may go unnoticed and never enter conscious awareness and therefore, never become formulated in language. Unlike repressed experience, which has been formulated and encoded, the unformulated is not retrievable as such. The result is a psychic consistency at the expense of assimilation of new experience and expansion of the mind. Psychopathology is here defined as a kind of rigidity and a fear of novelty and the psychoanalytic process as enrichment and expansion of experience (Levenson, 1983). According to Stern and others, a stable sense of self is established in the context of significant self-other integrations; new experiences that are too inconsistent with this may simply go unattended and not register. This may involve traumatic events like sexual abuse or far less extreme contradictions with one's familiar sense of self. Singer (1970) and Searles (1979) extended Sullivan's notion of self-threat (see Fiscalini, 1991) to include the universal wish to preserve attachment to loved ones. Experience that may prove a threat to cherished relationships may also go unattended and fail to become assimilated into the psyche. Often this may involve selective inattention to phenomenon that may hurt or otherwise contradict the desires of the loved other. This loving sacrifice referred to by both Searles and Singer can readily take the form of dissociating contradictory experience and thereby narrowing one's breadth of exposure. Psychopathology is here defined as a clinging to rigid and old modes of being, motivated by protection of stabile self states and also by protection of both attachment to loved others and the others themselves.

Bromberg (1994, 1996) has addressed a variation of this theme in explicating a notion of multiple self states. In contrast with a historical emphasis on a singular self, Bromberg views one's internal world as a combination of self-other integrations, not necessarily adding-up to one integrated self. These independent configurations may have no articulatible connection with one another and it is one aim of the analyst to stand in the spaces between these multiple self states. This connection of the gaps does not lead to a singular self but to a greater sense of internal coherence. Self states are dissociated from one another in the first place because of internal conflict between key self-other configurations. These multiple self-other internalizations emerge in the transference and analytic inquiry into them help patients' raise questions about contradictions and conflicts that had been inaccessible to consciousness.

Still another kind of unformulated experience refers to the very fabric of interaction with significant others. I refer here to the process of identification per se, and the subtleties of intimate engagement that forms the stuff of internalized self-other configurations in the first place (see Hirsch, 1994). In this earlier article I referred to such formative and key experiences as dissociative, largely because such phenomena happen without verbal articulation or conscious awareness. That is, we do not know that we are identifying when that is in process, nor do we recognize when we are internalizing self-other experience. They just happen and the particulars are within us but not articulatable. In reexamining Stern's contributions, however, it now seems more apt to use the broader term "unformulated," in accounting for phenomena that are not encoded yet are not necessarily conflictual. To reiterate, the term "dissociation" seems to best apply to unformulated experience that is based on conflict. There is, however, so much highly significant life experience (such as identification) that cannot be directly retrieved or reproduced in psychoanalytic inquiry that the mutative notion of the recovery of the repressed no longer seems to be a psychoanalytic first priority for many.

Before addressing the fitting therapeutic action that corresponds with conceptions of dissociation and unformulated experience, I wish to underscore that these phenomena can reasonably be addressed as universal. That is, the long association between dissociation and severe pathology only does not make full sense in light of recent literature on the subject. Both unformulated and dissociative experience play a major role in the development of all personality and as well, all unconscious or intrapsychic experience. The same defensive psychic operations that lead to severe restrictions and psychopathology, under kinder conditions, lead to normal or neurotic problems in living. It is not a matter of repression (neurotic) versus dissociation (character pathology) or repression (later development) versus dissociation (earlier difficulties). Indeed, it is more a matter of degree—some environments are more profoundly conflictual. Therefore more experience needs to go unattended, by both dissociating and repressive processes, in order to maintain some psychic equilibrium within oneself and between oneself and the significant, loved others.

As noted, in the psychoanalytic situation one may address repression as well as dissociation or unformulated experience; there is no mutual exclusivity. Analysts from different theoretical perspectives, however, tend to emphasize one or the other in search for developmental essences and for mutative therapeutic action. Ironically, many interpersonal and relational analysts use the more traditional term, "repression," to describe analytic inquiry into dissociated or unformulated experience. The conception of repression is, indeed, best suited to the classical psychoanalytic model. The core data of psychoanalysis are feelings that are drive derivatives and that were originally not acceptable to the significant others in the environment. These biologically derived affects are, therefore, compromised and distorted in order that they gain some expression. This expression is disguised both to the patient and to the others in the patient's world. Many compromises require such convolutions Symptoms are formed in order to contain otherwise irresolvable conflict. Anxiety exists lest the affect states emerge and neurotic symptoms may stay entrenched to hide the very same affects. The prototype conflict is Oedipal and psychoanalytic inquiry often revolves around the machinations one goes through in order to keep Oedipal wishes from awareness and in check.

The psychoanalytic method focuses on the analysis of transference—the patient's disguised expression of repressed affect toward the relatively blank screen and neutral analyst. In the form of dreams and both direct and indirect communications to the analyst, hidden feelings emerge into full view of the analytic gaze. These feelings are linked to their original familial sources while the passion of the immediacy of the transference is in full sway. Repression is lifted and freedom is achieved in two distinct ways: Affect is expressed directly in an accepting atmosphere, and historical conflict is understood. A clear link is made between current conflicts in the transference and historical conflicts with parent figures. Through the transference, the past is reconstructed in order that the patient both sees and reexperiences the original affects and the accompanying conflicts. Theory dictates that there is essentially a one-to-one connection between past and present affect states and conflict states. The past can be reasonably veridically reconstructed through the transference and repressed desires reactivated, more or less, in their original form. It should be clear that what is repressed is primarily memory of conflicted affect in relation to significant others and not necessarily concrete moments in history. Because the analyst is viewed as a relatively objective and minimally participating other, what emerges in the transference is the intrapsychic world of the patient in as pure a form as possible. The concept of repression rests on the belief that what is recovered in the analytic dyad belongs only to the patient and is by and large a relatively veridical replica of the patient's historically conflicted affect tates.

In light of recent trends in the literature on recovered memory of sexual abuse (e.g., Frawley-O'Dea, 1996; Harris, 1996), it is interesting that Freud's original conception of repression was in relation to specific moments or events in history. His original theory was a trauma theory and repressed incidents of trauma were believed to be the key factor in symptom formation. Psychoanalysis followed the hypnotic paradigm with the emphasis on reliving with the analyst the traumatic moments in history. Memory of specific events was seen to lead to a symptom-ending catharsis. Freud's early twentieth century shift to a model that deemphasized the actual input of others and instead focused on drive-based fantasy, moved the concept of repression from actual events to intrapsychic ones. Except for the tendency to search for primal scene memories and to use this external event as an important explanatory factor in development, the classical conception of repression rarely focuses on memories of others interacting on the patient. Currently, those analysts interested in psychic trauma such as sexual abuse tend largely to align with nonclassical psychoanalytic points of view, while carefully searching for specific moments in history that were *either* repressed or dissociated. It is also worth noting that popular media often still portray Freudian psychoanalysis as primarily addressing repressed traumatic moments.

The strongest criticism of the classical conception of repression has come from psychoanalysts who believe that veridical recovery of any sort of memory is not possible. Some of these critics are Freudian analysts (e.g., Schafer, 1983; Spence, 1982) but most identify themselves as interpersonal or relational (e.g., Aron, 1996; Hoffman, 1991; Stern, 1996) and are often referred to as constructivists or perspectivists. They describe the classical model as archaeological in that genetic interpretations made from transference experience are assumed to resemble the original experience, in a one-to-one correspondence. This is viewed as an untenable leap for a few reasons. For one, much time has passed between the present and the repressed affects of the past. Time leaves room for considerable elaboration based on intervening life experience. Also, as Spence argues convincingly, the theory of the psychoanalyst has a profound effect on the content of patient's memory. Analysts unwittingly influence memory in a manner that conforms to the preferred theory of the analyst. In examining the recovery of repressed experience, one finds dramatic parallel in the way patients present their storylines and the prototypical narratives that reflect the theoretical perspective of the analyst. Finally and perhaps most significantly, constructivists view the concept of transference as reflecting a two-person psychology. The analyst is always a participant-observer, if not an observing participant in the patient's transference (Gill, 1982; Hirsch, 1996; Levenson, 1983). In addition to participating by virtue of having a theoretical bias, analysts unwittingly interact with patients and this reflects the psychology of both parties. As well, the analytic interaction is seen as bidirectional; patients and analysts influence one another (Aron, 1996). From this perspective, one may never assume that recovered experience is anything resembling an exact replica of past experience. At best, patients and analysts mutually construct narratives that make sense of patients' histories and approximate the content of what is assumed to be repressed.

Constructivism and perspectivism has always been in conceptual harmony with the participant-observation model and that psychoanalytic model's attention to the power of countertransference (Maroda, 1991). It is inherent to this schema that the influence of the coparticipating analyst effects the data sufficiently enough so that past and present cannot be distinguished with objectivity. If past experience that has been encoded and then forgotten cannot be retrieved with exactitude, it is plain to see that dissociated and/or unformulated experience certainly cannot veridically be revived. For interpersonal and relational analysts, the essence of psychic development lies in the ongoing interactions with significant others and these internalized experiences are generally not put

into words as they unfold. Conflict between contradictory internalizations, threat to sense of self and to loved others, identifications and the
like, tend to be experiences that were never formulated in language in the
first place. Such ongoing historical experience, conflictual or otherwise,
is only on occasion isolated into specific memory units. This dissociated
or unformulated experience is not so much spoken about but lived out in
current life and most pointedly, in the transference. All of these experiences emerge in the transference-countertransference matrix and usually
are *mutually* enacted (Hirsch, 1996; Stern, 1987, 1989). Because both
parties are subjectively involved, the past history of the patient can never
be reconstructed, only co-constructed in a social context. Constructivist
philosophy is entirely in harmony with a participant-observation model
that places unformulated and dissociated internalized relational experience at the heart of psychological development. This is contradictory
with the notion of repressed affect states only to the extent that so much
of what occurs developmentally is never encoded in memory to begin with.

In summary, unformulated and dissociated developmental internalizations largely occur when *not-me* experiences are selectively inattend-
ed because of initially external and subsequently internal conflict, when
contradictions exist *between the spaces* of disparate self-other configurations and as a function of the ubiquitous process of *identification*. All of
this is part of normal development and by no means restricted to the life
experience of those diagnosed with extreme psychopathology, though
dissociation is often linked in the literature with such cases. In the pro-
ceeding text I use brief vignettes to illustrate these processes as they characterize the lives of individuals who generally function quite highly.

CLINICAL VIGNETTES

Case I

At a point rather early in analysis I confirmed to Mr. A, that I, like
most others, thought he was smart and good-looking. In the next session
he was quite angry that. like his parents, I accented his intelligence above
all. I reminded him that I also called him good-looking and at first he had
no recall of that comment. He had selectively attended only to my second
compliment.

A.'s core sense of self is built around his intellect, which he exer-
cises both in his work and in his very spare private life. There is little in
his world in the way of personal relationships. He is a loner and main-

tains a profound sense of isolation and separateness outside of the work-related relationships he cultivates in his rather successful career. His singular source of esteem in his large family was his intellect. He was quite different from all of his siblings, who tended to be very outgoing, boisterous, and avidly competitive athletes. He grew up believing that he must have been adopted. His siblings were very much in the mold of his parents with the exception that A.'s father was an avid reader as well as heavy drinker and athlete. His sole source of esteem and belonging came from whatever intellectual achievements he was able to share with his father. When I told him that he was smart I was doing what his parents did—valuing only one aspect of his being. If he had heard me comment favorably on his appearance, it would have contradicted his core sense of being a *mind* only. Truly hearing or beginning to integrate this other aspect of self could have lead to a destabilizing anxiety; what is he to do if he really has a worthwhile body as well as a mind? Will he experience the strong conflict of a temptation to move out of his position in the family—the creative but weird intellectual loner who shares some unique interests with father? Will he experience the anxiety of longing for human contact and being most uncertain about how to achieve this? In not hearing my compliment about his body, A. also protected his parents. If he was nice looking, why didn't they emphasize this?

In A.'s eyes, although he was hurt that his parents did not acknowledge more of him, he did not really believe there was much more to him that was admirable. He has been protecting his parents from their deficiencies and from his anger. If I could acknowledge his body, there is risk that he may begin to incorporate not only a broader range of self-experience but a clearer picture of parental shortcomings. A.'s selective inattention to my comments reflected a lifelong inattention to others' interest in his body and to a confrontation with a range of dissociated feelings toward his parents. His reaction to my referring to his good looks, among other things, did not lead to an uncovering of repressed experiences so much as it helped us construct a narrative about aspects of A.'s development and its sequalae.

Case 2

Mr. B. and I were more than 1 year into analysis and I could feel no more for him than periodic commiseration. Most of the time I actively disliked him and his persistent idealization of me both perplexed and annoyed me. I found him silly and psychologically dense, dominated by denial that his world was caving in. He seemed oblivious to my contempt and clueless about how to be with me in a way that could make me emotionally giving to him. With much questioning I was able to obtain what I thought to be a reasonable sense of B.'s life history. This led me, during one of my moments of contempt toward him, to rhetorically ask if he knew how much his now-deceased father had hated him. He was shocked, just as he would have been if I had directly disclosed my similar feelings. He had never articulated his father's hatred, just as mine had not consciously registered to him. He protected both of us and himself as well. He argued that his father, though more active with his siblings, had always been responsible and never mean or punitive. I too, had done my job and concealed my feelings verbally. B.'s stable sense of self was based on trying to get the important men in his life to adore him and treat him as special, while not attending to the fact that his efforts actually served to repeat past disinterest. He had no articulated sense that he was disliked and could not begin to know what was necessary to address this situation. He also, of course, had no conscious sense of his father and his analyst as bad and destructive. We were idealized and protected from B.'s counteraggression and from feeling that we really had hurt him profoundly. The hated self was "not him" and his cute and smiling denial lead me and likely B.'s father to the at least temporary conclusion that we were not especially destructive and indeed, doing our utmost to tolerate a rather unlovable individual. This transference-based construction of history helped B. expand his sense of self and articulate both pain and anger that he had never before consciously attributed to rightful sources. Both father and I lost the flimsy but persistent idealization that B. used to protect us, and himself as well.

Case 3

Mrs. C was warm, friendly, affable, and had much that was important to say to her analyst who thought that analysis was going smoothly. She spoke very openly and almost exclusively about extratransference material. I rationalized the absence of articulated transference expression as a function of her many important practical concerns related to her large family, demanding career, and health crises with elderly parents. I felt it was important for her to have my concerned and empathic ear, until something she said moved me to ask how important our meetings were to her. In a polite and matter-of-fact way she informed me that she found me very intelligent and sensible but thoroughly unemotional. Further, she had no personal connection to me whatever and was beginning to feel that analysis was a purposeless intellectual exercise. This was related with no apparent anger, though my insides felt like they had been yanked out.

C. was a girl in a family who was only interested in the academic and athletic achievement of its sons. Though she was smarter than her brothers, her currency was her affability. She made herself easy to be with and was never angry, demanding, or rebellious. In her relations with her original family, as with me, she felt more a cold emptiness than anger. This coldness was reflective of C.'s parents' and brothers' barrenness and lack of passion in relation to her. On one hand, C. internalized a self-other configuration of cold detachment, and on the other a superficial warmth and friendliness that served her well in her family of origin and in her professional and social life as well. C.'s emotionally disconnected self and her warm and friendly self were dissociated from one another. Prior to the emergence in the transference of both characteristics, she had never before wondered about the juxtaposition of these two aspects of internalized self experience.

Case 4

In a short time, I had helped Mr. D. emerge from a profoundly disorganizing depression, characterized by withdrawal and peculiarity that threatened to destroy a successful career. Prior to this acute episode, precipitated by a loss of a woman, D. had been work oriented and had little else in his life. His opening himself to love was almost his downfall. In short shrift, D. began to function far better than he had prior to the breakup. He began to care more about his clothes and general appearance and began to look more dapper and handsome than he ever had before. He became more conscious of earning money for he now had a wider and still-expanding range of interests. He was always intelligent but now D. began to get into intellectual interests that had long been dormant. For the first time in years he rekindled the athletic involvements of his childhood and started to work his body into more healthy and attractive condition. He forgot about his lost love and began to meet women at a more frequent pace than ever before. I, of course, felt like a most potent analyst. I was high enough on my achievements that I overlooked the extent to which a number of D.'s new interests reflected my own.

The degree to which D. and I were involved more in persuasion and identification than cure (see Levenson, 1983) began to be clear to me when I saw certain parallels in his relation to his father. D.'s father was a profoundly selfish man whose wife and only child existed to inflate him. Father was king and the two other serfs played to his tune in a way that became frankly masochistic. For example, though D. was an outstanding student his father forbade him to do anything but full-time blue-collar work on graduation from high school. This was highly unusual in their cultural milieu, where education was strongly valued. Were his father not so narcissistically self-absorbed, D. would not have been able to surreptitiously complete his schooling at night. Despite allowing himself to indulge in this one ambition, D. identified with his mother's submissive depression and unquestioningly twisted his life to conform to his father's wishes.

In the transference, I largely was D.'s father to his own mother-identified self. D. was my girl-boy, existing to enhance my own potency. Though my desires for him differed from that of his father, the formal configuration was similar. D. had never before spelled out the degree to which he repeated his mother's submissive life and existed to please his father. From his blunted perspective, he had believed that he had no choice in the cards that were dealt to him. His rapid cure reflected both his submissiveness to me and his proneness to quick identifications. This identificatory process, like so many self-other internalizations, was never formulated in the first place and D.'s patterns had been doomed to repetition.

In conclusion, I have tried to suggest that although repression and dissociation or unformulated experience are by no means mutually exclusive, the latter concepts may account for more of the variability in human development than the former. In part, the domination of the concept of repression is an artifact of this country's historical domination of classical psychoanalytic theory. Many relational analysts have not yet incorporated the terms "dissociation" or the newer "unformulated experience" into their lexicon when discussing relatively high-functioning patients. In addition, the concept of repression offers the emotional security of the possibility of veridicality, whereas the idea of unretrieveable experience may conflict with the wish for certainty. On the other hand, the growing literature that emphasizes a broader conception of the unconscious in tandem with a rapidly growing constructivist mentality reflects a changing landscape.

REFERENCES

Aron, L. (1996). *A Meeting of Minds*. Hillsdale, NJ :Analytic Press.

Bromberg, P. (1994). "Speak that I may see you": Some reflections on dissociation, reality and psychoanalytic listening. *Psychoanalytic Dialogues* 4:517–548

——— (1996). Standing in the spaces: The multiplicity of the self and the psychoanalytic relationship. *Contemporary Psychoanalysis* 32:509–535.

Davies, J., and Frawley, M. (1994). *Treating the Adult Survivor of Childhood Sexual Abuse*. Basic Books: New York.

Fiscalini, J. (1991). Expanding the interpersonal theory of self-threat. *Contemporary Psychoanalysis* 27:242–264.

Frawley-O'Dea, M. (1996). Supervision amidst abuse: The supervisee's perspective, in M. Rock (Ed.). *Psychoanalytic Supervision*. Northvale, NJ :Aronson, pp. 313–329.

Gill, M. (1982). *The Analysis of Transference*. New York: International Universities Press:

Greenberg, J., and Mitchell, S. (1983). *Object Relations in Psychoanalytic Theory*. Cambridge, MA: Harvard University Press:.

Harris, A. (1996). False memory? False memory syndrome? The so-called false memory syndrome. *Psychoanalytic Dialogues* 6:55–187.

Hirsch, I. (1984). Toward a more subjective view of analyzability. *America Journal of Psychoanalysis* 44:169–182.

——— (1994). Dissociation and the interpersonal self. *Contemporary Psychoanalysis* 30:777–799.

——— (1996). Observing-participation, mutual enactment, and the new classical models. *Contemporary Psychoanalysis* 32:359–383.

——— & Roth, J. (1995). Changing conceptions of unconscious. *Contemporary Psychoanalysis* 31:263–276.

Hoffman, I. (1991). Discussion: Toward a social constructivist view of the psychoanalytic situation. *Psychoanalytic Dialogues* 1:74–105.

Levenson, E. (1983). *The Purloined Self*. New York. Contemporary Psychoanalytic Books.

Maroda, K. (1991). *The Power of Countertransference*. New York: Wiley.

Schafer. R. (1983). *The Analytic Attitude*, New York: Basic Books..

Searles, H. (1979). *Countertransference and Related Subjects*. New York: International Universities Press.

Singer, E. (1970). *Key Concepts in Psychotherapy*. New York: Basic Books.

Spence, D. (1982). *Narrative Truth and Historical Truth*. New York: Norton,.

Stern, D. B. (1983). Unformulated experience. *Contemporary Psychoanalysis* 19:71–99.

——— (1987). Unformulated experience and transference. *Contemporary Psychoanalysis* 23, 484–491.

——— (1989). The analyst's unformulated experience of the patient.

Contemporary Psychoanalysis 25:1–33.

———— (1994). Conceptions of structure in interpersonal psychoanalysis. *Contemporary Psychoanalysis* 30:255–300.

———— (1996). Dissociation and constructivism. *Psychoanalytic Dialogues* 6:51–266.

Sullivan, H. S. (1953). *The Interpersonal Theory of Psychiatry,* New York: Norton.

Prologue to Chapter 8:
ANALYTIC INTIMACY, ANALYZABILITY AND THE VULNERABLE ANALYST

Though I only met him personally a handful of times, I have experienced Harold Searles as a mentor of sorts—maybe more of an analytic hero than a mentor. This paper originates from a panel held at a Division 39 of the American Psychological Association conference—the panel was entitled, "Honoring Harold Searles" and I was delighted to have an opportunity to honor him.

In the very early days of my career I worked psychoanalytically in a day hospital and the patient population consisted mostly of people below age 30 who had recently been hospitalized either because of a schizophrenic break or a serious suicide attempt. In this setting and in those days there were still a subset of psychoanalysts that believed that psychosis was more related to personal factors than biological predisposition. Parenthetically, I still do believe this as had Searles until is retirement and ultimate death. Indeed, no one had written about psychoanalytic work with psychotic patients more extensively and profoundly than Searles, though neither he nor anyone else believed that this work was as easy as working with well functioning patients. The day hospital context was a particularly fraught one for therapists, since virtually all of our patients left for home at 4 PM and were not in treatment over weekends. There was consistent fear that any given patient might make another suicide attempt or relapse into another acute schizophrenic break.

During these almost four years I read everything that Searles (e.g., 1965, 1979) ever wrote and could never have sustained working psychoanalytically without him at my side. His work provided a sense of optimism that significant progress can be made under conditions of serious dysfunction accompanied by the anxiety of even more dysfunction. He, in tandem with some colleagues, taught me to see that symptoms made psychological sense—the serious troubles that patients experienced were adaptive and related to very difficult life experience. As well, Searles help teach me that I was not dealing with disease, but as Harry Stack Sullivan originally put it, problems in living. In my efforts to help my patients make sense of why they tried to kill themselves or why they fell apart and went crazy, I saw therapeutic movement in many of them. To this day there is little more satisfying to see a patient who has fallen apart to acute dysfunction, reconstitute and move toward a productive life.

This type of work was what Searles loved best and what became his professional devotion. Circa 2018, few mental health professionals believe that psychotic experience is anything but biologically grounded and Searles work has, unfortunately faded into the psychoanalytic background. For those like myself who believe otherwise, Searles remains an icon, a beacon of hope for patients that meaning can be made of all symptoms and that this can lead to meaningful change. As I learned from Searles, the view that patients are intrinsically damaged and subsequently treated more like sick patients than fully human and unconsciously motivated human beings, creates a self-serving hierarchy in our field. That is, Searles introduced the idea that many therapists have a personal stake in seeing their patients as far more "sick" than themselves, and that this dynamic helps keep patients dysfunctional. He emphasized throughout his writing how crucial it is to respect patients' strength and to be careful about overly pathologizing them in ways that are often condescending. In his writing, Searles was more open with regard to his countertransference experience than perhaps anyone else in the psychoanalytic literature. From examination of his own subjectivity he learned about his own malevolence, concluding that to deny this likely leads to enacting it with patients. Too few psychoanalysts have headed Searles's warnings about the dangers of maintaining an excessive hierarchy of, healthy analyst—sick patient split. No one in our literature exemplified the analyst as more human and more flawed than otherwise than has Searles and in this context situated patients and their therapists on a more level playing field.

REFERENCES

Searles, H. (1965). *Collected Papers on Schizophrenia and Related Subjects.* New York: International Universities Press.
———— (1979). *Countertransference and Related Subjects.* New York: International Universities Press.

Chapter 8

ANALYTIC INTIMACY, ANALYZABILITY AND THE VULNERABLE ANALYST*

In the spirit of Harold Searles, I will begin with a personal anecdote. One year prior to my wish to start psychoanalytic training, I decided to begin personal analysis. My paltry postdoctoral fellow's stipend required me to see a therapist who needed a training case and a colleague recommended someone whom he was seeing at a very reduced fee and who apparently needed one more training patient in order to complete his psychoanalytic training. The institute was a prestigious one and the man was an experienced therapist and not especially young. The externals sounded good to me, we met and had what I felt to be a fairly innocuous but certainly not unpleasant interview. At the end of the initial meeting I was informed that my prospective analyst could not see me as a training patient; indeed, he did not view me as analyzable since his diagnosis of me was "narcissistic personality disorder" (this was pre-Kohut). He went on to say that such a diagnostic category precluded analysis and recommended that I seek psychotherapy—elsewhere. I thought that my desired career as a psychoanalyst was over until the conclusion of my next meeting with another analyst. When he accepted me as a patient I nearly jumped into his arms.

My *directly* personal revelations end here. Whether or not I was or am currently a "narcissistic personality disorder" is secondary. The analyst in question, I am convinced, did not like me as a person and certainly did not wish to spend years with me darkening his doorstep four times each week, at a low fee to boot. This experience was the first which led me down a theoretical path of perspectivism and away from the view of psychoanalysis as objective science. Judgements of fitness for analysis are based on the subjectivity of the analyst as well as the external criteria belonging to the patient. Diagnosis as well may be readily influenced by the personal sentiments of the diagnosis maker. Someone who liked me better, for example, may have called me an obsessive character and deemed me a prime candidate for personal analysis. He or she would have been no more objective in his or her prescription than the antagonist

---

*Hirsch, I. (1998). Analytic intimacy, analyzability and the vulnerable analyst. *Free Associations.* 42:250–259.

in this personal vignette. Harry Stack Sullivan's strongest and most radical contribution to clinical psychoanalysis, the participant-observation model (see, for example, Sullivan 1953), was the first organized psychoanalytic point of view which captured the full meaning of a perspectivistic or relativistic approach to psychoanalytic data. The observer is always part of the observed; the analyst can never escape subjectivity. Though Sullivan's own reserved and suspicious personality led to his ultimate retreat into the role of "expert" observer, he laid the groundwork for contemporary interpersonal theorists (see, for example, Levenson 1991; Singer 1970; Wolstein 1964) to extend his thinking to a more truly participatory one, something closer to observing-participation (see Hirsch 1992). By deeming himself an "expert" in *extra*-transference interpersonal relations, Sullivan failed to exploit the full implications of his radical field theory; the rather equal investigation of both participants in the psychoanalytic dyad. The study of countertransference, the analyst's subjectivity and the unwitting participation in the transference-countertransference matrix, was taken up in the USA by those who were directly influenced by Sullivan. Harold Searles, particularly in his collected papers published in 1965 and 1979, is perhaps the United States' most significant contributor to the countertransference literature.

Searles's focus on analysts' intense emotional responses and unwitting enactments with their patients highlights the vulnerability of the analyst who does not retreat behind the protection of prescribed technique or of presumed objectivity. As Greenberg (1991) has noted, participant observation is not a prescription but a description of what occurs in any social relationship, including that between psychoanalyst and patient. Hoffman (1983) summarized an informal school of thought, which at the time he called "social constructivism," wherein the analyst essentially becomes enmeshed in mutual enactments and relies in part on the patient's perceptions of this countertransference, to use the interchange productively. Mitchell (1988) has distinguished the contemporary interpersonal position from others partially based on analytic observation occurring post-enactment. Hoffman (1983), Greenberg (1991) and Mitchell. (1988) have followed the pioneering lead of Levenson's (1972; 1991) and Searles's (1965; 1979) portrayal of the analyst as often lost within the transference-countertransference matrix. For these two theorists, the analyst begins as a reserved questioner, observer and interpreter, but before long is immersed as a second party in the patient's internalized interpersonal world. While Levenson emphasizes Racker's

(1968) concurrent countertransference interaction, Searles also includes Racker's concordant countertransference; the analyst's identification with the patient. For them and others, the analytic playground becomes an arena for repetition of the patient's life history with the analyst less as an observer and more of a participant in the patient's transference (Gill, 1982; Wolstein, 1964).

The concepts of transference and countertransference take on new meaning in this paradigm. The terms become inseparable and are converted into Sullivan's two-person field, the transference—countertransference matrix. Transference is no longer viewed as belonging solely to the internal world of the patient but as a combination of the patient's historical stamp on the analytic dyad and the way the particular analyst interacts with the psyche of the patient. Countertransference is a combination of those personal qualities that each unique individual analyst brings, in interaction with what is evoked in the interactional field. For Searles and others, countertransference is not simply feelings which should be used to understand the patient but actions which are both initiating and responsive. Searles has noted, for example, that the vaunted Oedipal configuration may just as well begin with the parent/ analyst's sensual interest in the child/patient as the traditionally assumed reverse. Aron (1992) has described the fullness with which the analyst participates, as captured in the term 'mutuality', and credits Sandor Ferenczi for introducing this spirit into psychoanalysis. The willingness of the analyst to be used or influenced (Feiner,1977) by the patient and not to retreat into the presumed objectivity of prescribed technique reflects the vulnerable analyst.

The vulnerable or co-participant analyst (see Wolstein 1964) who participates with considerable mutuality can be said to engage at what Ehrenberg (1992) has called 'the intimate edge' (see also Hirsch 1983; Wilner 1975). An acknowledgment that the patient is not a naive observer but, as Gill (1982), Hoffman (1983), Levenson (1991), Searles (1965; 1979) and Singer (1970) have stressed, is astutely aware of the analyst's participation, strips much of the hierarchy away from the traditional doctor-patient relationship. The person of the analyst is viewed here as not only visible to the patient but as having no greater comer on truth or objectivity than the patient. The analyst and the patient are seen having two distinct perceptions of each other and of events and neither one can be considered reality and/or distortion. The notion of the patient's transference as pure distortion or projection has protected analysts for some time from the power of the patient's perceptions. Gill's reworking (see, for example, Gill1982) of the key concept of transference has indeed led to a change in that concept from one implying a distorted impulse to that of a perception (Greenberg 1991). The patient's observations are seen as just as "real" or plausible as the analyst's. Searles, in his numerous articles on countertransference, had noted the patient's ability to read and respond to the analyst's participation long before Gill's significant changes in the concept of transference.

Searles has always been a master at turning widely accepted or hackneyed psychoanalytic conceptions inside out. In each such instance, he challenges the role of the analyst as the strong, healthy or objective party and the patient as the weak, sick and distorting party. I have already briefly noted this with regard to the origins of the Oedipal configuration. In Searles's brilliantly ironic paper on what he calls the "dedicated physician," he attempts to explode the myth of the strong and benign doctor ministering supplies to the weak and helpless patient. This theme most dramatically emerges in work with severely disturbed patients where the therapist can more readily assume the role of the kindly provider of therapeutic supplies. In this prototype, Searles notes that it is often the patient who is the stronger of the two parties. The patient, through considerable dexterity in living, may have traversed an extraordinarily difficult path to have arrived at his or her "illness." This "illness" may be a compromise that someone only with a powerful survival instinct could have negotiated. This position may have been so hard won, and therefore so deeply entrenched, that the patient will not be moved. Searles has observed that people sometimes love their pathology. Rather than seeing this position as a function of weakness or lack of ego, Searles views it as an example of enormous resilience and stubborn will; a kind of compromise of conflict. His view of the therapist as "dedicated physician" is that of one who responds with a pseudo-kindness and pseudo-strength, in the face of absolute impotence.

Faced with the task of a resilient and willful patient who may refuse to budge, rather than honestly facing weakness, the therapist may sadistically turn the tables and condescend to the patient. The analyst's sadism can readily be expressed by a view of the patient as a deficient, weak, egoless or arrested as a child. The analyst defends against impotent rage by treating the patient as if he or she is a helpless, pitiable child and by acting with a cloying kindness which is not at all genuinely experienced. This sadism may be enacted by repeated portrayal of the patient as passive and receptive or it may lead to punitive actions such as excessive use of medication or ECT, "for the good of the patient." Searles's recognition of the therapist as compensatorily sadistic in defense, reflects a marked reversal of what is normally outlined. However, only by recognizing personal impotence and helplessness can the analyst appreciate the patient in fullest dimension; not someone simply sick and in need of help, but someone in conflict who stubbornly holds on to a viable compromise. Searles's vulnerable, weak or "sick" analyst is a mutual enactor in the analytic field; a far more intimate co-participant than the defensively strong, objective doctor.

Another example of the intimately engaged and mutually participating analyst is detailed in an article which Searles has referred to as his most profound; "The patient as therapist to his analyst." Once again, Searles is responsive to the stronger side of the patient and to the neediness and vulnerability of the analyst, a theme that runs through his work. He views as the essence of all psychopathology, the patient's love and devotion to the family of origin, which ultimately leads to a potential "compassionate sacrifice." For Searles, the role of the sick member or designated patient in a family is to enable the rest of the family to survive relatively intact. The so-called sick individual is like an Atlas, carrying his or her world on strong but burdened shoulders. This Atlas is thus paralyzed; he or she can do nothing in life but attend to the needs of loved ones. The family, in this reversal of the usual prototype, selfishly allows the patient to engage in profound sacrifice, and acts as if this Atlas is really the weakest of the lot. The "sick" patient stays sick so as not to separate and leave behind the needy family. Herein lies another of Searles's reversals; psychopathology is based more on love and strength than on hate, deprivation or weakness. It is the patient's loving attachment that leads to paralysis; an unwillingness to expand and enrich life and to leave loved ones in the dust.

The analytic relationship becomes the likely playground for repetition of this theme, with highly functioning patients as well as poorly functioning ones. Just as within the original family, the patient is likely to become attuned to the needs of the therapist. As the relationship develops, transference love may take the form of embedding oneself in the therapist's life in order to aid the therapist to feel like a worthwhile therapist and/or a more healthy and whole person. The patient's own strivings for personal idiom and for separation may be overshadowed by sacrificial transference love. This configuration is likely to be almost as difficult for the analyst to recognize and to bring to light as it was for the original family. The vulnerable analyst wants the patient to love him or her by aiding the analyst to feel strong and whole. The patient's healthy separation, however, can only be advanced by the analyst's sacrifice. The analyst must develop the strength to allow the patient to separate and to leave the analyst behind and alone. The therapist cannot do this unless he or she recognizes that this transference- countertransference configuration exists in the first place and begins to appreciate the patient's sacrificial gift. If the patient's loving generosity can be accepted directly, the patient may no longer need to exhibit it sacrificially. Searles speaks of what he calls the universal need to give to another. When this wish to be generous towards loved ones is thwarted, indirect means of giving become dominant. It is this indirectness which often takes the form of sacrificial love or compassionate sacrifice. The intimate analyst is more likely to recognize his or her own role in the patient's sacrificial love, accept the love directly and free the patient to pursue a more selfish life of personal enrichment.

Searles's emphasis on the strength and/or generosity of the patient and the weakness and/or self-centered aspects of the analyst underscores his full, co-participant, mutual view of psychoanalytic engagement. Analytic intimacy refers to an interaction where both parties are exposed by virtue of their unwitting enactments. The analyst is weak, needy, selfish, malevolent and a benevolent helper, while the patient is not only a recipient of analytic help, but also strong, willful and a therapist to the analyst. The genuinely intimate therapist does not hide behind the role of the exclusively healing, objective participant. The analytic model which has been referred to as observing-participation (see, for example, Hirsch 1987) allows the therapist temporarily to lose the observing function and become transformed (Levenson 1972) by the patient and enmeshed in the patient's internalized relational configurations (Mitchell 1988). Countertransference here refers not only to feelings but also to enactments. Both the analyst's personal qualities and the stamp of the particular patient are evident, and analytic observation occurs most therapeutically post-enactment. Another way to describe this is that each analyst, in his or her unique individual way, enacts both the old and bad internalized objects and, hopefully, new and perhaps better relational experience. From this perspective, the therapist cannot be the exclusively good object. If therapeutic change is at least partly a function of new interpersonal experience with a good-enough analyst, this cannot be achieved unless the therapist is first part of the patient's bad internalized experience. That is, the therapist must unwittingly become a part of the old and the bad and, with the patient's help, recognize this repetition, and only then should an attempt be made to wind out of it and form a new relationship (Hirsch 1987). Analytic intimacy thus always involves the analyst's malevolent or destructive aspects in interplay with the patient's repetitive pull for harmful experience. As Levenson (1991) has succinctly observed, we cannot not be sadistic with a masochistic patient.

In an earlier article (Hirsch 1983), I have described "pseudo-intimacy" as similar to Searles's portrayal of the "dedicated physician." Psychoanalytic models where the therapist is purported to be exclusively the good object convey only a surface intimacy. The analyst may believe that he or she is able to avoid both expression of personal malevolence and/or being transformed by the patient into role-responsive (see Sandler, 1976), bad, old object enactments. From this perspective, analytic participation is one- dimensional. The role of the analyst in that single dimension may be to provide missing supplies to the patient in a manner which resembles an effort at re-parenting; what Mitchell (1988) has called replacement therapy. In what has been called "the developmental- arrest model" (see Hirsch 1987), the patient is viewed as a child who has been thwarted in his or her growth. The analytic role is to supply what was originally missing. This may take the form of gratification, empathy or offering oneself as an object for identification. The patient is viewed as fundamentally deficient and through the above-described modes of analytic participation these deficiencies are compensated. Another mode of participation in which the analyst is purported to remain outside of repetition in the transference-countertransference mix is that of the therapist as a holding environment. Here, too, the patient is viewed as an insufficiently developed child and the therapist as able to maintain the optimal distance between loving presence and intrusiveness, to allow for the stunted development of the so-called "true self" to emerge. The analyst as transitional object is exclusively a good object. Though there may be considerable merit in these models, the role of the analyst is prescribed to stay out of enmeshment in the patient's old and bad repetitive patterns and to be present only as a new or good object. It is always easier to view a child as lovable and, in turn, to be generous and benevolent to the child. In my own and what I believe to be the Searles's conception of analytic intimacy (Hirsch 1983), the therapist must unwittingly enact the full range of personal dimension of self in interplay with the patient's key internalized figures. The patient is viewed as an adult; albeit, perhaps, with some regressive features. For Searles, this is the therapeutic symbiosis through which patient and therapist must evolve before anything new or potentially better may be reached. Prescribed analytic technique wherein the analyst is able to stay outside of the transference-countertransference matrix lacks the subjectivity inherent in intimacy of any kind.

It is the analyst's awareness of subjectivity that leads to openness, honesty and authenticity and brings me back to the question of analyzability. The factors which comprise decisions to accept one patient over another are based on the analyst's theory, personality and his or her unique personal reactions to any particular patient (Hirsch 1984). Also, each patient enters analysis with repetitive patterns which are prone to evoke concurrent countertransference responses. For example, patients who were hated or rejected by key family members may readily evoke such responses from prospective analysts. Conversely, patients who were seen as special or especially nourished and adored in their families may often be viewed as ideal candidates for analysis. *As* a rule of thumb, the more successful one has been in work and in personal relationships, the more likely it is that one will be successful as an analytic patient—or anything else, for that matter (Hirsch 1984). Since most analysts, like everyone else, prefer success to failure, given a choice, highly functioning individuals will be accepted as patients more readily than their counterparts. Patients who are more likely to cause the analyst strong feelings of failure, fear, anxiety, pain, hatefulness, boredom or personal inconvenience are the least likely to be "good analytic patients.". Patients who act-out, threaten suicide, have psychotic breaks or intrude into the analyst's private life are likely to be avoided if the analyst's economic circumstances allow him or her to be choosy.

These responses are nothing but very human. It is only natural that most of us prefer the likelihood of success to that of failure and prefer to spend intensive and extensive time with patients with whom we might otherwise be friends, to those whom we would probably avoid socially or otherwise dislike. The analyst who acknowledges subjectivity and effectively integrates countertransference is more likely to confront the real reasons for preferring some patients over others. This personal honesty can be used as a legitimate reason not to see certain patients, or, indeed, to work with difficult people, productively using one's negative countertransference to help the patients. The latter is most emblematic of

Searles's work. The worst thing that an analyst can do, on the other hand, is to invoke seemingly objective criteria to rationalize personal choice. Some analysts may feel unprofessional if, even privately, they acknowledge their own "bad" feelings and thus need to fool themselves as well as try to hide them from their patients. Nonetheless, it is important to convey to prospective patients that there is a very large subjective element to decisions about analyzability. If an analyst does not wish to work with a particular patient, then that patient should be told that it is not because he or she is unanalyzable, but because the analyst does not think he or she could be useful (thus at least implying that someone else may). Analytic intimacy in the realm of the question of analyzability lies in the avoidance of a retreat into prescriptive criteria and in an effort to view the patient in deeply personal terms and to respond as a second party in the observing-participant matrix (Hirsch 1984).

As most psychoanalysts are aware, Searles is one of the very few who has worked analytically and extensively with schizophrenic patients. He has found exciting what most of us find daunting and unbearable. His unique ability is more a function of his unique person than his technical skill. Among his remarkable personal talents are his uncanny attunement to himself, his ready use of that attunement and a willingness to be honest and to share what he sees in himself and in others. He treats his patients as equals and never looks down upon them. He is fully present as a flawed person. He says what he sees and knows that it is fully subjective. He does not hide behind prescribed technique and pseudo-objectivity. His observations are obviously personal and are felt by his patients as such. He admires his patients' strength and willfulness and recognizes ways in which he is weaker or more troubled than they are. He is the embodiment of Sullivan's "We are all more simply human than otherwise." He seems to thrive on the freedom to be himself that seriously disturbed patients afford him, and in turn he gives himself to them in all the mutuality and subjectivity of true intimacy.

REFERENCES

Aron, L. (1992) Interpretation as expression of the analyst's subjectivity. *Psychoanalytic Dialogues,* 2:475–509.
Ehrenberg, D. (1992) *The Intimate Edge.* New York: W.W. Norton.
Feiner, A. (1977) Countertransference and the anxiety of influence. *Contemporary Psychoanalysis,* 13:1–15.
Gill, M. (1982) The interpersonal paradigm and·the degree of the therapist's involvement. *Contemporary Psychoanalysis,* 19:200–37.

Greenberg, J. (1991) Countertransference and reality. *Psychoanalytic Dialogues,* 1:52–73.

Hirsch, I. (1983) Analytic intimacy and the restoration of nurturance. *American Journal of Psychoanalysis,* 43:325–43.

——— (1984) Toward a more subjective view of analyzability. *American Journal of Psychoanalysis,* 44:169–82.

——— (1987) Varying modes of analytic participation. *Journal of the American Academy of Psychoanalysis,* 15:205–22.

Hoffman, I. (1983) The patient as interpreter of the analyst's experience. *Contemporary Psychoanalysis,* 19:389–422.

Levenson, E. (1972) *The Fallacy of Understanding.* New York: Basic Books.

——— (1991) *The Purloined Self.* New York: Contemporary Psychoanalytic Books.

Mitchell, S. (1988) *Relational Concepts in Psychoanalysis.* Cambridge, MA: Harvard University Press.

Racker, H. (1968) *Transference and Countertransference.* New York: International Universities Press.

Sandler, J. (1976) Countertransference and role-responsiveness. *International Review of Psychoanalysis,* 3:45–7.

Searles, H. (1965) *Collected Papers on Schizophrenia and Related Subjects.* New York: International Universities Press.

——— (1979) *Countertransference and Related Subjects.* New York: International Universities Press.

Singer, E. (1970) *Key Concepts in Psychoanalysis.* New York: Basic Books.

Sullivan, H.S. (1953) *The Interpersonal Theory of Psychiatry.* New York: W.W. Norton.

Wilner, W. (1975) The nature of intimacy. *Contemporary Psychoanalysis,* 11:206–26.

Wolstein, B. (1964) *Transference.* New York: Grune & Stratton.

Prologue to Chapter 9:
Seinfeld's Humor Noir: A Look at Our Dark Side

As I noted in my prologue to chapter 5, writing about fictional characters is the writing I most enjoy. This particular article is unique for me for me in two ways: it is the only thing I've published in other than psychoanalytic book or journal; it is co-authored with my daughter and this for me is particularly special in a very emotional way.

The fiction that I've written about and have been most drawn to focuses on the candid and unapologetic portrayal of the dark or noirish side of people: Portnoy, Tony Soprano of *The Sopranos,* Don Draper of *Mad Men,* and now, the four *Seinfeld* characters. My affinity, for example, of American cinema noir of the 1940s, the comedy of Lenny Bruce, early Woody Allen movies, *The Wire* series, the *Breaking Bad* series, and Larry David's (the primary author of *Seinfeld*) *Curb Your Enthusiasm* are representative of the direction I lean in my tastes. It also thoroughly reflects my attitude and approach to my work as a psychoanalyst, that is, a view of myself as inherently neither emotionally or morally superior or better off than my patients. My daughter, a psychologist as well, for better or for worse, may have identified with my appreciation of these noirish leanings, though if not, she certainly is sensitive to them.

A key question we raise in writing about *Seinfeld* refers to the puzzle of why there has been such a wide American popularity of a series which focuses on four New York characters who are either Jewish or who live in a dominantly Jewish, urban culture. The best speculation we have is to point to a broad resonance to a cynical humor that is astutely attuned to the darkness that lies within all of us. Were this not genuinely funny and focused on a narrow subset of the population, enabling many viewers to not own such malevolence as their own, this darkness might be emotionally difficult for wide audiences to appreciate and to digest. The four characters involved are unabashedly narcissistic and venal, with ill will toward all, even one another. The absence of any desire for love or intimacy and any trace of altruism is expressed casually and candidly and without any apparent guilt or conflict. These characters acknowledge openly and with total consciousness, the dark and ugly aspects of all of us. Most people either suppress, repress, dissociate or just hide and lie about the sentiments about which the *Seinfeld* characters trumpet—actually brag. Though never physically violent, they appear to have no conscience and serve as a mirror to the amoral aspects that lie within all people. They have no redeeming qualities and they are perfectly okay with this. Served on a plate with brilliant and sarcastic humor, audiences can, perhaps, on one hand, attune to their own malevolent dimensions while on the other hand, dissociate these qualities as belonging to alien characters on the screen.

Chapter 9

SEINFELD'S HUMOR NOIR: A LOOK AT OUR DARK SIDE*

Schwarzbaum of *Entertainment Weekly* calls *Seinfeld* the most unabashedly Jewish show ever to reach a wide television audience. Greenberg, too, has referred to this sitcom as overwhelmingly Jewish in its ethos, and compares it in this regard with the films of director Woody Allen. Allen's movies, however, for the most part do not appeal to a wide American audience and often fail economically despite acclaim from critics. Jerry Seinfeld et al. are consumed by vast audiences in the United States, *despite* the troupe's very thinly veiled ethnicity. The primary purpose of this article is to offer some speculation about possible causes for this success. In other words, we want to articulate the profoundly personal issues that this show touches on that may account for its widespread resonance among a diverse American and even international audience.

The themes addressed in *Seinfeld* must be sufficiently tuned in to some cross-cultural issues to transcend its New York, Jewish bias and appeal to so-called middle America. We suggest some key issues that connect emotionally to so many: immaturity and the changes to gender relations that have precipitated prolonged adolescence, later marriages, and normative divorce; narcissism and unrelatedness; and venality. The show's brilliance and its resonance with audiences rests in its ability to address these themes in ways that are normally unspoken in the public forum. The four main characters are quite different from one another in their respective personas but bear great similarity with regard toward their shared immaturity, amorality, narcissism, unrelatedness, and general ill-will toward others. There is insufficient data for a pychogenetic of these individuals, although their manifest characterological qualities are vividly portrayed.

This series has been referred to by its creators and by some critics as "a show about nothing." We believe, to the contrary, that the series is about very important "somethings." This high quality black humor is a satirical examination of the universality the dark characteristics that lie within all of us and are comically and cynically exemplified by these four

Hirsch, I. & Hirsch, C. (2000). Seinfeld's humor noir: A look at our dark side. *Journal of Popular Film and Television* 29:116–123.

beautifully drawn characters. As reprehensible as these four are, a vastly diverse population of viewers has closely identified with them. For those unfamiliar with the show, we will briefly describe Jerry Seinfeld, Elaine Benes, George Costanza, and Cosmo Kramer.

Jerry allegedly plays himself, a well-known stand-up comic who uses his real-life name and essentially hosts his three friends in his Manhattan apartment that serves as a clubhouse. Jerry is successful, the only career-directed member of the group. He is vain, neat, and attractive, always casually dressed, generally in tight jeans. He is virtually always aloof, cool, confident, and profoundly sarcastic and cynical in all social situations. Because he earns a good living and is the least hysterical of the foursome, he gives the strongest appearance of normality. However, he has declared, "I hate everybody," is phobic about germs, obsessed with neatness and cleanliness, and utterly uninterested in intimately loving another person. Any excuse is acceptable for ending relationships with many appealing and considerably younger women. "Love" is an unutterable word.

Jerry is an only child and is in relatively close contact with his rather normal and sympathetically portrayed, stereotypically middle-class Jewish parents. One can speculate that Jerry's narcissism may stem in part from their adoring oversolicitousness, but the degree of his venality and unrelatedness is hard to link with what we see from his interaction with family. The ever-sarcastic Jerry never expresses a kind or sympathetic feeling toward anyone and the only sincere things he ever says are penetrating and often humiliating criticisms. Relationships are games, and he has the requisites to be a winner-nothing ever hurts him.

Elaine is a "shiksa" who attracts Jewish men (among others), including a thirteen-year-old bar mitzvah boy and the presiding rabbi ("shiksappeal"). Elaine and George both are New York Jews in all their inflections and mannerisms, although they are designated as non-Jews to attract a wider audience that might not warm up to an entirely Jewish foursome. Elaine is dark, petite, pretty, and stylish, speaking in a subtle accent associated with affluent New York suburbs. She is outspoken, verbally aggressive, confrontational, uninhibited, and adventuresome. Elaine has an active sex drive, just as active a sex life, and is as unabashed about this as any woman on prime-time television. Like the male prototype and her three male buddies, she is thoroughly lustful and enjoys sex for the sheer pleasure of it. Also like her friends, she has no real interest in a serious relationship, marriage, or children. Like Jerry, she will use any excuse to break off a relationship with a boyfriend. Unlike Jerry, her lovers are almost always inappropriate losers and rarely match her wit and intelligence. As articulate and perceptive as Elaine is, she has no ambition and uses her wiles to avoid serious work. There is not, however, any sense of her wanting to be taken care of in a long-term relationship. Although sexy and feminine in manner and appearance, she is more like "one of the guys." There is little distinction made between her own attitudes and values and those of her three male friends. Elaine reflects a play on gender parity, a contemporary world where upper middle-class men and women are more alike than at any time in modem American history.

George, in counterpoint to Jerry, is a self-described loser: "short, fat, and bald" ("I am king of the idiots!"). Everything that can go wrong for him usually does; he is as awkward and abrasive as Jerry is smooth and seductive. He has no sense of any interest or realistic talent that may evolve into a career and attempts, in his jobs, to get by with day-to-day misguided trickeries. He states that he comes from a long line of quitters and that he was raised to give up. He is stingy to an extreme, totally dishonest ("I lie every day"), and thoroughly selfish, as are his three cohorts. This is best illustrated in an episode where he runs over children and old people to escape what he thinks is a fire. He comes close to marriage, but his fiancee dies ironically, directly related to George's petty frugality. George and his friends are quietly pleased when the doctor announces that she has died.

Through considerable exposure to his parents, we see George more closely than the rest. They are Italian Americans from Queens who have all the prototypical characteristics of Jews from previous generations in Brooklyn or the Bronx. They give the audience a look at the genesis of George's miseries. Mrs. Costanza is loud, abrasive, critical, and overbearing. It is known that she has never laughed. Mr. Costanza, who is even more loud and hysterical than his wife, is also suspicious of everyone. They have no sense that their son's life is troubled and do not worry about his misery or lack of aim. Bickering among themselves and with others is their primary commitment in life.

Although based on a real-life friend of the show's writer and co-creator Larry David, Kramer is the least realistic of the four. Kramer is a clown in appearance and behavior. He has electric, frizzy hair, a constant startled response, and wears peculiar retro 1950s outfits. He is constantly involved in physical pratfalls, more cartoon figure than a person. His temperament is less cynical than his friends' and, unlike them, he is never bitter, depressed, or sarcastic. He is perennially and naively optimistic, yet every scheme is a disaster, and he destroys everything that he touches. Although he appears relatively benevolent in attitude, one may infer from the way he destroys others' life, limb, and property that he shares his friends' malevolent qualities. Kramer appears to be in his mid-to-late forties, yet he too has no career (actually no job and no visible means of support at all) and no apparent interest in even moderate-term dating, much less marriage and family. In our way of thinking, he is the least substantial of the main characters—he comes closer to a clown figure than to a person we can identify in ourselves or with others in our lives.

Extended Adolescence

All four main characters, although at least in their middle thirties, live like late adolescents. They make every effort to rebelliously mock and flout rules of propriety (mocking themselves as well), and any view of life that is not "gamey" is viewed as weak and foolish. As Jerry proclaims in regard to dating, ''Without games, how do you know if you're winning or losing?"

In a classic episode, all four primary characters have a contest to determine who can abstain the longest from masturbating. No one is very successful. Their narcissistic involvement takes clear priority even in their close friendship with one another. This onanism (being "masters of their own domain") becomes crucially important to them in order to maintain other than full involvement in any relationship. The adolescent nature of the four friends' involvement in masturbation is most clearly accented by George. On one occasion George is "grounded" by his parents after having been detected masturbating on their bed. On another occasion, he is caught masturbating in his parent's bathroom. Although masturbation is common throughout life, it is rarely addressed in the media as an adult phenomenon. On one hand, it is just this sort of speaking about what is rarely addressed that makes this series so special. On the other hand, the preference for masturbation over sex with partners underscores the relative immaturity of the four friends.

For this group, sex and friendship are defined as mutually exclusive; relationships are characterized by one or the other. In a brilliant repartee, Jerry and Elaine discuss the possibility of becoming lovers again and conclude that it would destroy their close friendship. They decide it must be either "this or that," not sex plus warmth and closeness. George independently struggles about whether or not to introduce his girlfriend to his three friends, as he wishes to keep these worlds separate. He concludes that there are two Georges—the "relationship" George and the "independent" George—and does not wish his "worlds to collide."

The four friends live in a clubhouse atmosphere. They spend an inordinate amount of time in both Jerry's apartment and a local luncheonette. Career and work remain secondary both in time spent and in emotional commitment. Jerry rarely seems to prepare for his gigs and, on a play of being a comedian, he essentially mocks his own work—its comedy on comedy. The only one of the four who takes anything seriously is George. Despite his dishonesty, George has desires (e.g., women, food, notoriety, money, more hair, and thinness), and it is this that leaves him frequently hurt, disappointed, and humiliated. Jerry, Elaine, and Kramer desire little beyond casual sex and short-term projects in pleasure. Their ability to constantly mock themselves as well as others makes them emotionally invulnerable.

The immature antics of these four caricatured late adolescents are reflective of a number of contemporary psychocultural developments. The way they live and their interests are supposed to reflect contemporary middle to upper middle class urban life, with a strong Jewish accent. Particularly in urban areas and among all social classes, there are many more unmarried individuals than in earlier eras. The rate of divorce has increased markedly, and marriages among the more educated and professional groups are occurring at considerably later ages than during other periods. Consequently, childbearing tends to begin later in life. Later marriage and pregnancy have much to do with the dramatic increase in the number of women who stay in school to pursue advanced degrees, ambitiously engage in demanding careers, and compete relatively equally with men in the professional, economic, and courtship marketplace.

With many middle and upper middle class women and men taking longer to complete education, young people tend to remain economically dependent on their families of origin much later into life than in prior generations. Many such parents are second-generation Americans and have achieved reasonable affluence and career success. Whereas these middle-aged parents were expected to surpass their parents in education and achievement, their children often find it daunting to surpass their parents' sometimes highly impressive careers and financial holdings. This configuration can conspire to stretch adolescence and dependency, financial and otherwise, well beyond what adolescence originally represented.

The *Seinfeld* characters are a bit old for the first wave that suggests this phenomenon—they are more reflective of young adults now in their middle to late twenties to middle thirties. Their more advanced age may represent the exaggerated and caricatured nature of comedy and satire, in this case, the portrayal of forty-plus-year-old adolescents. The extension of adolescence so effectively satirized here resonates most directly with young adult, urban, Jewish audiences. This is the background, explicitly or otherwise, of the four leading performers and the characters they play. Nonetheless, as noted earlier, the show is enormously popular among very diverse populations of viewers.

The extension of adolescence seen in today's young adult population, despite the dependency conflicts that are implicit, may be the envy of a wide range of people who are not engaged in this way (as well as resonating with those who are). The four characters manage to live in very comfortable circumstances and engage in interesting and diverse activities, by and large, without needing to either work diligently or earn significant income. Their lives are more leisure than otherwise. Nothing is to be taken seriously, including oneself. This ethos not only applies to men (as is more traditional) but to women as well. There is no traditional distinction between the genders here. In this respect the show is very much on the pulse of developments in changing gender configurations (Dimen; Goldner; Guarton; Harris) and the growing equality between genders. The Seinfeld characters represent an exaggeration of this contemporary phenomenon. They touch the fantasized desire of so many who wish never to grow old, to be free of commitment, to be eternally able to play with friends (Fogel, Lane, and Liebert; Hirsch "Men's Preference"), and to have sex with multiple attractive partners (Stoller).

Narcissism

The celebration of pure narcissism as it exists in the educated, upper middle-class, Jewish male is well illustrated in Philip Roth's (1968) classic *Portnoy's Complaint* (see Hirsch "The Analyst's") and in Woody Allen's movie *Deconstructing Harry* (1997). Both Portnoy and Harry are unabashed and almost gleeful in their pursuit of selfish pleasure (particularly sexual). Not only do they have absolutely no regard for the ill consequences their behavior has for others, but it seems clear that injuring others, particularly women, is an important, albeit unconscious, aim. Although both characters differ from Seinfeld and friends by virtue of their strong career ambitions, all six care only for their own immediate pleasures. The acclaim of the book, the movie, and the television series is, in part, reflective of the resonance that these normally unspoken narcissistic desires have with a wide audience. It also suggests that these qualities are not exclusive to the well educated, Jews, or even men. The narcissism that Portnoy and Harry deny as consciously intended to hurt others is not simply openly acknowledged by *Seinfeld's* crew, it is gloriously celebrated. It cannot be underestimated that so many of these ugly "truths" emerge from Elaine. In contrast to the work of Philip Roth and Woody Allen, women here have parity of desire and of selfish interest. In these respects, Elaine is even more aggressive than her friends and this, we believe, has much to do with the popularity among women of this otherwise misogynist show.

The four main characters are inordinately involved with their respective bodies. None wishes to give his or her body or soul to another in any loving way. Sex with the same person over time is invasive, and pregnancy distorts the female body, making it unattractive to men. The *Seinfeld* body of work stands out among its peers for articulating narcissistic body obsessions that are common for many but rarely highlighted in film or television.

We have already addressed the frequent allusion to adult masturbation. In addition, this series makes extensive references to male baldness and the anxieties and concerns about adequacy that are related to hair loss. George perpetually laments these body states and is certain that most women find him unattractive. Toilet habits also are addressed here more so than in any other television program. Issues of amount of time spent in the toilet while defecating, reading rituals during defecation, post-toilet hand washing, and frequency of visits to the toilet are examples. In one episode, George is forced to purchase an expensive art book after taking it into a bookstore bathroom to read while defecating. There is reference, as well, to nose picking, a subject commonly avoided in media.

Episodes are also devoted to two aspects of the body that we have never before seen addressed yet are noticed and thought about by most people under relevant circumstances. The first is the observation that scrotums and penises shrink when men are in cold water for extended periods. This is raised in the context of worry about male potency and adequacy as defined by penis size. The second is the incidence of fleshy chests or "breasts" in some men and how this, as well, may lead to anxiety and doubt about masculinity. In one episode, Kramer and Mr. Costanza, who has "breasts," scheme to develop a male bra, "the Bro" or "Mansierre" for men who wish to restrict their chests from jiggling.

Another major focus of the characters' narcissism is centered on romantic relationships and sex. Jerry and Elaine attract the most partners and are quite vocal about these matters. Jerry is clear that he does not want a serious relationship, and his excuses ring of consciously intended insincerity and mockery of intimacy: not laughing at his jokes; not kissing him by third date; being too altruistic; having had too many other sex partners; not giving him a massage; "shushing" him while watching a television program; being too much his soulmate; not letting him play with her collection of antique toys; finishing his sentences. He wants to publish his own "relationship Monopoly" game, highlighted by a "get out of relationship free" card, which can be "superseded only by an eight more months of pain, torture, and guilt card." The closest Jerry has ever come to exclaiming love was when he was dating a woman (a stand-up comic) who was a facial look-alike. The reference to self-love was not at all a subtle one.

All the characters are prideful about their inability to love and their emotional barrenness. In becoming involved with an affectionate woman who tries to engage him in a "touchy-feely" relationship, Jerry mockingly exclaims, "I'm open [to feelings], there's just nothing there." All agree that they are interested in partners only when the partner is not reciprocally interested or when someone else is interested and has the partner's priority. Elaine is noted for her instant break-ups as soon as any of her peculiar set of boyfriends shows any interest beyond the purely erotic. About one rare reasonably appropriate man, she asserts, "He's a wonderful guy, but I hate him." All also agree that "you can't have sex with someone you admire." This principle guarantees optimal emotional and physical separation from their lovers.

As noted earlier, none of the four friends has any interest in raising children. When one of George's girlfriends is apparently pregnant, he is initially overjoyed that he is not sterile ("My boys can swim"). The theme of aversion to marriage and children is most strikingly brought home by Elaine, the lone woman. In describing one's wish for marriage, Elaine states, "It's a barren, sterile relationship that ends when you die." In reference to having children, her pithy and contemptuous remark, "It's been done to death," reflects both a sentiment rarely articulated by a woman in the media and an unusual parity between the sexes in the *Seinfeld* series. In Woody Allen's words and particularly applicable to the characters in this series, "Marriage is the death of hope."

The narcissistic involvement with the self and the inability to connect with others are lovingly portrayed in comically caricatured extremes. Such character traits, however, are not restricted to so-called "narcissistic personality disorders"; they exist somewhere along a continuum in most or all of us (Hirsch "Ubiquity and Relativity"). Most individuals, when honest with themselves, see something of the parodied selfishness and self-involvement exhibited consistently by Seinfeld and his friends. It is far more common than usually acknowledged, for instance, to be preoccupied with the body and body functions. Concerns about physical attraction currently pervade our culture. Never before have so many had elective plastic surgeries and engaged the range of diets to achieve bodies that resemble models and movie stars. Men and women alike seem consumed by their perceived physical inadequacies related to weight, height, baldness, hair quality and color, penis size and erectile potency, breast size and shape, length and shape of legs, and so on. In addition, fears and preoccupations about health are more typical than extraordinary. *Seinfeld's* absorption with toilet functions reflects, among other things, the obsessive worry that often accompanies any variation in usual bowel functioning. The creators and writers of this series are unusually well attuned to common narcissistic body concerns, and so many viewers seem to see this as a parody on their own body quirks.

In a similar vein, *Seinfeld* sensitively addresses the difficulty many men and women have in loving, staying in love, and remaining sexually faithful to lovers[1]. All of the *Seinfeld* characters are exposed to numerous attractive sexual partners, even "short, fat, bald" George. This titillates the fantasies of viewers who may imagine such benefits if only they were free of commitment. The awful things that are said about serious relationships and the valuation of interpersonal cruelty, detachment, and utter selfishness resonate with some of the wishes, if not the behavior, of most people. The never-married status of these characters also reflects, as already noted, the increased level of "singleness" in our culture. Of course, many who are single wish to or do become attached. Nonetheless, through formal separation and divorce, more individuals have been

---

[1]It is noteworthy that the strongest attachments and fidelities displayed are among the four friends. This interconnection is generally quite strong, although these four narcissists can also be very cruel and selfish toward one another.

choosing periodic separation over the older ethos of trying to make accommodations and work out matters. Seinfeld speaks to those who secretly wish to shed commitment, to those who simply fantasize about this, and to those who actually have done so. The sadistic thoughts and feelings expressed repeatedly about the nature of sexual fantasies, the loss of sexual passion toward intimates, and the wish for emotional distance effectively tune into the minds and feeling states of an enormous audience. Almost everyone can relate to at least some of *Seinfeld's* cynical observations about love and sex, and it is liberating to hear stated what is normally muted.

Venality

If the dominance of narcissistic sexual desire void of both commitment and reciprocity lends credence to Freud's besieged drive theory, unmitigated destructiveness and hurtfulness may be used to nail down this theory's validity. This article, however, will not be a vehicle to argue the relative merits of drive and relational etiologies of sexual preoccupation, aggression, and primitive exploitativeness. We know far too little about these characters' families and life histories (except, perhaps, for George) to understand their respective psychogenetics. A drive discharge understanding is easy here,[2] for Seinfeld and friends indeed are brutally unfeeling at best, and hateful at worst.

This thoroughgoing exploitative and unprincipled position is most clearly captured in the series' final episode (May 1998) and in the last show of 1996, although there are examples in every one of the 168 segments. In the long-awaited final episode, the foursome witnesses the mugging and robbery of an effete, obese man. Instead of coming to his aid or calling for help, they laughingly enjoy the spectacle and verbally mock the man's obesity and victim status. They are subsequently arrested based on an obscure bad citizen's law and put on trial. Many of the people they scorned and hurt over the series' duration return to testify to their destructiveness, and all four are convicted and sent to prison. In the brief prison segment of this finale, Seinfeld and friends show no remorse, fear, or worry; their life proceeds in prison as it did outside as they cynically denigrate their fellow inmates and the prison system. One of the unusual and

---

[2]Were we to search for genetic understanding of these characters, we would be personally biased to look more toward their unique interpersonal histories than in the direction of their unchecked drive states

creative twists of this last episode is its deviation from the traditional happy ending. One would think, based on film and television tradition, that these characters might recognize their unmitigated venality and arrive at some more humane place or they would be forgiven and then reform in loving reciprocation. *Seinfeld's* uniqueness lies in its relentless cynicism and its absence of any positive values in its corrupt characters.

The finale of 1996, we believe, reflects *Seinfeld's* most powerful example of these qualities. In this episode, George is absolutely miserable in his cowardly inability to wiggle out of his engagement to a lovely woman (Susan). His three friends are brutal in their efforts to portray the deadly life toward which their compatriot is headed. The dependent George agrees fully with his friends' prognosis; he is less consciously attuned to his dependency and to his wish for union than he is toward his narcissistic pseudoindependence. This ambivalent romance goes on through many episodes until the shocking finale when Susan becomes seriously ill, is briefly hospitalized, and dies. She is apparently poisoned by the cheap glue used on her wedding invitation envelopes, chosen by her frugal fiancé who thus inadvertently (?) kills her with his cheapness and ambivalence. The most shocking moment of all is reserved for the final fadeout. The four friends are in the waiting room where the doctor somberly tells them of Susan's death. They look at each other without expression except for the slightest trace of subtle smiles. They say nothing to the doctor or one another, shrug, and leave the hospital to resume their normal routines. The stunning absence of the normally expected response was dramatic and perhaps the most profound statement of the series.

Less dramatic examples of destructiveness and absence of core good will toward others are legion: People with infirmities are routinely the butt of humor; George gets into a fight with the Bubble Boy, a child who lives in a sterile tent because of an immune disorder, and accidentally destroys his bubble, almost killing him; Elaine wants to know what is the proper etiquette when an older beau has a serious stroke so she can gracefully abandon him; the group invariably parks in spaces reserved for the handicapped; Jerry's nastiness to an elderly great aunt precipitates a fatal heart attack; immediately after a friend of Jerry's attempts suicide, Jerry dates the friend's girlfriend. Tragedy is used as a vehicle for seduction: "There's nothing like a funeral to advance a relationship [sex]. She's crying, you put your arms around her to console her; it's like three dates in one shot."

Seinfeld exposes the human destructiveness and lack of principle and morality that exist to some degree in all people. Perhaps only the late

Lenny Bruce has done this better. It is convenient for most of us who live reasonably sophisticated, nonviolent, middle-class lives to attribute venality, harmful intent, and immorality to the obviously criminal or to the physically violent, those designated as evil by virtue of their overt criminal acts. *Seinfeld* artfully exposes the evil that lies even within a subgroup that is often associated with political liberalism, concern for others, high moral standards, peace, equality, freedom, and brotherhood. Although upper middle-class Jews are often associated with these "good" humanitarian values, *Seinfeld's* popularity with a broad audience suggests a wider net. People of all backgrounds from diverse parts of the country identify with the venality that is celebrated in each episode.

Seinfeld holds a mirror to our ugly, amoral aspects and makes such qualities seem all too familiar and human. In an earlier era, Lenny Bruce was persecuted for doing something similar. His martyrdom paved the way. It is a tribute to advances in civil liberties that *Seinfeld* can now exist in the medium of the "common man."

Conclusion

The absence of redeeming, positive, humanistic values of the characters in *Seinfeld* sets them apart from other sitcom series. The genius in the writing is the creators' awareness that viewers *identify* with the immaturity, narcissism, and venality of *Seinfeld*. The primary characters reflect the worst civilized (nonviolent) qualities that exist within most people, and these are flaunted with cynical humor. The message given by the creators is that this represents an exaggeration of what most middle-class, educated, and apparently evolved people are like. They seem to have succeeded in getting audiences to acknowledge their similarity with these characters, to resonate with and to accept some universally shared inhumane qualities, and to develop a sense of humor and acceptance about this darkness. *Seinfeld* is most decidedly *not* a show about "nothing"; it is a show dedicated to the exposure of some of the worst and most hidden aspects of the neat, well-manicured majority.

REFERENCES

Dimen, M. (1991.). deconstructing differences: gender, splitting, and transitional space. *Psychoanalytic Dialogues* 1:335–52.

Fogel, G., F. Lane, & R. Liebert. (1996). *The Psychology of Men*. New Haven: Yale UP.

Goldner, V. (1991). Toward a critical relational theory of gender. *Psychoanalytic Dialogues* 1:249–72.

Greenberg, H. (1996). Trivial pursuits: Seinfeld on the couch. *Psychiatric Times* 13:18–19.

Guarton, G. (1996). Masculinity, femininity and change in psychoanalysis. *Journal of the American Academy of Psychoanalysis* 24:691–708.

Harris, A. (1991). Gender as contradiction. *Psychoanalytic Dialogues* 1:197–224.

Hirsch, I.(1993). The ubiquity and relativity of narcissism. *Narcissism and the Interpersonal Self.* Ed. J. Fiscalini and A. Grey. New York: Columbia UP, 293–317.

———— (1994). The analyst's participant-observation with the special patient. *Comparing Schools of Analytic Therapy.* Ed. P. Buirski. New York: Aronson, 107–37.

———— (1997). On men's preference for men. *Gender and Psychoanalysis* 4:469–86.

Schwarzbaum, L. (1998). The Jewish question. *Entertainment Weekly* May 4:80–81.

Stoller, R. (1975). *Perversion: The Erotic Form of Hatred.* New York: Pantheon.

———— (1979). *Sexual Excitement: Diagnosis of Erotic Life.* New York: Pantheon.

Prologue to Chapter 10:
ON IDEALISM AND SOBERNESS: FOUNDING AND MAINTAINING A PSYCHOANALYTIC INSTITUTE

When I learned of the plan for *Contemporary Psychoanalysis* to publish a special issue on the broad subject of psychoanalytic institutes, I immediately asked permission to be a part of this. I had been one of seven colleagues to form a new institute in 1981, and administering and teaching at this institute has been a significant part of my professional identity and as well, an important part of my social life.

From the beginning, this experience has been an emotional roller coaster for me and this special issue felt like an opportunity, perhaps, to help resolve both some of my mixed feelings and my intense feelings about this undertaking with which I was still quite involved. Of course, this was difficult to do without getting personal in my writing, though being self-revealing in my writing was not new to me. I also hoped that others who were thinking of starting a new psychoanalytic institute might benefit from some of the difficulties I addressed, though I do acknowledge that writing this was more for my own potential benefit than anything else. However after stating this and after reading my first draft, I was pleased that this to be public article provided a history of the Manhattan Institute for Psychoanalysis and that there was possible value for those involved with this institute, present and future, to have a sense of this history.

The title, "Idealism and Soberness," captures some of the hopes, compromises and disappointments that I experienced and that I imagine anyone who has been a part of a project like this has felt. The older I get the less idealistic about anything I have become. The experience of being one of the founders of an institute has been one contribution to this development, though as I try to make explicit toward the end of this article, the net experience for me and I hope for many involved with the Manhattan Institute, has been far more life enhancing than it has been hurtful. Living life with a certain sobriety or even a sense of the inevitability of darkness, combined with caution about idealistic expectations, has been for me a useful lesson, or at least, an adaptive one.

Chapter 10

ON IDEALISM AND SOBERNESS: FOUNDING AND MAINTAINING A PSYCHOANALYTIC INSTITUTE*

It is highly likely that most of us who have founded a psycho-analytic institute or have been responsible for administering one have approached this responsibility with something that approximates idealistic hopes and dreams. As with most other significant commitments in life, however, one soon finds that perfection does not exist, and one begins to adjust to aims and goals that fall short of the original ideals. Even within the most successful and well-respected institutions, administrators must recognize the necessity for adaptive compromise.

The Manhattan institute for psychoanalysis admitted its first class in the fall of 1981, and I was co director and one of seven founders. All seven of us were not far beyond our own graduation from the New York University Postdoctoral Program in Psychotherapy and Psychoanalysis. Each of us was identified with the interpersonal track at NYU,[1] and we wished to spread our wisdom to potential analytic candidates who either could not or wished not to matriculate at NYU or at the William Alanson White Institute. These bastions of the Interpersonal tradition in psychoanalysis did not admit those colleagues who were licensed in social work, and we believed that this subgroup, having no place with a core Interpersonal orientation to train, would comprise the significant majority of our body of students. This turned out to be true in Manhattan Institute's initial class and is so to this day. To varying degrees all seven founders knew and liked one another, believed that we viewed psychoanalysis through a similar lens, and respected one another's talents as clinicians and as psychoanalytic thinkers.

We all felt strongly attached to our collegial connections and to our teachers at NYU, though we were aware of some flaws in this program and hoped to improve on it. In addition to the exclusion of clinical social workers without doctorates, NYU at the time had two serious shortcomings. The NYU Postdoctoral Program was fundamentally divided between two orientations, or tracks, Freudian and Interpersonal. Since

---

*Hirsch, I. (2009). On idealism and soberness: Founding and maintaining a psychoanalytic institute. *Contemporary Psychoanalysis* 45(3):330–344.
[1] The Relational track at NYU did not yet exist.

the program's inception, there had existed between these groups a strong antipathy that pervaded the atmosphere and at times erupted into rancorous administrative battles.[2] We idealistic founders of a new institution believed that we could establish an environment characterized by harmony and generous good will.

An additional shortcoming existed within the Interpersonal track alone. Although the quality of the clinical supervision of candidates was often outstanding, there was a singular absence of scholarship in the Interpersonal curriculum.[3] That is, almost every course in the Interpersonal curriculum was a clinical seminar, duplicating individual supervision with what amounted to group supervision. Many of the faculty were charismatic teachers and magnificent supervisors, and I believe that many of us received outstanding training in clinical praxis. Unless a student was ambitious enough to read the analytic literature on his or her own, however, one could graduate with virtually no scholarly exposure to either the historical literature or contemporary writing. Those of us who were students in the Interpersonal track had more fun than our Freudian colleagues, though we were often jealous of their intellectual rigor. The seven founders of the Manhattan Institute set out to duplicate the intellectual rigor of the NYU Freudians, while maintaining a core point of view that is best described as contemporary Interpersonal theory. We designed a curriculum that taught psychoanalysis from a historical perspective, and included courses that studied all the significant traditions in psychoanalysis, and were taught by faculty identified with these schools of thought. Correcting this scholarly deficiency in our own training proved to be an easier task than creating an atmosphere of social harmony at the new Manhattan Institute.

On a more directly personal "I" note (in contrast with a "we" designation), I believed that spending time on institutional administration would be a rich and rewarding experience. I was very active on committees as a candidate and young graduate at NYU and believed that having ultimate administrative responsibility would provide for me an excellent balance to seeing patients, teaching, and supervising. I believed that I would be a leader (co director) who would help create an egalitarian atmosphere[4] where community members at all levels

---

[2]This unpleasant situation was rectified some years ago.

[3]This problem has long since been corrected at NYU's Interpersonal track.

[4]This was one of the best features of NYU's Postdoctoral Program.

were free to speak their minds and that this freedom would lead to harmonious relationships among and between faculty, candidates, and eventually, graduates. I also felt that I was highly responsible, organized, and disciplined and that these were useful qualities for an administrator. Indeed, they proved valuable to a new institute but creating an environment where all were at peace with one another proved daunting for me. In our naive efforts to establish an ideal psychoanalytic institution, my colleagues and I originally shared some specific ideals, some of which were partially actualized while it was difficult to approximate many others.

Ideals

A. Money was not an important ingredient in running a psychoanalytic institute. Income would come from student fees and naturally from charitable contributions once it became publicly apparent what a stellar program we had developed.

B. All seven founders would continue to get along with one another, and rivalries, dislikes, and other pedestrian forms of engagement were beneath us.

C. All administrators would work equally hard and assume responsibility with equal rigor.

D. We would be able to be highly selective in choosing from an abundant supply of students, and faculty and supervisors would be pleased with the work of the vast majority of these candidates.

E. Students would be uniformly pleased with the quality of their courses, teachers, and supervisors.

F. A largely fulfilled body of students would become very active as graduates and thus help expand what the institute offers and happily slide into teaching, supervising, and administrative positions.

G. Referrals for private patients would be at least reasonably abundant, and no one at any level would want for earning a respectable living.

Students and graduates expected that their teachers and supervisors would admire their clinical work and in response fill their practices. Faculty and supervisors anticipated that their admiring students would refer to them their friends and family members.

H. If we did not institute a training analyst system (paralleling our experience at NYU), more students would apply since they would not be required to switch from an analyst outside our program to one of our own appointed analysts, or they would have a wider berth of analysts to choose from.[5] Further, we did not wish to create competition and a hierarchy among our faculty and supervisors, and we wanted to be able to offer our graduates (post five years) the possibility of working analytically with candidates and with potential candidates.

I. Offering faculty and supervisory positions to our colleagues from NYU, White, Adelphi Postdoctoral, and elsewhere would create good will among those designated, and those who were not invited would understand that there needed to be limits on how many could be involved. With regard to ultimately selecting graduates for faculty and supervisory posts, those not invited would generously understand that not everyone could be asked and that some graduates were just consensually thought of (by peers and by teachers) as simply better students than others.

Soberness

Aside from issues of physical health, there is little in life that gets one down more than having insufficient money and the ability to enjoy the amenities that relative prosperity allows. None of the seven founders of Manhattan Institute had any reasonable idea about how much money it took to run a not-for-profit institution, nor had we thought seriously about how this money was to be raised and how difficult this might be. In retrospect, this sounds absurd, but we assumed that, because we all had relatively decent practices and were diligent and hard-working professionals, money would come to our institute, somehow, as it had come into our independent practices. That is, the broader community would recognize the quality of our institution and relative economic security would inevitably follow. None of us had any interest in bothering with the pedestrian task of raising money, nor did we even think of incorporating a person who knew how to do this. We wanted to own, preferably, or at least rent quarters where classes and meetings could be held, where students and faculty could socialize with one another, and where administrative and secretarial personnel could be housed. We wanted enough money to advertise sufficiently and publicize our new program; we wanted enough secretarial help so that we would not be responsible for every administrative detail; and we wanted to pay our faculty for teach-

---

[5]Our only requirement in this regard is that a candidate's analyst be five years post graduation from a bona fide psychoanalytic institute.

ing. Nonetheless, during the two years of meetings to plan the setup of Manhattan Institute, almost all our time was devoted to matters of scholarship and educational organization (e.g., course sequence, course content, requirements for admission and for graduation, choosing faculty). We almost never spoke about economic planning. Before we began to collect fees from students, when funds were needed, the seven founders would simply give or loan the money to the institute.

In retrospect, we did everything backwards, and in so doing we created financial struggles that exist to this day. Indeed, before addressing the more interesting matters of courses and recruitment of teachers and candidates, we should have raised money to fund this enterprise to function in the style toward which we aspired. Since we ourselves all detested fund raising activities and, in particular, asking friends and acquaintances for contributions, we should have seen to it that someone else initiated those activities *before* we opened our doors to candidates. Many of our own and our professional colleagues' ideals do not include the pragmatic significance of material comfort, but a less head-in-the-clouds and more sober attitude is advised for any other group that considers beginning a nonprofit educational organization. Indeed, the founders of the Manhattan Institute knew nothing about initiating and running an organization, and such deficiencies, as will be seen, were not restricted to financial administration. Though our institute 27 years post founding is vibrant and thriving in most respects, we are still financially marginal and live with the minimum of economic security. And, though we have now incorporated persons who know what they are doing with respect to raising funds and administering these funds, there is much catching-up that is still needed. Most glaringly, the Manhattan Institute still does not own its own space, nor does it rent space sufficient to hold classes and meetings. If we had such space I believe that we would be an even greater magnet for students than we have been, and the institute would thrive all the more. The ideals of academic immersion cannot preclude the pragmatics of financial security if one wishes to create a truly ideal psychoanalytic institute.

Economic matters were not the only arena where the seven founders of the Manhattan Institute proved to be naïve. Though a few of us did have some experience in the administrative end of psychoanalytic or other mental health organizations, none of us were students of organizational psychology, nor, as it turned out, were we especially talented at managing an organization. Emblematic of our innocence was our failure to consider whether or not seven equal administrative partners could possibly run any organization efficiently. We assumed that all seven founders would be motivated to work equally hard and take the initiative to assume responsibilities with equal vigor. In retrospect, of course, this was impossible. Indeed, from the beginning there were great differences among us on this count, and inevitably this variable was a source of tension in the group.

Even more fundamentally naïve, however, was the expectancy in the first place that seven individuals would all continue to get along with one another and enjoy working together in a peaceful and harmonious group process. From my current vantage point this seems nearly impossible. The configurations of the relationships were quite different from one another, and the quality of each dyadic combination varied enormously. For example, one pair was a married couple, another pair had been close friends for years, another pair hardly knew each other, and another pair never really liked each other soon after the beginning of regular meetings. Four of the seven founders initiated the idea of starting an institute and deliberated considerably about whom else to invite to form the core planning and administrative group. Everyone involved was initially respected by the others both as a person and as a psychoanalytic professional. But none of us considered how different configurations of personal intimacy would lead to fractures and the formation of sub groups. As well, we failed to predict that in the course of a few years of intense contact, people who initially thought well of one another would not necessarily continue to feel this way. As should have been expected, some pairs or subgroups of the seven became close or closer, while others developed antipathies.

I think that all seven founders were looking for a close professional family, both among the seven of us and in the institution that we were forming. Our naïve expectancy that rivalries, factions, resentments and dislikes would not happen left us ill prepared to cope with these unpleasant matters when they eventually developed. Were we even reasonably exposed to training in organizational development, we would have expected the problems that arose and been better able to negotiate inevitable personal problems. Nonetheless, the Manhattan Institute survived these disruptions. A couple of the seven founders became less involved (or uninvolved) with the institute, a couple stayed active but withdrew from administration, and a few continued to be active on all fronts including in leadership positions.

Unfortunately, some resentments still quietly linger, though fortunately, the institute has found many second-generation leaders from within the corpus of graduates and faculty or from importing respected outsiders. None of the seven founders currently holds any important administrative position, and never again has the program been led by more than a trio of co directors. There has actually been no repetition of the disruptive strife that I reported among the founders, although nobody expects institutional harmony across the board. Whether one is looking for a professional family or for simply a professional affiliation, consistent ideal loving relatedness will not exist. Psychoanalysts are no more free from rivalry and petty or profound dislikes than is any other group. I have concluded that there is no ideal institute any more than there is an ideal national group, religious group, or political group. Every one of us is deeply flawed as an individual, and every organization has at least fairly serious internal problems. The approximation of the ideal can be reached only when there is sober recognition that there is no such thing as an ideal psychoanalytic institute any more than there exists an ideal human being.

It is also naïve to assume that cultural, economic, and societal conditions remain constant. As we have been reminded in recent years, when the stock market is booming or the real estate market is rising consistently, one ought not expect that this straight upward trend will continue. In the late 1970s the practice and the teaching of psychoanalysis in the United States was still flush from the exuberant popularity of the profession during the 1950s and 1960s. Insurance companies still reimbursed psychoanalytic patients reasonably well, and analysts and analytic institutes both experienced no dearth of patients interested in multiple-times-per-week treatment. The laws of supply and demand favored analytic institutes, and most programs were in a position to be quite selective in choosing candidates for admission. Many able candidates were turned away from their primary choice of institute and were forced to apply to their secondary choices. There were very few analytic institutes nationally, and, although New York City had far more programs than any other city, there did not seem to be enough slots for all those who were interested.

This lack was especially marked if one was from the social work profession. In response to this supply-and-demand configuration, a number of new institutes developed or were developing around the same time period. A number of these new programs, as well as older and more established ones, were delighted with the quantity of applications through the early 1980s. The Manhattan Institute was able to be highly selective in admissions policy, and classes of between 8 and 12 were normal in these beginning years. Income from course work and student fees was sufficient to allow the administrators to live with the illusion that we did not need to raise more money from donors. The relative abundance of candidates also allowed us to expect that market conditions for candidates would remain constant. Of course, this expectation proved not to be the case for either new or long-established psychoanalytic training programs.

It is difficult to know whether economic reasons, the advent of managed care, and the promotion of shorter term, symptom-focused treatments led to a decline in patient interest in entering analysis or whether simultaneously cultural interest in psychoanalysis was waning independently. I suspect both factors conspired to produce a decline in the numbers of patients interested in or able to afford to see analysts at a minimum of three times per week. Largely because of the growing shortage of multiple-times-per-week patients and the greater economic uncertainties in practicing analysis, applications to institutes across New York City declined considerably. The laws of supply and demand began to favor applicants and worked against the desire of analytic institutes to both be highly selective and admit large classes. By the mid- to late 1980s, it seemed that too many new institutions had been initiated and that some might not survive.

From then on, the class sizes at the Manhattan Institute were decidedly smaller, and we could not be as selective as we had been if we wanted to have a viable class each year. Nonetheless, over the years we are fortunate to have admitted what has turned out to be, for the most part, a highly talented student body. The strongest compromise the Institute has made in admissions has been in the realm of clinical experience prior to admission. That is, whereas in our early years we often suggested to applicants that they expose themselves to more clinical work and then reapply, beginning with the middle 1980s we often could not afford to do this.

It is difficult for me to discern if our early candidates developed into analysts who were superior to those who followed, although if they did, the difference has not been dramatic. I am not sure that I can explain the reason for this, since it is somewhat counterintuitive. Perhaps more recent candidates, entering the field of psychoanalysis in a less than ideal time period, needed to be more highly motivated and devoted than their predecessors were. This era has not been an ideal time to pursue a career in psychoanalysis, and analytic institutes often have been forced to have far less than ideal class sizes and to choose from a small pool of applicants. Times change and compromises with the ideal are made by necessity. Even under ideal conditions of supply and demand, not all candidates who are selected turn out to be pleasing to their teachers and supervisors, that is, "good" analysts as judged by both informal and formal peer and teacher assessments. Though it is naïve to expect judged excellence across the board, the idealism and grandiosity involved in beginning a new institution somewhat blinded my colleagues and me to this sober reality.

While administrators, faculty and supervisors were learning that the candidates were not ideal, candidates found that their teachers and supervisors could also be disappointing. I will say more about this process later, but for now I will note that the seven founders of the Manhattan Institute, being very careful to choose teachers and supervisors who represented diverse psychoanalytic orientations, spent an enormous amount of time selecting who among our many colleagues to invite. This was painstaking a task and was also often quite hurtful to friends and close colleagues who were not invited to join us as teachers and supervisors. In our naïve idealism, we were convinced that each course would get excellent reviews from students who would be uniformly pleased with the learning process in supervision.

Of course, that was not what happened. As time went by some supervisors were no longer requested by students, and some teachers were asked by the administration not to teach any longer. This process was very difficult and, for rejected teachers and supervisors, very hurtful. An ideal institute would be composed of teachers and supervisors who are uniformly adored, but in reality in every institute some classes are dull and some supervision is disappointing. I like to think that Manhattan Institute's teachers and supervisors have higher than average ratings as compared with other programs, although even then the learning process will always fall far short of ideal. Indeed, teaching in particular is very hard, and a certain percentage of classes in any educational setting of any sort will be found to be boring and unproductive. Careful selection processes will never fully control for this any more than such processes can select invariably excellent students.

I was very active in my early years after graduation from NYU Postdoctoral, both in volunteering for administrative responsibilities and in trying to build a society of graduates. This was also true for most of the seven founders of Manhattan Institute, and we all hoped that our candidates would be grateful for their excellent education and contribute to the growth and development of their cherished institution. I expected that institute graduates would actively attend colloquia, form committees, or join committees, in sufficient numbers to share the increasingly tiresome administrative burden of running an institute, and initiate the fund-raising dimension of administration so phobically avoided by their seniors. In an ideal institute every graduate would stay involved, and, even if some did not assume responsibilities, all would at least attend meetings and parties and "stay in touch." It did not take long for soberness to set in. Some graduates were not pleased with their education and never again had anything to do with Manhattan Institute; others did not feel sufficiently recognized by their teachers, were hurt, and decided to disconnect; and still others were simply involved with personal commitments that far overshadowed institute loyalty. My idealism had not led me to expect this lack of continuing interest in the institute, and I was disappointed. Although one need only look at older and more established institutes to see that a certain percentage of graduates will always be either disaffected or uninterested in remaining involved, idealism creates a certain blindness. I wanted a community where there was universal good will and intense involvement, and this was not a sober expectation. Not every graduate felt grateful to me and to my co founders for creating an ideal culture.

Nonetheless, though far from my ideal, Manhattan Institute's graduates have come to contribute greatly in many ways. Many now teach and supervise and present at colloquia, and, in large part, our graduates have become the institute's primary administrators. There is now an active society of graduates who initiate new programs and assist in the running of the institute in every way. In a sense, the institute now belongs to its graduates, and even though to me this is wonderful, it is not ideal. Too many no longer are a part of this community and see our institute as too far from ideal.

Among the disappointments of disaffected graduates, as well as many graduates who are strongly committed to Manhattan Institute (and most other institutes too), is the sobering fact that it is difficult for most analysts to earn a comfortable income in full-time practice in New York City. There is simply an insufficient number of potential patients interested in long-term treatment, much less multiple-times-per-week analysis, to satisfy the professional and economic needs of what has evolved into a probable oversupply of trained psychoanalysts. This situation is, as I mentioned, likely related to a few key factors: declining insurance reimbursement, the emergence of popular shorter term treatments, including dramatic advances in psychopharmacology, and the decline of psychoanalysis' cultural cachet. Despite the declining numbers of newly trained analysts, too many analysts still complain about considerable financial uncertainty and anxiety, and this dilemma is also often true for many senior analysts.

I and almost everyone I know, regardless of generation, entered analytic training anticipating, or at least hoping, that their teachers and peers would refer enough patients so that a strong practice would develop. Indeed, most analytic candidates have the fantasy that their teachers are prosperous and have an overabundance of referrals that they cannot absorb and that candidates will benefit. Though such referrals do occur to some degree, most usually fall far short of most candidates' hopes, and this disappointment often results quickly in the training process. This dearth of referrals is sometimes the first significant jolt to students' conception of an ideal training situation. At first, candidates may feel that their teachers do not deem them worthy of referrals, but before long, in dialogue with peers and or/supervisors, it can become clear that the senior professionals have far fewer than expected referrals to dispense. And many referrals that are made go from senior analysts to their senior friends and colleagues. Because referrals are not abundant for so many at all levels of our profession, referrals are often made to those who are most likely to refer back. Candidates' desires to be taken care of with referrals are not at all unreasonable. It is often disillusioning, indeed, frightening to recognize that the road to economic security may be a very difficult one and that one must become independently imaginative and creative in an effort to achieve it. Many candidates, newly trained graduates, and even senior practitioners not only suffer from a paucity of multiple-times-per-week patients in their practices, but also find themselves practicing in ways that are not analytic in order to meet financial obligations. Some stop practicing in an analytic vein entirely so as to make financial ends meet.

It has become clear to me over the years that we who strive to teach and supervise at analytic institutes are as much motivated by our own quest for economic well-being as are analytic candidates. In becoming part of any institution one inevitably hopes that referrals will come from peers as well as students. Indeed, in those institutes that have a training analyst system, students are required to become patients of a select group of senior analysts. I believe that this is the single biggest motive for maintaining such a hierarchical system (I will say a little more about this later). Even absent a training analyst system, however, teachers and supervisors hope to see candidates as patients and also hope to get referrals from the roster of friends and family of their admiring juniors. This is as much of a fantasy for faculty as is students' desire to be looked after by senior teachers.

In an ideal institute, candidates and graduates would get the referrals they need to practice analytically and to earn a good income. One could argue that institutes ought not admit students without being able to help them build their practices. And, in an ideal institute, teachers, and supervisors will have a steady stream of referrals from many sources and not be dependent on their students to be their patients or to supply referrals to them. In an ideal institute I believe that faculty should take care of candidates' and graduates' financial needs, so that graduates can concentrate on becoming better analysts and not compromise their attention with non analytic therapies in order to earn a decent living. Achievement of this goal is far from our situation at Manhattan Institute, as well as in the other four institutions where I teach or supervise and, I believe, in most analytic training centers in New York City and probably nationally as well.

Economic considerations are seldom far from conscious awareness when one is addressing most professional matters, though in an ideal world and in an ideal analytic institution such considerations might be in the background rather than foreground—an expectation that is highly naïve. To get a flavor of the scope of importance of matters economic, one need only read one of Freud's biographers (e.g., Gay, 1988), and see how central financial concerns were to the founder of psychoanalysis. Money matters are usually discussed among peer friends, and most analysts, young and old, are not keen on making public the degree to which such concerns are central to them (Hirsch, 2008). The wish to attend a psychoanalytic program as a student and the ambition to participate in an institute as a teacher, supervisor, or administrator cannot be viewed as independent from financial considerations. Certainly these considerations are as potent for most faculty, supervisors, and administrators as they are for students. The wish for financial well-being makes administrative decisions related to faculty and supervisory appointments inevitably a very loaded and controversial issue.

Even though the seven founders of the Manhattan Institute were aware that the selection of faculty and supervisors was a thorny matter, we were, nonetheless, naïve about the degree of personal difficulty that might result from selecting some people and not others. Our initial effort to tackle this matter was to reject a training analyst system. Having trained at NYU Postdoctoral and appreciating the benefits of their liberal policy for who can serve as an analyst for candidates (any graduate, five years post graduation from an approved analytic training program), all seven of us agreed to adopt this standard for our new institute. Though many have argued that a "good" analysis by a "highly capable" analyst was a crucial candidate experience for both personal growth and learning to be an analyst, we did not believe that, even with the noblest of intentions, could a truly equitable system be devised to determine who was good and who was not quite good enough to analyze analytic students. We knew that the personal biases of those who do the choosing can never be separated from such choice and that it was audacious to suggest otherwise. We further observed that institutions with tiers of training analysts and others who wish to be training analysts and are not, create an unfortunate hierarchy, where a minority of graduates walk with a certain swagger of success but a majority have the stooped posture of dysphoria or feelings of bitterness or inadequacy. We also felt that it was unfair to create a situation where a minority of analysts had not only a distinct bump in status but also a considerable economic advantage as well.

With our shared heritage from the left-leaning NYU Postdoctoral Program, this was one of the matters about which there was total accord. To this day, those of us who are still active at the Manhattan Institute are very pleased with the decision not to institute a training analyst system. Although some of the analysts chosen by our candidates over the years have, in my own personal estimation, been far short of ideal, I cannot say that this percentage is any different from candidates who have gone through institutes with a training analyst system. Anecdotal discussion with many of my colleagues points to not infrequent dissatisfaction with their initial official training analysis, and many in our field return to treatment and choose a different analyst (Tessman, 2003). This of course proves nothing, and a controversy will always exist in our field. I am convinced, though, that the absence of a training analyst system at Manhattan Institute has made our program closer to the unreachable ideal than it might have been.

Unfortunately, though inevitably, other subjective selections need to be made in any educational institution; the results of these choices are imperfect, and some individuals are always injured. An institution will never be ideal while some colleagues may feel chosen and adored and others abandoned. A certain percentage of the latter group will invariably become disaffected with or antagonistic toward their more "in" colleagues. In this way alone an institution can never even approach the ideal of a uniform happy population. The founders of the Manhattan Institute failed to appreciate how strongly some of our friends and colleagues would react to not being invited to become the initial group of teachers and supervisors for our candidates. We had assumed that because these people would be eligible to analyze our candidates in our non training-analyst system they would be happy to be affiliated with us in this less formal manner. In retrospect it was naively idealistic, even foolish to believe that colleagues with whom we had been friendly would not be terribly hurt by seeing peers included while they were not. How could this rejection not be perceived as a harsh judgment of their basic competence? Though there were no obviously recognizable consequences within the community of the Manhattan Institute per se, some of us who were founders and selectors made enemies for life. The institute did suffer to the extent that those colleagues who felt hurt and excluded did not refer candidates to us and some even steered them toward rival institutes.

The process of selecting faculty and supervisors from within the community of Manhattan Institute's graduates has caused tension and discord in much the same way that the ordaining of training analysts has in other institutions. Unfortunately, there is no way to avoid this problem, though, fortunately, not every graduate wishes to engage in the sometimes grueling preparation and stress that often accompanies teaching. Parenthetically, almost every graduate of a training analyst system wishes to become a training analyst. Those who make it clear that they are not interested in teaching are obviously less likely to be wounded than their counterparts who wish to become faculty and are not invited. Manhattan Institute has evaded the often equally thorny question of choosing supervisors. No one has been chosen to be just a supervisor, the initial selections having been made when the institute was formed. Since that time, our policy for becoming a supervisor has been linked to teaching. More specifically, if one is selected as a teacher among the pool of interested graduates or outsiders, and if, after teaching there is a favorable written set of evaluations from the class, the teacher becomes both a member of the faculty and a supervisor. Many of our graduates, as well as graduates of other institutes, would like to supervise without first having engaged in the more laborious activity of teaching, and the chore of making such selections would likely create enormous hurt and resentment both within and outside our community. Although such a decision seems to me close to an ideal one, there is no way to circumvent the problems involved in inviting some and not others to join faculty. Because such choices need to be made, there will exist a population of injured parties, further confirming that there is no possibility for an ideal situation in any psychoanalytic community.

Concluding Remarks

I feel very proud to have been one of seven founders of the Manhattan Institute for Psychoanalysis and to have been the co director and then director for the institute's first 11 years. Twenty-seven years later this "boutique" institution, though struggling in ways that so many analytic programs are struggling these days, is also a vibrant and thriving community. By accenting primarily the darker or more sober elements of organizational life that fall short of anything called ideal, I worry that I have failed to portray how rich the experience of forming a new institute has been for me and how vital a community we created for so many wonderful psychoanalysts. I am very proud that our graduates received a strong scholarly education and were exposed to a range of theoretical points of view. Indeed, many found other schools of thought more compelling than the Interpersonal perspective and felt free to pursue these lines of thinking while candidates. More than anything, I am grateful to all the people I have met and come to know (students, graduates, faculty) whose path I might never have crossed were it not for the existence of the Manhattan Institute. Many of them will be highly valued relationships for life, and I appreciate that many in this community have formed configurations of personal relationships and can say the same. We tried to form an ideal institute, and we established one that, though far from ideal, has added significantly to the well-being of so many in the analytic community and so many patients who have been served by them. A certain level of soberness will always shade unfulfilled ideals, though the potential for richness in striving for certain ideals makes the project decidedly worthwhile.

REFERENCES

Gay, P. (1988). *Freud: A Life for Our Time*. New York: Norton
Hirsch, I. (2008). *Coasting in the Countertransference: Conflicts of Self-Interest Between Analyst and Patient*. New York: Routledge Analytic Press.
Tessman, L. (2003). *The Analyst's Analyst Within*. Hillsdale, NJ: Analytic Press.

Prologue to Chapter 11:
IT WAS A GREAT MONTH: NONE OF MY PATIENTS LEFT

This title was taken from a quote from a colleague, published as part of a chapter on money, in my first book (Hirsch, 2008). The editors of the book where this current article was published were very taken by this quote, since it seemed to capture for them how worried so many analysts are about the ability to earn a good, upper middle class livelihood. Indeed, as I have observed, analysts' moods may very from despair to elation, depending on current patients terminating or potentially new patients calling for an initial appointment. And, even when a termination is planned based on therapeutic success, the loss of income involved often creates a down mood.

I have referred to analysts' financial concerns as the biggest problem in our field (Hirsch, 2008). This anxiety often leads to patients being encouraged to remain in therapy longer than warranted, creating a mutual dependency that is excessive and destructive to our patients. There are many other potential consequences that are based on analysts' need for income, to sight a few: pushing-out prematurely patients who pay a low fee; seeing patients one session per week at a high fee rather than the analytic preference to see people multiple times per week (which often involves a lower per session fee); determining that a patient *needs* therapy for life—I've heard the term, "lifer" used to justify this regressive forecast; analysts' failure to address patients' darker sides, fearing that this may make more conscious patients' anger and that this anger will lead to anger at the analyst and precipitate premature termination; seeing patients for double sessions rather than inconveniencing them by the expectancy that they physically attend multiple sessions per week; and for similar reasons, settling for telephone or Skype sessions when a patient may be able to attend in person; accepting referrals from patients of those close to them rather than suggesting referral to a colleague.

I would not be attuned to the destructive aspects of analysts' financial needs were I not guilty of such compromises myself. The only way to combat this problem is to recognize with candor that we selfishly need money for many reasons, not least of which is to feel successful in a very competitive profession. It is normal to desire a comfortable life and to wish for the esteem of success, the latter so often defined by money. Any absence of analysts' candid self-awareness of these matters makes it more likely that therapeutic compromise will occur.

REFERENCE

Hirsch, I. (2008). *Coasting in the Countertransference: Conflicts of Self-Interest between Analyst and Patient.* Routledge: New York & London.

Chapter 11

It Was a Great Month: None of My Patients Left*

In this chapter, I will attempt to expose my psychoanalytic profession and myself as simply human when it comes to money and to greed. I believe that an analyst's awareness and acceptance of his own disquieting characteristics are likely to lead to more productive use of these feelings in our everyday analytic work. When we analysts deny our shameful or personally discordant feelings and strivings around money and project them into patients, we lose touch with them and are at risk for doing harm in our work.

A number of years ago, shortly after I left my hospital job and began full-time independent practice, I ran into a former supervisor of mine who I had not seen for some time. She was with her lawyer husband, and after she congratulated me for making the bold move into private practice, something she had been reluctant to initiate, her husband asked me bluntly how I dealt with the conflict between my patients getting better and leaving and the loss of income that followed. He implied quite clearly that his psychologist wife, senior to me and more qualified, had chosen the professional high ground by continuing to see her patients on a hospital salary basis. His commentary was not only pithy, but also profound and jarring. It was a distinct departure from the normal congratulatory, well-wishing responses to which I had grown accustomed. I had no intelligent answer to his question, and I recall mumbling something about recognizing that this was a problem, and that I hoped my successfully discharged patients would be satisfied consumers and refer others to me.

I had a similar encounter some 30 years later while I was in Germany for a conference. At a dinner with a few German colleagues I had just met, I learned that national insurance paid 100% of psychotherapy and multiple times per week psychoanalytic fees for prolonged periods of time. I was further told that because of this coverage, virtually every analyst had a full practice and a waiting list for new patients. My jealousy was palpable, although tempered by their lament that the fees that I and

*Hirsch, I. (2012). It was a great month: None of my patients left. In: B. Berger & S. Newman, Eds. *Money Talks*. New York & London: Routledge, pp. 13–20.

other American analysts were charging were roughly two to three times what they received. Parenthetically, the issue of fees and busyness of practice is a primary subject of discussion whenever I travel, as soon as a drink or two loosens tongues.

One of my German colleagues, when learning from me that the practices of the vast majority of American analysts were not full, and that the competition for patients in the marketplace of supply and demand was often considerable, asked the same question put to me 30 years earlier. He wondered how I could try to help patients when an ultimate positive outcome would lead to my losing income. This time I was more prepared and had a better answer. I had already coauthored an article identifying economic conflict as the single greatest problem in our profession (Aron & Hirsch, 1992), and I was in the planning stages for a book dealing with issues such as these (Hirsch, 2008). I essentially told this man that I believed his system created far better conditions for productive analytic work, and that despite my enjoying much higher fees, I believed I would be both less anxious and a more useful analyst in their system.

Economic anxieties plague all but a very few analysts I know, especially in large American urban areas like New York City where the supply of trained analysts is voluminous, and the relative number of potential patients who can afford preferred analytic fees creates considerable competition among analysts. Most colleagues are elated when a new referral comes and depressed when a patient leaves prematurely. Sadly, even after a successful analytic experience, it is often difficult to feel satisfaction and pride only, without this being tempered by anxiety and regret in relation to lost income. This is best captured by an interchange I had with a colleague. "How's it going?" I asked him when I ran into him one day in the street. "It's been a great month-none of my patients left," he responded.

The degree to which we are dependent on our patients both to exercise our skills and to create economic security is powerful, and although this is preoccupying, it is rarely addressed in the literature or as part of formal panels and conferences. Analysts' economic dependence on patients leads to an inherent and profound conflict between self-interest and patient interest, and this conflict always has the potential to severely compromise analytic work. Indeed, I believe that analysts' financial concerns reflect the most vivid example of this conflict, and I believe that our anxiety about income is the single greatest contributor to compromised analyses.

There are many and often major consequences of worry about money. Perhaps the most common one is the problem of keeping patients in treatment for too long and the excessive mutual dependency that inevitably arises. I have no actual research data to support this, but my own anecdotal observation is that many patients remain these days in analysis for a staggering number of years. This appears to be more common than it was in previous generations. Contemporary patients (many of whom are analysts themselves) often seem to remain in analytic treatment for 10,15, 20, or even 25 years, with the same analyst.

A related effect of analysts' economic interests emerges in the number of times per week that patients are seen. With most analysts, I also believe that at least three sessions per week is optimal for good analytic work. But analysts' motives for seeing patients multiple times each week are sometimes unrelated to this analytic ideal. Some patients who are seen frequently are not necessarily being treated in an analytic context with analytic aims. That is, some analysts do supportive or maintenance-oriented work with patients who can afford this, and they behave as if they were conducting a formal analysis that actually requires the frequent sessions. Similarly, many patients who can afford high fees will be seen multiple times per week for many, many years, long after analytic goals still prevail. One colleague has said to me, without shame, that a couple of his patients are so troubled that he anticipates that they will be "patients for life." Another well-respected colleague proclaimed at a clinical meeting that she and all of her colleagues have what she called their "lifers," patients who allegedly "need" to be in analysis for literally their entire lives. Shockingly, this statement was not challenged by others at the meeting.

In these situations, "analysis" has become a vehicle for the creation of mutual attachment and dependent ties, and the rationale for this centers around biased assessments of patients' psychopathology. The very idea of adhering to the patients' original analytic goals or aims is forgotten too often. Maintenance of the analytic relationship can, and frequently does, become an end in itself.

Another compromise precipitated by analysts' anxiety about money occurs when the analyst strives to be liked by his or her patients so that they remain in treatment. This takes the form of analysts being overly supportive and complimentary or striving to be helpful in ways that do not correspond to the analytic aim of facilitating autonomy. They may avoid challenging patients when this would be potentially useful, or they may duck uncomfortable transference themes, particularly those related to anger and disappointment. Analysts may be too tentative so patients' anxiety, even productive anxiety, is kept to a minimum. They may use deliberate self-disclosure to gratify patients' wishes.

I also believe that certain theoretical points of view are sometimes embraced more because they are gratifying than because they are likely to effect ultimate separation and autonomy. Both analytic reserve and analytic challenge can be eschewed for fear that these attitudes may provoke patients to quit, while measures that are more traditionally associated with supportive psychotherapy serve to maintain patients in prolonged attachments.

It is my view that analysts will be more likely to conduct briefer analyses, and analyses that foster independence, when they are more willing to let patients leave and bear the loss of income. Unfortunately, this does not occur enough in our current analytic culture. When it does, it may be a function of an analyst's practice being full, the analyst having new patients waiting, or the patient's fee being so low that the analyst does not wish to prolong this commitment at such a reduced fee. I am not suggesting that the willingness to see patients leave is always good. This also can easily be misguidedly based on wishes for higher fees or to see someone new or perhaps more interesting. Keeping patients for many years and seeing them frequently can of course be appropriately based on what is genuinely best for patients or be evidence of a strong and ultimately fruitful attachment. However, analysts' financial needs carry much weight in the myriad judgments and choices we make daily in our clinical work. These choices are often quite conscious on our part.

There are several other money-driven practices that have become somewhat common even among the most ethical and respectable among us. They concern the ways in which the modality of psychoanalysis is often compromised and other treatment modalities are collapsed into each other in confusing and potentially damaging ways. For example, when an appealing patient who is highly motivated (someone with whom an analyst wishes to work) can afford to pay only a demarcated amount of money, the analyst often opts for a higher fee to see this individual once or twice weekly. This is selected over dividing the dollar amount by three or more sessions per week or referring the patient to someone whose fees are lower, an analyst who could provide a more optimal psychoanalytic experience. Another example of this occurs when it is difficult for a patient in analysis three or more times weekly to commute to an analyst's office. Such a patient might be offered a double session at double the fee, thereby defeating some of the original aim of the psychoanalytic frame that occurs multiple times per week. This co-constructed "deal" between analyst and patient maintains for the analyst the advantage of receiving payment for an ideal number of sessions.

More recently, telephone sessions have also attacked the analytic frame. They have become a way to reduce inconvenience for busy patients while maintaining the patient's consistent willingness to stay in therapy. An analyst may cooperate with this to maintain the patient in therapy or to secure optimal income. Finally, although it has long been recognized as poor practice, analysts might accept referrals from patients who are either close friends or family members of their patients. They may also see a patient while regularly doing couples therapy with that same person and the person's significant other.

It is clear to me from all that I have struggled with personally and seen practiced in my field that we psychoanalysts are no more noble as a group when it comes to financial greed than are our counterparts in the financial sector, the "business world," law, and medicine. In denying to ourselves our own financial ambitions, psychoanalysts often have little to offer by way of understanding to people in other fields who make headlines for their so-called disregulated affect or compulsive irrationality.

Fundamentally, I do not believe that psychoanalysts' frequent criticisms of individuals in the word of business, often veiled as semi-diagnostic designations, are warranted. I think that the wish to earn maximum money and to be recognized as successful or powerful is but a variant on normative ambition. Any human quality, like ambition, that can be seen as productive for individuals and for society at large can also in extremis cause harm. The desire for recognition, power, and status is normal across disparate cultures, and the degree to which any individual possesses these qualities lies on a bell-shaped curve. Because many psychoanalysts and others in the helping professions deny having such personal needs to any significant degree, strong ambition and greed are often projected onto those "bad" others in different professions. These "others" then become demonized in the best way that psychoanalysts do this—the designation of diagnostic labels that conveniently lead to a "good and noble me and bad them," binary.

In private conversations, at committee meetings, in published articles, and in the context of clinical presentations of patients, those others outside our profession are often discussed as living on a moral low ground in comparison with the prototypical psychoanalyst, allegedly in aggregate embracing higher moral standards with respect to money and other forms of ambition. Because psychoanalysts belong to a helping profession for which fees and income may on average be lower that those of other professionals mentioned, and because most psychoanalysts, at least in large urban centers in America, lean leftward in their political beliefs, analysts may readily deceive themselves and deny that ambition for status and money plays a role in their aims. This superior moral attitude, indeed, often disguises what is actually a sense of weakness and inferiority toward those who earn appreciably bigger incomes or have more social power and stature, including many of the patients whom psychoanalysts treat.

There exists a clear irony in the fact that psychoanalysts invariably prefer to see patients who can afford what we call a "full fee" (the analysts' maximum fee), and that this fee, often barely or not at all covered by insurance, is more than the vast majority of people can afford. Without considerable income, family money, or rarely available terrific health insurance coverage, only a very small percentage of people can engage in a psychoanalytic process even once weekly. Once-weekly treatment, however, is only one third to one fifth of what psychoanalysts desire. And, as is well known, these sessions one to five times weekly often last for many years. It is rare that an analytic patient who is productively engaged in treatment and who can afford to keep coming will spend less than 5 years "on the couch." Of course, as already noted, 10 to 20 or more years are not at all uncommon. Although many analysts may reduce their fee from their full fee to a lower one to accommodate analyses multiple times per week, the total income accrued from such therapy is likely quite significant. And yet, with all the education and years of study and personal analysis, analysts' income is often less than counterparts in other professions like medicine and law. It is especially less when compared to those earning incomes in the world of finance, banking, and private business.

I see great hypocrisy in analysts' distinct preference for patients who are wealthy enough to help support them and simultaneous denigration of those patients for their greed, mercenary values, and economic ambitions. Most contemporary analysts have integrated Harry Stack Sullivan's now famous phrase, "We are all more simply human than otherwise," (Sullivan, 1940, p.16) and have embraced the value that Racker articulated so well: "The first distortion of truth in the analytic situation is that analysis is an interaction between a sick person and a healthy one" (Racker, 1968, p.132). The best analysts are those who readily acknowledge their subjectivity and their personal flaws, and view themselves as neither objective observers of specimen patients nor inherently more psychically healthy because of being in the role of healer. The term, *wounded healer* has been widely embraced by contemporary analysts, who largely have been increasingly free to speak and to write publicly of their most intimate feelings and foibles.

Although economic greed is a shortcoming that analysts share with many others, I have observed, paradoxically, that this remains one area wherein analysts commonly differentiate themselves from their patients and in their remarks about public personalities. That is, I have noted that when speaking or writing about wealthy patients or public figures, analysts often split off and deny their own financial and power-related ambitions, while emphasizing, in a condemning and pathologizing manner, these qualities in others.

I do not have many speculations regarding why this happens. I previously suggested that analysts often feel inadequate in comparison with patients whose ambition has led to far greater material success and comfort than that available to the purportedly stronger person in the analytic dyad—the analyst. An analyst's ambition for, or envy of wealth and power may be quite painful in this context, so these uncomfortable emotions may be attributed to belonging to the patient only and then be regarded as immoral or pathological characteristics. Such attribution not only pathologizes a patient (or a public person), but also pumps up the analyst so that he or she may then feel more like a powerful healer. In the analyst's eyes, he or she is now in a position to cure the allegedly sick patient of the latter's pathological greed and ambition and moral and personal failings, allegedly inferior to the qualities of the supposedly healthy and moral analyst. Here, the analyst positions him or herself not only as more powerful by virtue of heartier mental health but also as stronger through an attribution of moral superiority. This positioning, clearly not useful to patients, is supported often by left-leaning political beliefs shared by a majority of psychoanalysts, beliefs that often encourage suspicion of dishonesty toward almost anyone whose ambitions have led to an accumulation of wealth and power.

It is my view that those analysts who are most successful in achieving either relatively high income ·or public professional recognition have ambitions quite parallel to others outside this profession. I further argue that many analysts who do not feel successful along these dimensions are soothed in their disappointments by denying their thwarted ambitions and attending to the ambitions of others only as pathologically excessive.

For example, the term *mania* is often used in our field to describe people who work long and hard and with much energy to reach very high aims or reap strong economic rewards. Other designations, such as *type A personality* or *workaholic,* are also common. Mania comes from the colloquial *maniac* or, more respectfully, from the severe psychiatric diagnosis, manic-depressive. The connotation of these terms is most negative, although I believe personally that when harvested productively, a fair touch of mania is often highly productive both for the individual and for what the results of this mania may produce for society. I have long believed that many people who have contributed greatly to the human race have been driven in ways that could be called manic. This designation could be viewed as either "healthy" or pathologic depending on the eye of the beholder and his or her motives, conscious or unconscious. Leaders and pioneers in the arts, the sciences, philosophy, business, politics and yes, even psychoanalysis, have been motivated by ambition for recognition, power, and sometimes wealth. They could be called workaholic, manic, or both in either the productive or the pathological sense of the words.

In conclusion, the economic realities of psychoanalytic practice in America create choices that I believe very few of us would make were we working for a salary at a clinic or under the German national insurance system. Some analysts opt for therapeutic configurations that constitute, or come close to constituting, unethical conduct. I believe that almost every analyst makes some decisions about the basic physical structure of the analytic relationship that reflects compromise that falls short of analytic ideals. Such decisions can only be controlled when they are acknowledged and made without self-deception. However, even in full consciousness, I suspect that most analysts will make some basic frame decisions that are affected by financial self-interest. The more that these realities are embraced, the less they will be projected onto ambitious or wealthy patients such that these patients become demonized or pathologized for qualities that we analysts share with them.

REFERENCES

Aron L. & Hirsch, I. (1992). Money matters in psychoanalysis. In *Relational Perspectives in Psychoanalysis.* N. Skolnick & S. Warsaw (Eds.), Hillsdale, NJ: The Analytic Press, 239–256.

Hirsch, I. (2008). *Coasting in the Countertransference: Conflicts of Self-Interest between Analyst and Patient.* New York: Routledge.

Racker, H. (1968). *Transference and Countertransference.* New York: International Universities Press.

Sullivan, H.S. (1940). *Conceptions of Modern Psychiatry.* New York: Norton.

Prologue to Chapter 12:
GOING DEEP, GOING WIDE

This paper expands on my inclination to view dissociated or unformulated experience as a vehicle to understand how unconscious motivation is key to comprehending the connection between early development and adult ways of being in the world. As already noted, Freud's archaeological model is a depth model. Repressed instinctual material is layered underneath consciousness and when discovered in the transference, it may rise to consciousness and modify the defensive system that is causing constriction and symptom formation. A model of dissociation is more of a width model. What is unformulated is not thought to lie *beneath* consciousness but alongside of consciousness. Both systems emphasize unconscious motivation as the central psychoanalytic tenet, though a concept of depth prioritizes the explanatory "why," while the dissociative model emphasizes the question of "what."

What is meant by "what" is the emphasis in the analytic situation on recognizing and describing the consistent patterning that characterizes how people engage their world. The "what," as seen on the surface runs parallel to the "what" that is dissociated. Our unconscious beings are fundamentally the same as "what" is lived out in consciousness. The past is always in the present (Levenson, 1983). Unconsciousness is not seen as deeper but different—it lies parallel to consciousness. In most psychoanalytic systems the recognition of what is unconsciously motivating is thought to expand choice and to create an acceptance of the multiple dimensions of self. In the model that I attempt to describe, these dimensions are thought to be lived-out in the context of the transference-countertransference matrix, patient an analyst mutually enacting key internalized relational configurations. These configurations are thought to reflect and to figuratively duplicate earlier and significant internalized object relations. Recognition of this patterning and the unconscious motivation to repeat what is most known, offers patients the opportunity to possibly engage differently with a new significant other. This *width* model emphasizes the expansion of experience and the acceptance of dimensionality.

The use of two acclaimed television series to illustrate my thesis is consistent with what I've done in a number of my published articles. This both reflects my personal interests and makes writing less grueling and more recreational. *The Sopranos* and *Mad Men* are two of my favorites and in my opinion, two of the best series ever produced. What is special for me about them and to a degree, any other film or literature that is of high quality, is the very recognition of the multidimensionality of people. We are all more simply human than otherwise (Sullivan, 1953)—both good and bad. Lesser writing often fails to recognize this, creating the binary of all good heroes and all evil villains. These two television series, as well as others, like *Breaking Bad* and *The Wire,* vividly portray the width of people—the coexistence of badness and lovingness. The analytic situation lends itself to the in vivo living-out of what has been dissociated. This allows patients a first hand view of their range of self states and in this context, promotes both the awareness and the integration of the widest breadth of experience.

REFERENCES

Levenson, E. (1983). *The Ambiguity of Change.* Northvale, NJ: Jason Aronson.

Sullivan, H.S. (1953). *The Interpersonal Theory of Psychiatry.* New York: Norton.

Chapter 12

GOING DEEP, GOING WIDE*

Contemporary theories of psychoanalytic action have for the most part shifted from an archeological model, analyst as objective scientist/detective in search of patients' deeply repressed affective experience, to analyst as often unwitting co-participant in a relationship ultimately designed to broaden patients' awareness and acceptance of their varied internalized self-other configurations. These sometimes dissociated configurations often emerge in the context mutual enactments between patient and analyst.

INTRODUCTION

Aside from any sexual connotation, where "deep" or "going deep" tends to have a clearly positive valence, for me the reference has been largely one related to sports. More specifically, "he hit the ball way back to *deep* center field" or "the receiver ran a stop-and-go pattern and went *deep* down the sideline" or "the guard stopped his dribble and pulled-up for a *deep* jump shot, well beyond the arc." Depending on which baseball, football, or basketball team I am rooting for, and if the ball was caught or the shot made, the connotation of "deep" may be pleasing or disappointing to me. There is no intrinsic value attached, good or bad depends entirely on my allegiances and affiliations. "Deep,"[1] as I have most frequently used it, is a descriptive term, suggesting neither anything inherently good or bad, profound or superficial.

Similarly, the term "wide" has a normally positive sexual referent as well as a distinct meaning in the three sports just mentioned. In the former, wide may refer to preferred sexual positioning or it may suggest engaging in an expanded range of sexual behavior. Indeed, in sports this term usually refers to broadening the field of play and/or using as much as of the field as possible. Once again, the successful deployment of a wider field has a positive or negative valence depending on similar allegiances. In life outside of sex and sports and in my professional life in

---

*Hirsch, I. (2014). Going deep, going wide. *Psychoanalytic Dialogues,* 24(3): 317–331.

[1]From this point on I omit the quotation marks and italics from the word *deep* and after initial quotation marks for the word *wide,* there will be no more.

particular, I am more likely to embrace conceptions of width than of depth. I hope to elaborate, of course, but at this juncture I just note that expansion of awareness and of repertoire or flexibility of experience is absolutely central to what I consider core aims of the psychoanalytic process.

I have not infrequently encountered notions of depth (though not width) in reference to three other interests of mine: literature (fiction), film, and so-called "high-end" cable television. In these avenues there usually is a value placed on the term. Deeper is seen as distinctly more profound. For these media, deep is often juxtaposed with its alleged counterpoints, superficial or shallow. What is considered good quality writing in literature, film, or television often refers to the presence of intended symbolic meaning that lies beyond the merely descriptive. As I argue more specifically when my discussion turns to psychoanalysis per se, for me the quality of knowing, understanding, or effectively capturing moments or capturing people lies not in conceptions of layering surface and depth or employment of the symbolic. Aside from the technical aspects of writing, what in my judgment makes for quality is the ability to evoke affect and identification in the reader or the observer. I am often asked why I liked a particular movie, piece of fiction, or television series, or why I proclaimed that a different work was meaningless to me. This is usually difficult for me to answer, and most of the time all I can say is that the piece spoke to me or that I personally resonated with the characters or the story line. That is, it not only evoked some affective experience that I could relate to but also provided a resonance with elements of my own life or my own thought processes. In addition and of no small importance, good writing in literature, film, and television can expand the experience of the reader or viewer. That is, it can provoke us to look at aspects of ourselves that we prefer to lie dormant, unspoken, "not me" (Stern, 2010; Sullivan, 1953), and in the broadest sense, unconscious. I hate to use the phrase "confrontation with truth" to describe what I mean, since I firmly believe along with most of my contemporary colleagues that these words cannot be used with any sense of objectivity. This said, what I think of as quality in writing *feels*, indeed, like a capturing of a very personal truth or facing truths about ourselves or the world around us that we have avoided examining. For me, the power of any high-quality fictional portrayal lies in presenting for me a sense of clarity, a bringing to life in the page or the screen something that I could not readily or effectively articulate myself. In short, I can say that such exposure is expansive to the reader or viewer. To say any more about esthetic quality in any of the arts is well beyond my personal abilities or the scope of this paper. I do, however, proceed with two illustrations of what has been uniformly reviewed as of high quality in contemporary cable television series. I argue throughout that clarity of description and expansion of both dimensionality and awareness has greater moment in capturing the esthetics of writing and of understanding the people we see in psychoanalysis than binary dichotomies of surface and depth.

TWO ILLUSTRATIONS FROM CABLE TELEVISION

Tony Soprano, the lead character in the universally acclaimed HBO series *The Sopranos*, is a man designed by writers to capture the complexity and the multiple aspects of most people. One can use the currently popular psychoanalytic conception of multiple self-states (e.g., Bromberg, 1998; Stern, 2010) to describe this. Of course, as in most fiction, characters are presented in exaggerated form, both to affectively illustrate a theme and to be entertaining to audiences. Tony is a gangster, a leading light in organized crime, quite at home with murdering, stealing, and cheating. Violence and dishonesty is integral to his existence and to his personal heritage. Under most circumstances he has little conflict about his way of life and has no interest in altering his criminal ways. He is evil by most humanistic standards, though this is not all he is.

Though Tony cheats sexually on his wife, he appears to love her, and despite all of the very sexy younger women available to him he has no interest in leaving his wife. He has a difficult relationship with his son, but there is little question that he loves him too, and is fiercely protective of him. His Oedipally tinged relationship with his daughter is less conflicted—he is both crazy about her and proud of her. In one of the most renown episodes, he takes his daughter on a college tour and while there he encounters a fugitive enemy and proceeds to strangle him to death. The juxtaposition of being both a devoted upper middle-class father and a violent criminal is magnificently captured. Tony is portrayed as a typical family man, as part of a family with the usual set of high moments and considerable battles, struggles, and heartaches, especially the sort of difficulties that most of us who are married and/or who have had adolescent children can identify with. And he is also a violent criminal, living by a code that defies all traditional standards of morality and of stable family life. This said, his family does have stability, and aside from sexual infidelity he is loyal and committed to his wife, as he is also with a close circle of fellow mobsters. He will never betray them so long as he is not betrayed by them. If he is betrayed, of course he will murder his betrayers.

Peculiar for his line of work and his culture, Tony begins analytic therapy with an attractive woman analyst and fellow Italian American, Dr. Melfi. This unusual move is precipitated by a series of what can be called anxiety attacks and hysterical blackouts. Melfi, as well as much of the audience, interprets these symptoms as reflections of conflict about his violent ways. There are scenes rich in symbolism where the imagery of birds suggests the unconscious wish to be free of his past and of his criminal life. We learn much about his history, the criminal father with whom he identifies and whose mantle he assumes, and his despicable and destructive mother, who at one point tries to kill him and who in turn Tony flirts with murdering.

Dr. Melfi, a basically traditional and ethical professional, finds herself quite drawn and attracted to Tony's masculine power. She is tempted to violate sexual boundaries yet does not, though when she enlists Tony to take revenge on a man who tried to rape her, therapeutic boundaries are severely compromised. Toward the end of the series Melfi cruelly drops Tony as a patient, allegedly because of some pseudo-scientific piece of psychoanalytic literature claiming that "people like" Tony, diagnosed as sociopathic or psychopathic, are intractable. She bows to this bogus diagnostic rhetoric and to pressure from her supervisor and peers, and in my own mind unethically rejects her profoundly hurt patient. Most viewers likely believe that this ugly decision was based more on fear of her attraction to Tony than anything else, diagnosis serving as a seemingly legitimate and professional rationale. The good doctor proves not to be a very good person, not literally violent like her patient, though evil in her context as a healer/doctor.

This all-too-brief synopsis, as I intend it, is an effort to illustrate that human complexity and multiplicity has little to do with layerings of surface and depth. What brings *The Sopranos* to life and contributes to its acclaim is the portrayal of the expanse of its characters, a broadening of the psychic elements of all of the primary players in the story. We get to know each character in his or her darkness and lightness and develop a way of seeing these fictional people in a wide range of what is currently referred to as self-states. Most of us contain good and bad, malevolent and benevolent aspects, and embracing our various dimensions, conscious and unconscious or split-off, is one way of characterizing the expansive aim of any psychoanalytic enterprise.

Looking at the analytic process both as one of expansion of awareness and of personal dimensionality in no way should conflict with notions of unconscious motivation, the centerpiece of psychoanalysis since its inception. Unconscious need not be seen as anything deeper or more real or profound than consciousness. Who we are consciously, manifestly, and currently is just as much our "real" selves as those parts of ourselves that we cannot recall (repression) or formulate (dissociation). Our present is just as profoundly significant as our past. Indeed, we all are motivated by internal forces that we do not see or understand, though we are also motivated by forces that are visible and conscious. The former is harder to find and exerts great influence precisely because we are in less control of what lies beyond awareness. I suggest that one is not deeper or more profound than the other, just different. Discovering what we have not formulated consciously (Stern, 1997), leads to a broadening of the surface. It is not necessarily a greater truth than much of what has been on the surface.

As important as the significance of the unarticulated past is, the human tendency is to repeat that past, for better and for worse. That is, what currently motivates people to repeat what may be a troubled and unhappy past is just as significant as conscious recognition of elements of that past. Tony, despite any conflict about continuing his violent and dangerous ways, is deeply wedded to his identification with his violent and criminal father and to the culture in which this is embedded. Independent to what risks and miseries this highly dangerous life brings, his unconscious attachments to his past compel him to continue living in the ways that he is most comfortable. As Levenson (1972, 1983) teaches us repeatedly, an ability to provide patients with a sense of clarity of patterning may be analysts' most important skill and talent. Observation of the consistency, past and present, in the way patients live can have greater healing significance than explanations or interpretations. As Levenson argued, description, sensitivity to the "what" of experience is more likely to have affective resonance than interpretations of the "why" of experience. Explanations tend to be wedded to cherished theoretical constructs and analysts' will usually find what our preferred theory tells us to look for and to expect (Hirsch, 2008; Spence, 1982).

It is the artful depiction of Tony, Melfi, and a bevy of other interesting characters in all of their contrasting complexity, the expansion of character as multidimensional rather than unidimensional, that makes *The Sopranos* a series of very high quality. As well, through the more singular and intense study of Tony, we can see how compelling it usually is to repeat even the most troubled of pasts, choosing comfort and familiarity in priority to the risk of new and unfamiliar experience. The writers have been able to capture the range of their characters self-states and the persistence of these conflicting states (Bromberg, 1998) in a way that provokes viewers to reflect upon their own wider breadth of being, in the context of continuing to live in the often limited ways that lends itself to consistency with the past.

Mad Men, the AMC cable television series, has been as highly acclaimed as *The Sopranos* series that preceded. The leading man, Don Draper is the centerpiece of a culture of highly attractive and business successful men who could be considered evil, or if that's too strong, immoral in ways different than Tony Soprano and his crew. These men are neither physically violent nor overtly criminal. They represent the advertising industry in New York City, centered on Madison Avenue from the middle 1950s through much of the 1960s. This subgroup were at that time the "Masters of the Universe," Tom Wolfe's (1987) term for what the men of Wall Street have represented from the 1980s until today. The men (almost exclusively men) of Madison Avenue were the men of wealth, glamour, creativity, charm, high fashion, good looks, and the power that comes with these qualities. As depicted, again in some exaggerated form and exemplified by Don Draper, they felt invincible and immortal. They could drink, smoke, and remain relatively sleepless with no ill consequence; have sex, in spite of being married, with as many attractive women as they could handle; neglect their children; treat their underlings, often female, with utter disrespect; and help market products that could be either useless or harmful, absent of any apparent moral conflict. So long as the business was prospering, Don and his colleagues were on a testosterone high, able to fly above any deleterious consequences or potential consequences of the way they lived. And, when there were consequences, they were resilient and able to rebound. Indeed, they were manic without being depressive (Hirsch, 2011, 2014).

More than with any other character, the writers give the audience a glimpse of Don's life history. He was raised as Dick, in a deeply fractured, abusive, and impoverished farm family; left home for the army during the Korean War; and took on the identity of his dead colleague, Don Draper, trading identifications so that he, Dick, was presumed dead. Though uneducated formally, he is exceptionally smart and creative and, as well, strikingly handsome and seductive. The new Don worked his way up to Madison Avenue, and a beautiful and sophisticated and better bred wife, and reached the pinnacle of his profession. Dick/Don re-created himself, he became "not him", the brand of Don was sold to the world, and his former self was hidden to all others and manifestly transcended by himself.

The Don we see most of is not a nice person. This is cable television noir—virtually all of the main characters have more darkness and badness in them than generosity or benevolence. There is no murder here, just profound selfishness and mistreatment of others. Yet through examining the life and life history of the leading man, we see what drives him. We have data to make inferences about his unconscious motivations as well as seeing his conscious ones. Knowing his harsh life history helps make him sympathetic in ways similar to how therapists often feel empathy for the wounded sides of their not necessarily very nice patients. In spite of Don's being a very hurtful human being, the audience is also charmed by his incredible good looks and his keen intelligence and creativity, and develops a strong crush. Like we do with Tony, we root for the bad guy. However, and here is the profound talent of the writers and actors, the bad guy is not simply bad—he has qualities that we find very compelling and are drawn toward. Most of the audience does not want Tony to be assassinated or Don to be discovered as Dick and/or fail in business. We as audience are expanded by the recognition that we too are both bad and good. We are complex and are helped to recognize this by recognizing the multidimensional qualities of Tony and Don. The wounded little boy, Dick, stands parallel to and will always be a part of the slick and ruthless Don. Indeed, Dick is not deeper than Don simply because of chronological ordering. Perhaps one difference between pedestrian and good writing is the absence of binary thinking—there are no absolute heroes, no singularly good guys or bad guys. I suggest that in most good writing the breadth of good and bad, dark and light, in the fictional characters reflects the range of most all of us.

Once again I suggest that issues of layering, of depth and surface, do not capture effectively the dimensions of lived life. What is unconsciously motivated and buried and what occurred in formative years is no more relevant or descriptive of who one is than what is conscious or lived-out in contemporary life. Indeed, the past is very present in current life and potentially visible to psychoanalysts, viewers, and others who closely and carefully observe. Don's way of treating others and the health risks he takes constantly jeopardize him—he cannot entirely stop being

Dick. Tony, Don, and most all of us are composed of our past and present, our unconscious motivations and our consciousness, and of course our good and our evil. The past is not deeper than the present because it also *is* the present. The more we can be aware of all of this, the more evolved we are as human beings, warts and all.

CONCEPTIONS OF DEPTH, WIDTH AND RELATED MATTERS IN PSYCHOANALYSIS

Wachtel (2003) already addressed and critiqued concepts of depth so thoroughly and clearly that I can only hope here that I might, at best, elaborate a bit further. Indeed, much of what follows takes off from and/or reiterates what he has outlined. Freud's (e.g., 1912, 1915) archeological psychoanalytic model, the discovery or recovery of repressed memories, thoughts, and affects set a tone for psychoanalytic thinking that persists to today. It is apparent that the distinction between the repressed and the conscious was vertically layered—consciousness was on top and unacceptable desires and experience were hidden on the bottom. Psychoanalytic process reflected a dig to find what was hidden and to see how this emerged in the transference, a place where it could be readily visible to a psychoanalytic patient. One can see how conceptions of surface and depth are very relevant and logical metaphors for this model of mind. I believe, however, that one unfortunate consequence of this model is the relative value attached to these binary dimensions, that is, unconscious became viewed as profound, the "nitty-gritty," with consciousness sometimes thought of as superficial or largely simply self-deceptive. Without diminishing the central significance of the psychoanalytic effort to articulate unconscious motivation, the unconscious dimension of mind need not be considered as deeper than consciousness. In efforts to clarify and understand human motivation, conscious and unconscious process can be viewed as complimentary—two elements of mind that exist on a vertical plain ranging from totally unarticulated to optimally clarified experience.

The relatively recent trend among psychoanalytic writers identified as Interpersonal or Relational (e.g., Bromberg, 1998; Hirsch, 1994; Hirsch & Roth, 1995; Stern, 1997, 2010) tend to think of unconscious process often as dissociated experience. This can serve to neutralize the binary notion of surface and depth. Most significantly, Stern speaks of unconscious process often as experience that has never been articulated—"unformulated experience." Looking at unconscious from this lens does not necessarily imply that some psychically painful or conflictual experiences have, indeed, been experienced consciously and then repressed. Stern adds to the idea of matters forgotten, which will require digging to get to, the idea that much experience in life was never put into any words that one might say to oneself. That is, some psychically painful experiences were too awful or conflictual to be articulated or formulated in the first place, or much experience occurred early enough in life at points when words did yet not exist, or many important life experiences painful or not at all painful occur outside of the context of any articulation. Very significant here are the universal processes of identification with significant caretakers and internalization of key self-other interaction. Though these processes are as central to personality development as any can be, they invariably develop outside of any description in language.

What has not been articulated is not inherently deeper than what has been, it is different and in a different place along a horizontal continuum. We can never discover what has not been formulated or articulated in words, we can only guess or speculate what might have been experienced, by observing the repetitive nature of current experience. I suggest that people are consistent and re-create their present to conform to the past. I soon say more about this. Psychoanalysts can never *discover* the past, we can only make inferences to this based on observation in the present. Of course, the transference–countertransference matrix is the ideal forum for the establishment of narratives designed to draw isomorphic parallels between past and present (Levenson, 1972, 1983; Spence, 1982). In this context the psychoanalytic emphasis may be seen largely as a way to expand and enrich patients' personal data more so than a process of discovery of repressed truths. This involves a greater emphasis on description, the "what" of experience, than it does on interpretation, the "why," the cause-effect explanation of experience. A horizontal model aims toward a broadening of the present while a vertical model is geared toward discovery of past secrets that may serve to liberate the present. Certainly there are multiple ways that psychoanalysts can help their patients.

The contrast between a focus on discovery or on expansion need not reflect a psychoanalytic binary, though it does reflect a different emphasis. Interpretation is the sine qua non for discovery while description prevails for expansion (Levenson, 1972, 1983). The former most values the "why" of experience, while the latter most values the "what." These foci by no means need to be mutually exclusive, in spite of some different theoretical assumptions made by different schools of thought. In absurdly brief synopsis, the archeological model (primarily traditional Freudian and traditional Kleinian) conceptualizes that consciously felt early desires, largely in the incestuously sexual or violent dimensions, are too threatening to children's basic survival and therefore must be repressed. The compromises between expressing these forbidden wishes and expressing them in some disguised form may lead to symptoms. The discovery of these repressed desires, projected onto a relatively neutral analyst and thereby subject to interpretive clarity, may lead to an acceptance of them, to remission of symptoms and potentially to a fuller life. The dissociation or unformulated experience model (e.g., Interpersonal, Relational) places unacceptable sexual and aggressive drives and drive derivatives in a far secondary status. What *are* most seen as causing problems for people are troubled familial relationships and the identification with and internalization of these. These experiences tend to be internalized and not articulated, but instead they are lived out and repeated throughout the life cycle of any individual. This psychoanalytic situation is the ideal vehicle for the expression of these repetitive themes. When analyst and patient invariably become engaged in mutual transference–countertransference enactments, parallels are drawn between this interaction, presumed childhood configurations, and current extratransference ways of engaging.

In the latter model, there indeed is an assumption (and therefore an element of interpretation) that inferred earlier experience has a distinctly precipitating effect on later experience. The potential value of such interpretation is not lost on most analysts who identify as Interpersonal and Relational. However, what is different from a more vertical model of surface and depth is that earlier is not viewed as deeper as much as it is viewed as isomorphically parallel to current ways of being (Foehl, 2008; Levenson, 1972, 1983). Earlier is viewed as temporally different but not qualitatively different. The 40-year-old in our office is living out with us a variation of the 4-year-old at home and the 40-year-old with his spouse. To the extent that the attuned analyst can describe current transference–countertransference patterning and clarify this for the patient, one can say that the patient has been enriched. Indeed, enriched because he has a view, albeit in the context of a very subjective narrative (Levenson, 1972; Spence, 1982), of the continuity of past and present, and as well and of extreme importance, how he unconsciously shapes his current life to conform to the troubled past.

A brief note is merited here about trauma, since this has been much the focus of our literature in recent times (e.g., Bromberg, 1998; Davies & Frawley, 1992) and is relevant to our discussion of surface and depth, repression and dissociation. I say only that profoundly traumatic experience like sexual or violent abuse or exposure is sometimes consciously put into words and subsequently forgotten because of the horror, and sometimes because of that same horror never consciously articulated in the first place. Of course, what constitutes trauma is subject to differing opinions, though what I refer to here is what most mental health professional would call egregiously horrific and threatening to psychic and/or physical survival. If we infer that traumatic experience was repressed, the archeological method of recovery seems quite relevant in efforts to help patients integrate earlier experience. If we infer that trauma has never been formulated in words, the best analysts can do is help patients construct a narrative about what may have been experienced and to help them see how they may be unconsciously recreating variations of such trauma in their current life.

Much of what most of us analysts see in our practices most of the time is likely not the results of horrific trauma but of some combination of the statistically normal range of good and bad internalized relational configurations (Mitchell, 1988) with our significant caretakers. As I have suggested, these internalizations become our patients' internal template, and there is the tendency to shape current experience to repeat and to conform with what is most familiar and familial (Mitchell, 1988; Thompson, 1950). In this context I find the all-too-common distinction between pre Oedipal and Oedipal problems, earlier and later pathology, fixations at early stages of development and arrested development, like Wachtel (2003), as specious and largely rhetorical. Indeed, earlier experience, before words in particular, is more difficult for analysts to get to, though I see no reason to refer to this as any more deep than later experience. Actually, for most people, later experience is quite similar in quality to earlier experience. Parents who relate to each other and to their children when the child is age 2 are the same parents with usually the same patterns of relatedness when the child is age 6. Troubled patterns of relatedness are as troubled as they are because they tend to be consistent and persistent. What was troublesome for our patients (and for us as people/patients) at 2 is likely to be troublesome at 12. And the troubled patterns that we identify with, internalize and indeed repeat, usually stay with us in a pretty rigid manner.

As Wachtel (2003) discussed, what is often wedded to the idea that earlier is deeper is the conception that earlier troubled experience is sicker and/or more primitive (Klein, 1946; Kohut, 1971; Winnicott, 1958). I have just argued, as has Wachtel (see also Levenson, 1972; Mitchell, 1988), that there normally is consistency in nurturance across the years and that bad caretaking earlier may be no worse than bad parenting later, that is, consistently bad parenting across the developmental years is usually not restricted to these very early years. Many Object-Relational (see Winnicott, 1958) and traditional Self-Psychological (see Kohut, 1971) perspectives evoke the concept of "developmental arrest" to describe those who have failed to develop sufficiently because of inadequate parental holding or empathic immersion. I have no doubt that any child will be psychically injured because of these deficiencies, though like Wachtel (2003), I object strenuously to conceptions that imply an intrinsic stuckness and or psychic emptiness (e.g., "egoless"). Notions of "arrested development" have a long history in psychoanalysis, beginning with analogous references to patients being helplessly stuck at oral, anal, oedipal, or latency stages of development. Indeed, these patients were often spoken of as literal babies in adult clothing. Searles (1979), perhaps more that any other analyst, found such fixed diagnostic description as arrogant, disrespectful, condescending, infantilizing, and pathologizing. He believes, and I agree wholeheartedly, that such conceptions exist to help depressed and unhappy psychotherapists feel better than and more than their patients. To the extent that we view our adult patients as babies, primitive, egoless, stuck in anality or otherwise stuck or arrested, it is usually implied that we are not they, a potential antidepressant buzz for us to be sure, at the expense of our patients. Such designations also flies in the face of Racker's (1968), wonderful dictum that the analytic relationship is decidedly not one between a well analyst and a sick patient, and of Sullivan's (1953) best known words, declaring that patients and therapists are all more simply human than otherwise. Like the value-laden binaries of deep versus superficial and intrapsychic endogenous drives versus internalized interpersonal experience, notions of psychic emptiness and fixity of stages do little justice to both the flexibility of people and to their will and agency. I argue that a good deal of what composes unconscious process is the motivation to remain in those very emotional states that make us feel unevolved and miserable in a variety of ways. We may be victims of our early experience, but humans are responsible for the perpetuation of this all-too-comfortable and familiar experience. Our patients are not stuck at lower or deeper levels, nor are they egoless or otherwise empty. As Freud (1912) said, the domain of psychoanalysis is the problems that we make for ourselves. If I would call anything deep in tone, it is not the earliness or so-called primitiveness of pathology, or the absence of awareness of the repressed, but the ability of the analyst to help patients recognize the degree to which internalized configurations are perpetuated unconsciously, regardless of the degree of detriment to self and to others (see, e.g., Tony and Don). As Freud taught, the essence of the psychoanalytic process is the deconstruction and examination of how we repeat and perpetuate the very miseries we live with and about which we lament.

An alternative way to seeing deep or repressed experience as the root of neurotic problems follows from what I have been suggesting. Thompson (1950) described it well when she suggested that our problems do not lie in our past experience, regardless how bad this early experience was. The essence of personal problems of *all* levels of severity lies in the unconscious perpetuation of these problems in the present. She posited the challenge of understanding the motivation for doing the same things over and over again that caused misery in the first place (see Freud, 1912). She suggested that we continuously and actively, albeit usually largely unconsciously, shape our environment to conform to the past and to what we have internalized from our pasts. We are inclined to evoke responses from others that lead to interpersonal configurations that are consistent with our past relationships (Wachtel, 1982). This in and of itself plays a major role in repeating and maintaining old experience. In spite of what Freud described as the miseries we make for ourselves, old and internalized experience is more familiar, comfortable, and loyal to the environment we came from and to which we are profoundly attached than are any ways of being that to the outside world may look healthier. What is unconscious here is the intensity of connection to the old and the core conflict about separating from this (Fromm, 1941; Searles, 1979; Singer, 1965). In many respects it might be more therapeutically useful to our patients to see them as perpetrators of old patterns instead of helpless victims of past bad doings of significant others. The latter is very real, though it is not what keeps troubled lives going. Existential concepts (see, e.g., Basescu, 1988; Farber, 1966; Fromm, 1941; Hoffman, 1998) of will, agency, and choice have been very influential to this line of psychoanalytic thinking.

As alluded to earlier in this paper, the theory of therapeutic action that follows from this thinking is highlighted by contemporary notions of mutual enactment—the jointly constructed unwitting and repetitive engagement between analyst and patient (e.g., Bass, 2001; Hirsch, 1993, 1995; Jacobs, 1986; Levenson, 1972; Sandler, 1976; Stern, 2010). In a nutshell, since this conception is likely to be familiar to most readers, patients "nudge" their analyst into a role reciprocation where old patterns are lived out unwittingly between them. The analyst must become part of the problem in order to resolve it (Foehl, 2008; Levenson, 1983). Once this repetitive pattern is consciously recognized by either party, parallels are drawn between the analytic interaction, historical configurations, and current extratransference experience. In the best of all possible worlds the patient can see the degree to which he re-creates his old problems by unconsciously designing his current life to conform to the familiar and comfortable internalized past. In this context the opportunity exists for patient and analyst to engage in new ways, ways that might form new internalizations and generalize beyond the analytic relationship.

At the risk of being redundant, conceptions of depth have little moment here. More relevant is the idea of repetition and continuity. Earlier is neither sicker nor deeper but an unconsciously prescriptive pattern for the present and future. The successful psychoanalytic experience will help people recognize, as Freud has said, how they make their own problems, and in the context of the analytic relationship something new may develop from the mutually lived-through old. Indeed, it may be said that a psychoanalysis based on notions of depth is largely an interpretation-based psychoanalysis, while one based on valorizing width is more experience-based, with much currency given to the description of interactional experience. This distinction is not entirely dichotomous and need not rekindle the age-old debate about what is most mutative in psychoanalysis, insight or new experience. However, I would say that analytic emphasis on depth does lend itself to a more insight and interpretation model of mutative action, and an emphasis on width, to a model that focuses on the shifts in the mutually constructed analytic relationship, and the articulation of this process (Gill, 1982).

Before moving on to a clinical illustration, a brief word about psychoanalysis' love affair with complex theory. Mitchell (1988) used the term "physics envy," and more recently I (Hirsch, 2008) referred to "philosophy envy," to describe what seemed to be the tendency toward elaborate theoretical tenets to explain human matters that could be explained more simply. Mitchell suggested and I agreed that many psychoanalysts, uncomfortable with the utterly subjective and unscientific nature of this profession, feel the need to compensate by positing theories that sound either technically elaborate or philosophically profound. The pragmatics of understanding people can readily be lost in overly intellectualized formulation. I suppose that the greatest perpetrators of overly technical formulations have been many traditional Freudians and Kleinians, while the Lacanians and some postmodern theorists deserve the mantel for their often incomprehensible and overly intellectualized philosophical musings. In adding these thoughts to this paper I might be justifiably accused of being anti-intellectual or just plain too stupid to understand human complexity. Indeed, the history of pragmatism with the Interpersonal psychoanalytic tradition along with the tendency to be suspicious of strong theory have led this subgroup to often be accused of superficiality. I end this section, following Levenson (1972), in arguing once again that the surface of things reflects and captures the inside, and that current relationships tend to parallel early ones. Indeed, this is a very succinct way to summarize much of my own wordiness here in critiquing conceptions of depth in psychoanalysis. With some provocative hyperbole, Levenson (1972) extrapolates Oscar Wilde's aphorism that only superficial people insist on looking beneath the surface.

CLINICAL ILLUSTRATION

Robin, a Caucasian, single 33-year-old pediatric nurse, consulted me post-birthday, increasingly anxious about the prospect of never marrying and never having children. Robin had a very pretty face and dressed quite fashionably, yet was dramatically overweight. She conveyed to me that she loved her work, was very highly regarded, and had risen to a high-level administrative position. She had many women friends, though a number of these friendships were characterized by Robin's generosity and caregiving. Most of her friends, as well as her younger sister, were married and a number of them had young children. Robin was constantly baby-sitting and giving gifts, though when speaking of this to me she never conveyed a sense of imbalance in these relationships. Her own love life was dreadful. She claimed to have no sexual interest in women, masturbated with men in mind but never in her entire life had a boyfriend. Indeed, she did little or nothing to find romance. She had sex only a few times, each time while drunk and not even recalling in the morning the sex that happened during the night.

Robin has been enmeshed with her own mother, as was her mother with Robin's grandmother, for as long as she remembered. She shared her mother's thick body type, while Robin's sister was lean like her father. Her mother has been depressed and miserable in her marriage, again for as long as she can recall, and Robin has served as her mother's chief vehicle for both emotional support and complaint. Much of Robin's leisure time has been spent with her mother, shlepping out from the city to the suburbs, taking her shopping, taking her to the nursing home to visit her grandmother (her mother does not drive). Neither party seemed to recognize that days and evenings spent this way precluded any efforts to find the potential father for her desired children. The concept of "father" (as in father to her own children) was associated with her own father with whom Robin rarely spoke and who was the primary target for her anger. Like her mother, Robin perceived her father as a disgruntled, angry, cold, and verbally abusive man, though he has been able to provide his family with a comfortable upper middle-class, suburban life that has included numerous luxuries.

Though this did not at all carry over to how Robin functioned at work, both Robin and her mother were extremely volatile, crying powerfully or getting angry at the most subtle slight or injury. In the early going of our therapy she frequently cried hysterically at what she perceived as my critical commentary. I found this hysteria grating and all too often felt paralyzed by what seemed like total irrationality, and wished for our hour to end rapidly. I will, of course, say more about this. Robin's symbiotic-like involvement with her mother freed Robin's sister to pursue a far more autonomous and rich life, a life that included many romances and a recent marriage. Her sister felt absolute freedom to rarely visit her family or to listen to their mother's complaints. She also felt far more forgiving of their father's shortcomings and had a reasonable relationship with him.

From the very beginning it was very easy for me to see why Robin had no love life. She did virtually nothing to meet men or to lose weight. When she did pursue electronic dating sights, she easily became frustrated by the inevitable rejections and quickly withdrew. More dramatically, when a man expressed some interest, Robin usually did not follow-up with a response. When I questioned her about this she seemed satisfied with an explanation of "shyness." At more reflective moments she revealed that the prospect of spending extended time with an interested man felt claustrophobic to her. In her dissociated manner she did not put any of the above, including her maintenance of an obese body, together with her barren history with romance. She insisted that she just "could not catch a break."

As can be gleaned from the tone of my writing I was decidedly put off by her absence of self-reflection and how cautious I believed I had to be lest my patient become dramatically tearful and profoundly injured. Of course, this configuration reflected an enactment—I was yet another unsympathetic man who felt hurtful and, as well, sexually turned-off. If I maintained simply an empathic and supportive mode I was kind, though withholding of key observations about Robin, in and out of the transference. I hated this "walking on eggshells" way of being and, as well, I believed that it would take us beyond my patient's child-bearing years to establish a relationship where she was convinced that men could be decent human beings. Indeed, I was also convinced that this approach would inevitably prove futile, since my non-verbal, attitudinal, and right-brain to right-brain communications would belie my empathic and holding persona. Were I to bracket or "hold" my observations gleaned from a combination of my here-and-now experience and parallels from her life outside of our relationship I could be truly depriving my patient, confirming her belief that men give nothing.

Essentially, in Levenson's (1983) terms, I decided to do what is most comfortable for me and what I do best—I tried to address the question, "What's going on around here?" That is, I tried to draw parallels between Robin's way of being with me and our way of being together, and her way of engaging her father and other men. While maintaining what I felt as a genuine resonance with her loneliness and her profound fear of never having children, I conveyed to her how I most always felt in the role, like her father, of the bad and hurtful man. I observed to her that her ready flights into what I experienced as her intensely tearful and irrational hysteria left me feeling like she was disengaging from me. I noted that I expect that this resembles the way she is when with available men and that it likely leads to the quick ending of any such relationship. I took her at her word that she invariably feels a wish to flee when with a man, and with me as well, portraying her to herself as someone who neither trusts nor likes my gender. Essentially I tried to document how her wish for conventional marriage is in stark contrast with her dislike of her father, me, and most all men. I noted the many ways she artfully avoids getting to know men (spending most of her leisure time with her mother; her identification with her mother's hatred of Robin's father and men in general; her maintaining a level of obesity that likely turned off most men; in any case, rarely doing anything to actively meet men; and her avoidance of returning emails from potentially interested suitors when she did pursue electronic dating sights).

I readily linked these phenomena with her dislike of me, her feeling that I was more hurtful than potentially helpful, and her consistent wish to flee analysis for good. To Robin's credit she did stay with me and rarely missed sessions. She began to consciously connect with her dissociated yet profound identification/marriage with her mother and with the part of her that wants to have nothing to do with men (and me) in general. Robin gradually began to see that she was very skilled in keeping herself far away from me and other men and that she was not at all simply a victim of men's disinterest in her. Though I did refer to the causal "why" of her way of being (e.g., her mother's hatred of Robin's father; her father's general meanness), much of what I attempted to do was address the "what" of her life, that is, an effort at description of her way of being in the transference and in the world more generally. The "me" she had been most connected with was the woman who was the object of men's hurtfulness or disinterest. The "not me" was the woman who hates men and avoids them at all cost—the perpetrator, if you will, of her own loneliness and sense of being barren. I did not conceptualize Robin and her absolutely vacant love life as a reflection being stuck in some earlier phase of development or as function deficiencies in internal structure. My inclination was to highlight for her the degree of consistency in her own connection with familial significant others, that is, her parents and siblings way of being in their family was steady and predictable throughout Robin's life cycle. I let her know that I believed that she had internalized these relational configurations (Mitchell, 1988) and that despite her misery, organized her life, albeit unconsciously, to repeat and to conform to the known, familiar, and unfortunately miserable past. I believed that I helped broaden her sense of herself from that of victim of unfortunate family circumstance to an active agent in the contemporary re-creation of such familial configurations.

What I have described in this illustration may to some appear superficial—not sufficiently deep. Perhaps it is, since I made little effort to look for early memories or experiences or to conceptualize my patient's life as having gone through or have failed to go through specific stages of development. I saw with Robin a consistency from her earliest interpersonal memories and her up-to-the-moment way of engaging in and out of the transference–countertransference matrix. My emphasis focused less on specific causal moments of memory of the past or what was missing or deficient in her life experience and more on what *was* present. That is, my emphasis rested on Robin's unwitting perpetuation and her persistence in structuring her life to conform to what she knew best. The analysis of the enactment of my fulfilling the role of the hurtful man without either affection or sexual desire proved key. Robin ultimately responded—she became less hysterical with me and more reflective. Her way of looking at her life expanded well beyond herself as victim, to herself as active agent (Hoffman, 1998). She stopped crying at every small slight of mine, she began looking prettier to me, we became more flirtatious, and I developed a strong fondness for her. I cannot determine whether her "getting it" as a patient was responsible my feelings shifting or my affection for her precipitated changes in her psyche. I'd prefer to believe the latter; it better fits my theory of the salubrious impact of new experience with the analyst as new and internalized significant other. Either way, I became for her a kinder, softer, and more generous version of my gender, and it was not too long after this that she pursued romance more productively, met a kind and loving man, and married him. Robin and I both went wider, and my patient's expansion of her experience made me a happier analyst. My home team's productive use of an expanded field of play yielded an antidepressant-laced boost for them and for me.

CONCLUDING REMARKS

I do not claim that everyone I work with changes as much as Robin seemed to change. I wish that I could make this claim. However, in offering a way of thinking that is different than what is often considered a deeper and more profound psychoanalysis, it seemed to me that I had to present a clinical illustration that some might consider an example of superficial work, or maybe worse, not especially depth psychoanalysis. The Interpersonal psychoanalytic tradition of pragmatism and the existential theme that runs through this tradition are central to my emphasis that people's problems lie less in the past than in the unwitting perpetuation of that past. In this context, therapeutic action involves the analyst becoming part of the problems in order to resolve them (mutual enactment), and when aware of this descriptively portray "what is going on around here." A left brain discovery of repressed conflict-laden sexual and aggressive familial longings, in my way of thinking, does not capture the essence of the most significant elements of unconscious motivation. For me and for those who share my thinking, the most important element of unconscious motivation lies in our attachment to our identifications and internalizations of self-other familial configurations, and our fear of emotional separation and aloneness. The human inclination to maintain emotional equilibrium, to repeat and to structure our lives to resemble both the happiness and unhappiness that we best know, to not let go of our key attachments and thereby face separation and aloneness (Fromm, 1941; Searles, 1979; Singer, 1965), is what is most dominant in the dissociated human psyche. To the extent that the analytic situation can provide a mutually lived and described experience that evolves to some contrast with what is most familiar to the patient, we have successfully gone wider.

REFERENCES

Basescu, S. (1988). The therapeutic process. *Contemporary Psychoanalysis* 24:121–125.

Bass, A. (2001). It takes one to know one: or, whose unconscious is it anyway? *Psychoanalytic Dialogues* 11:683–702.

Bromberg, P. M. (1998). *Standing in the spaces: Essays on clinical process, trauma & dissociation*. Hillsdale, NJ: The Analytic Press.

Davies, J. M., & Frawley, M. G. (1994). *Treating the adult survivor of childhood sexual abuse: A psychoanalytic perspective*. New York, NY: Basic Books.

Farber, L. H. (1966). *The ways of the will: Essays toward a psychology and psychopathology of will*. New York, NY: Harper & Row.

Foehl, J. C. (2008). Follow the fox: Edgar A. Levenson's pursuit of psychoanalytic process. *Psychoanalytic Quarterly* 77:231–1268.

Freud, S. (1912). Papers on technique: Recommendations to physicians practicing psycho-analysis. *Standard Edition* 12:111–120). .

———— (1915). Papers on technique: Observations on transference-love (Further recommendations on the technique of psycho-analysis, III). *Standard Edition* 12:159–171).

Fromm, E. (1941). *Escape from freedom*. New York, NY: Holt, Rinehart & Winston.

Gill, M. (1982). *The analysis of transference* (Vol. 1). New York, NY: International Universities Press.

Hirsch, I. (1993). Countertransference enactments and some issues related to external factors in the analyst's life. *Psychoanalytic Dialogues*, 3, 342–366.

———— (1994). Countertransference love and theoretical model. *Psychoanalytic Dialogues* 4:171–192.

———— (2008). *Coasting in the Countertransference: coasting in the Countertransference: Conflicts of Self-interest Between Analyst and Patient*. New York, NY: Routledge/The Analytic Press.

———— (2011). Narcissism, mania and analysts' envy. *American Journal of Psychoanalysis* 71:363–369.

———— (2014). Narcissism, mania and analysts' envy of patients. *Psycho-analytic Inquiry* 34(5):408–420.

———— &Roth, J. (1995). Changing conceptions of unconscious. *Contemporary Psychoanalysis* 31:263–276.

Hoffman, I.Z. (1998). *Ritual and Spontaneity in the Psychoanalytic Process*. Hillsdale, NJ: The Analytic Press.

Jacobs, T.J. (1986). On countertransference enactments. *Journal of the American Psychoanalytic Association* 34:289–307.

Klein, M. (1946). Notes on some schizoid mechanisms. *International Journal of Psychoanalysis*, 27, 99–110.

Kohut, H. (1971). *The analysis of the self.* New York, NY: International Universities Press.

Levenson, E. A. (1972). *The fallacy of understanding*. New York, NY: Basic Books.

———— (1983). *The ambiguity of change*. Northvale, NJ: Aronson.

Mitchell, S. A. (1988). *Relational concepts in psychoanalysis: An integration*. Cambridge, MA: Harvard University Press.

Racker, H. (1968). *Transference and countertransference*. New York, NY: International Universities Press.

Sandler, J. (1976). Countertransference and role-responsiveness. *International Review of Psychoanalysis* 3:43–47.

Searles, H.F. (1979). *Countertransference and related subjects; selected papers*. Madison, CT: International Universities Press.

Singer, E. (1965). *Key concepts in psychotherapy: An introduction*. New York, NY: Random House.

Spence, D.P. (1982). *Narrative truth and historical truth: Meaning and interpretation in psychoanalysis*. London, UK: Norton.

Stern, D.B. (1997). *Unformulated experience: From dissociation to imagination in psychoanalysis*. Hillsdale, NJ: Analytic Press.

———— (2010). *Partners in thought: Working with unformulated experience, dissociation, and enactment*. New York, NY: Routledge.

Sullivan, H.S. (1953). *The interpersonal theory of psychiatry*. New York. NY: Norton.

Thompson, C. (1950). *Psychoanalysis: Evolution and development*. New York, NY: Thomas Nelson & Sons.

Wachtel, P.L. (1982). Vicious circles: The self and the rhetoric of emerging and unfolding. *Contemporary Psychoanalysis* 18:259–273.

———— (2003). The surface and the depths. *Contemporary Psychoanalysis* 39:5–26.

Winnicott, D.W. (1958). *Collected papers: Through pediatrics to psychoanalysis*. New York, NY: Basic Books.

Wolfe, T. (1987). *The bonfire of the vanities*. New York, NY: Farrar, Strauss & Giroux.

Prologue to Chapter 13:
NARCISSISM, MANIA, AND ANALYSTS' ENVY OF PATIENTS

Invited to write an article in a special journal issue on the subject of narcissism, I had the opportunity to expand on my earlier criticisms of diagnostic thinking, arguing once again that like all personal qualities, narcissism is not a disease but a quality within all people to some degree or another. That is, all personal qualities lie on a continuum and the extremes of any continuum are usually problematic—not constituting illness per se, but trouble for any given person who possesses that given quality, and as well, those other persons in close proximity. Indeed, I argue that like cholesterol, there is good narcissism and bad narcissism and too little of this quality is problematic in a different way than too much. And beyond this, who is to say with any objectivity what is too much—it is not a diagnostic/medical condition and there is no blood test to determine pathology. Indeed, I suggest there are many qualities that qualify as narcissistic and the broadest definition is analogous to plain old self-absorption. In this context, obsessive preoccupation and depressive self involvement qualify as narcissistic, though in a way quite different than the more flamboyantly bloated qualities like grandiosity, vanity, exhibitionism, and aggressive selfishness.

I suggest that the purpose of diagnostic thinking in our field is essentially an effort to provide clarity and structure to complex phenomenon for which this is incompatible and narrowing. Diagnosis obliterates unique individuality as well as productive curiosity. It implies fixed ideas about causality and the illusion that there is a one-size-fits-all strategy for treatment. And there is more: diagnosing a patient instead of describing the personal qualities of that patient is a statement that the patient suffers from an illness, with the implicit implication that the doctor/therapist, in contrast, is diagnosis-free and healthy.

I argue that many people with the more flamboyant qualities of narcissism also posses a touch of mania, and the combination of these qualities often make for very high achievement. I believe that it is common for analysts to be envious of such people, who indeed, may lead more interesting lives and reach far loftier goals of achievement than their analyst. In response to envy, analysts frequently pathologize these qualities, ignoring entirely the often highly productive achievements that result. In the acting-out of envy by pathologizing, an analyst may be compensating for how "less than" the analyst might feel in comparison. It is often difficult to deal with patients whose lives may be more rich and productive than our own. In this article, as I enjoy doing, I use examples from fiction and as well, draw on real life people (e.g., Freud, Bill Clinton) to illustrate that the combination of narcissism and a touch of mania can indeed result in making the world a better place, even though there may be a down-side to those in close proximity, e.g., spouses, children. I suggest further that most individuals who have had the greatest constructive impact on the world are likely to have significant narcissistic and manic qualities.

Chapter 13

NARCISSISM, MANIA, AND ANALYSTS' ENVY OF PATIENTS*

It is not uncommon for analysts to feel envy toward patients who have achieved significant rewards or acclaim for their work. Highly successful individuals in all fields often display both narcissistic and manic qualities. Analysts all too often destructively exaggerate these qualities into the realm of the diagnosed pathological as one way of dealing with this envy.

I begin with a gesture of solidarity with my Interpersonal psychoanalytic heritage, paying respect to Harry Stack Sullivan's (e.g., 1953) game-changing introduction of analysts' subjectivity (participant-observation) to the corpus of psychoanalysis. This, of course, is characterized by his well-known declaration that both analyst and patient are both more simply human than otherwise. In this spirit, let me initiate this article with a display of my own narcissism and grandiosity by citing and quoting liberally from the only previous paper I have published (Hirsch, 1993) which focuses exclusively on the characteristic called narcissism. In this earlier paper, I try to make clear that I have a strong antipathy toward the use of diagnostic categories in psychoanalytic thinking, and as well, the prescription of treatment directives that flow from any such categorizations. In this same edited volume, Fiscalini (1993) asserts that such apparent certainties are reflective of a pervasive narcissism among psychotherapists of most stripes. I argue that personality characteristics like narcissism, mania, depression, anxiety, and the like are ubiquitous, that is, these qualities are present in everyone, though certainly to varying degrees. Every personal characteristic can be seen as lying somewhere along a continuum, and the effort to medicalize psychology is narrowing and largely a defensive and constricting way to deal with the irreducible subjectivities (Renik, 1993) and pervasive uncertainties inherent to the psychoanalytic enterprise. Diagnostic categorization is antithetical to any notion of unique individuality (Wolstein, 1954) and an assault on the key psychoanalytic values of uncertainty (Stern, 1990; Hirsch, 1992) and of analysts' curiosity and the courting of surprise (Stern, 1990). Needless to

*Hirsch, I (2014). Narcissism, mania and analysts' envy of patients. *Psychoanalytic Inquiry* 34(5):408–420.

say, I believe this is also applies to any fixed notions of causality that alleges to explain the standardized genesis of the range of personality characteristics.

> One of the bastions of psychoanalytic absolutism has been the notion of diagnosis and the type of treatment, analytic or otherwise, that corresponds to a particular diagnosis. Though this is not universally accepted, the adaptation of the medical model to analytic work is still pervasive, and diagnostic considerations are still the focal point for a considerable body of psychoanalytic literature. The risk is, of course, that the categories and models of treatment get reified and uniqueness and nuance are overlooked. The psychotherapists' response (or formulation) may readily be to the group norm or diagnosis, and not to the unique individual. One can work with diagnostic categories without these categories becoming absolute, fixed entities, if indeed, the diagnosis is not viewed as such, but instead, as a personal characteristic of the patient. It can be used descriptively, more as an adjective than as a noun [Hirsch, 1993, p. 294].

And in describing why the diagnosis of narcissism has been so troublesomely important:

> Narcissism is pivotal because essential distinctions about personal development are often dependent upon whether the patient is deemed 'narcissistic' or at a higher level of psychological integration. Historically, patients have been divided into analyzable vs. unanalyzable (see, Hirsch, 1984) based, to a degree, on the extent of narcissistic involvement. Those individuals who were perceived as essentially narcissistic were considered too immature or developmentally arrested to benefit from psychoanalysis. Psychoanalytic technique was thought to be too austere and depriving, as well as too verbal for the more contact-hungry narcissistic patient. Further, it was believed that such (narcissistic) individuals could not form a transference to the analyst since they were not sufficiently personally related to do so. It often seemed tha t anyone toward whom the analyst could not relate was deemed narcissistic and unanalyzable [Hirsch, 1993, p. 295].

In this same paper, I note that the efforts of Interpersonally identified analysts like Sullivan (1953) Fromm-Reichmann (1959) and Searles

(1965) to work analytically with the extremes of narcissism were applauded, but did not capture the imagination of the large body of American psychoanalysts. The former group offered no new analytic technique to reach the hardest-to-reach patients at the narcissistic extremes, suggesting instead that vigilant awareness and use of countertransference subjectivity is key in being able to persevere in treatments that were highly difficult and often dominated by analysts' feelings of rage and futility. They suggested sometimes sharing these feelings with patients in an effort to breach the latters' affective disengagement, and such recommendations led some to easily write-off this sub group as *wild analysts*. Not until Kohut (1971) entered the scene was analytic focus on working with those deemed and diagnosed as narcissistic of central interest in the psychoanalytic field. Kohut, a highly respected member of the American psychoanalytic establishment, had much more credibility than those identified as Interpersonal, and he caused quite a stir. In very stark summary, Kohut, opposite to both his Freudian and Interpersonal colleagues in different ways, suggested that those patients considered and diagnosed as narcissistic were not able to deal either with analysts' austerity or subjectivity. He observed that many patients were inclined to quickly quit treatment in response to the reserve of classical Freudian analysts and the challenge of Interpersonal analysts. In contrast, Kohut suggested an empathically dominated analytic stance, essentially suppressing both analysts' interpretive and observational positions. He posited that, in light of patients' deficient early internalizations, empathy was the most likely road to the establishment of a stronger self and what followed, a relaxation of survival-based narcissism. As I discussed this absurdly brief historical survey (Hirsch, 1993) I suggested that the development of Self-Psychology had both positive and negative implications. The good news was that a far broader range of patients were considered analyzable, and the subject of narcissism became a central focus in the analytic literature. The bad news was the reinforcement of diagnostic thinking, and prescriptive treatment that inevitably follows. Kohut reawakened the field to the importance of empathy in contrast to theory-based interpretation or excessive challenge, though his approach smacked of the objectivism inherent in the attempt to distinguish diagnostically who fits into the category of narcissism and who has evolved from that lesser state of being. This overly medical thinking was compounded by the suggestion that there were two distinct forms of psychoanalysis, traditional classical Freudian for those deemed non narcissistic and Kohut's methods for the less-than narcissists.

Subjectivity, intersubjectivity, uncertainty, and surprise, qualities that drew me to my Interpersonal teachers, seemed to me foreclosed. In the more current parlance of one- versus two-person psychologies, the alleged objectivity of analysts' interpretations were replaced by the alleged ability to empathically know the experience of another.

Since the publication of what I have summarized, in the context of the broad Relational turn in psychoanalysis (e.g., Greenberg and Mitchell, 1983; Mitchell, 1988; Aron, 1996) the tone of the literature is such that Freudians have become less sure of their interpretations, Interpersonalists have been more modest in celebrating the accuracy of their countertransference observations, and Self-Psychologists less sure that their empathy is only about the patient and not also telling about the subjectivity of the empathizer. And Kohut's key clinical recommendations, the worthy effort to empathize optimally, were applied to all analytic patients, reducing the objectionable diagnostic divide between those deemed to be narcissistic versus those who were more developmentally evolved. Gabbard (1995) speaks about a convergence in the field around Interpersonal (or Intersubjective, or Relational) conceptions of mutual enactment (Levenson, 1972: Sandler, 1976; Jacobs, 1986; Hirsch, 1998). With regard to narcissism per se, Self-Psychology has evolved, for the most part, to Post Self-Psychology (see Fosshage, 2003) and no longer emphasizes either diagnostic certainties, prescribed modes of treatment, nor a dichotomy of the patient population into narcissistic and non-narcissistic categories. This salubrious development leaves one without a clear perspective on what narcissism actually is, and to the default position that the observation of this quality lies, to a reasonable degree, in the eyes of the implicitly subjective observer. And the observer/psychoanalyst may indeed, as evidenced by my so heavily leaning on my own previous writing here, be more worthy of the descriptive adjective, narcissistic, than any patient he or she might be engaging.

So, because I will be sharing some thoughts about patients (and analysts) who I will be describing as narcissistic, it is warranted here that I say at least a very brief something about what might justify this descriptive label. Lasch (1979), in a widely read book of his time, described the pure quality of narcissism as characterized by some or all of the following: vanity, exhibitionism, arrogance, grandiosity, and self-absorption. The otherness of the other is dramatically secondary to the centrality of *meeness*. Of course, all of these qualities are shared by most people to some degree or another, and only a small minority of individuals are pure narcissists in any one of these ways. Analysts and patients, alike, relate with others on some continuum of narcissism. Probably the most common illustration of narcissism lies in quotidian self-absorption, either at moments or as a general characteristic (see, Barnett, 1971; Fiscalini, 1993). Parenthetically, this is not the most common public perception of what constitutes narcissism. I believe that most of the lay population, if not also the population of psychoanalytic therapists, associates the term with an inflated, albeit defensive, feeling about oneself, closer to excessive vanity and exhibitionism. However, those who are obsessional most certainly also qualify as being narcissistically self-absorbed. Although many will disagree, I believe that depression, unfortunately also often used as a diagnostic category, is intrinsically inseparable from self-absorption. As just noted, most often in a professional context, the term *narcissistic* is used to describe those more colorful qualities like grandiosity, exhibitionism, vanity, and arrogance. This more common usage masks the fact that those who are depressed may be at least as, or more, not affectively present nor available for human engagement as their more flamboyant counterparts. This theme, however, may some day wait for another paper, for I fear, most narcissistically, that to publicly highlight the narcissistic aspects of common and especially severe depression may place me in a bad light with my colleagues and peers. Suffice it to say, that I do, sometimes intrepidly, address this observation with my depressed patients and friends.

In what remains of this article, I take the more exciting road and address the quality of narcissism as it intersects with qualities like arrogance and grandiosity. I run some collegial risk here too, as you may see, for I had thought originally of titling this article "In Praise of Mania." Like depression, hyper-mania is most often pathologized. However, given the choice, who would not opt for at least a reasonable touch of mania in preference to an analogous flavor of depression or even-temperedness? Just as a range of depression and obsessional self-absorption is prevalent in society, perhaps particularly among psychoanalysts, hyper-mania and the narcissistic self-absorption accompanying this characteristic are shared probably by a large, though probably smaller, number of more fortunate individuals. I have observed, and this will be the theme of my clinical illustrations, that the narcissism inherent in mania leads to a hell of a lot more personal happiness than that of depression. As well, and not a small footnote, I have observed and judged many narcissistic-manic people to be among the most productive to society. Every personal characteristic that tilts away from the center of the bell-shaped curve has its down sides for that person and for those who populate the life of that subject. I try, however, to illustrate some of the under-addressed productive side of a reasonable degree of manic narcissism. In considering this, I suggest that many in the psychoanalytic profession who have made the most public impact share this quality with their business, political, and entertainment counterparts. I also suggest that analysts' envy of such attributes in some of their high achieving patients can account for much of the pathologizing and diagnostic name-calling that one can see in the literature.

The highly successful cable television show *Mad Men* refers to the depiction of the advertising industry during its heyday—early 1960s New York. Many of the highly successful agencies were located on the elegant Madison Ave., and the industry was often referred to, and still is to some degree, by this street name. Again narcissistically, I begin this section with a personal anecdote, one that relates to my reference to *Mad Men*.

In the summer of 1962, I celebrated my college graduation by embarking on a three-month-long trip to Europe with a close childhood friend who had just begun what would later evolve into magnificent career in finance (Wall Street). His girlfriend at the time, a high school classmate of mine, like me, was about to begin a doctoral program in clinical psychology at a university distant from our shared and beloved heritage in Brooklyn, New York. My friend had some concerns about losing her to geographical distance and into the arms of a fellow graduate student, or more likely, to a lecherous psychology professor with a pipe and a goatee (the professorial prototype outfit at the time). This, however, was of minor concern to him, compared with his literal ongoing obsession about the likelihood of losing her that summer, for her summer job situated her at an advertising agency on Madison Avenue. My friend's potential glorious summer, two 21-year-old men driving around Western Europe, was severely compromised by visions of his cherished girlfriend seduced and ravished by impeccably dressed, clever, charming and older *Mad Men*. During this part of the 20th century, the men of Madison Avenue were the men of glamour, of style, of good looks, of power, of wealth, and of creativity. They were the romanticized "Masters of the Universe," a term that Tom Wolfe (1987), a number of years later created for the men of Wall Street, the banking and the investment professions. What Wall Street has represented from the latter part of the 20th century to this day, the men of Madison Avenue were, at least from the middle 1950s through the 1960s, the men associated with power, and the excesses and sense of invincibility that often accompany great power.

My friend had good reason to be worried, for as anyone who has watched *Mad Men* can see, the stars of advertising agencies sometimes lived life on a perennial high—invincible and immortal. As symbolized by the two handsome, elegant, self-assured, seductive, and brilliant lead characters, Don Draper and Roger Sterling, these men did not need to live by the constraints of conventional society, and they could have most anything they wished for. Don and Roger, both married with children and living in wealthy suburbs, were in a position to have sex with legions of beautiful, often much younger, women and took full advantage of this, with no apparent concern for any potential impact on their families. Don's wife, vain, immature, and dependent, was gorgeous and worshiped him, and put up, for some time, with powerful neglect and many nights alone, while remaining enamored. Ultimately, she found someone else to take care of her and she left him. Roger's wife was highly capable, strong, and nurturing of him, and he eventually abandoned her to marry a beautiful secretary almost as young as his daughter. Both men left child-rearing exclusively to their wives, one spouse capable and the other not all. The well-being of their children barely, if at all, seemed in focus. Neither Don nor Roger seemed to need sleep or rest. They could drink alcohol and smoke cigarettes to what now appears like incredible excess, with no anxiety about potential consequences. Even after Roger had two heart attacks in quick succession, he did not think of changing his smoking, drinking, and eating habits, nor his passion for sexual adventure.

Almost in caricature, the lead characters, as well as minor ones, consumed alcohol and cigarettes all day long. Although these were the days that most adults smoked, research was beginning to lead to serious warnings about health risks. The major client of the advertising agency of focus was a leading cigarette brand, and Don and Roger deliberated how they might minimize the public perception of these risks. In no way was this translated into personal danger—both characters had cigarettes in their respective mouths while addressing with their tobacco clients how health risks might be finessed. In discussing the advertising culture of this era with acquaintances who actually had worked in this industry, I learned that *Mad Men* exaggerated the degree of drinking that occurred at the office during the work day. They did confirm, however, that much alcohol consumption did occur during long business lunches. Actually, this is the origin of the prototyped *three-martini lunch.*

The somewhat exaggerated sex, drinking, and smoking in *Mad Men* reflects dramatic license, although like most good fiction it effectively captures significant essences of its subject matter. This show, about wildly high-achieving and charismatic men depicts beautifully the selfishness, manic energy, grandiosity, and sense of invincibility and striving for immortality that often accompanies great achievement. The capacity to work extraordinarily long hours, to barely relax, sit in quiet contemplation, engage in intimate emotional moments or focus on the well being of intimates may, indeed, often go hand in hand with extreme levels achievement. I suggest that the level of narcissistic desire toward ambition, whether to achieve money or power (more likely the latter) and the manic energy and sense of limitlessness that may accompany this, is characteristic of many, especially men, who reach the highest heights in the world of work.

Freud's analytic aims of fulfillment in love and work is hard to achieve, for often, what it takes to reach the highest accomplishments in the area of work do not mesh well with a life of personal intimacy. Freud, himself, worked endlessly—the volume of his written work, not to mention the quality of this work, is hard to fathom. There was cost to Freud's family of origin, some of whom he failed to save from the Nazi ovens, and as well to the family he developed. It seems well established now that Freud essentially had two live-in wives, his actual wife and her sister. Like his mother before them, these women apparently both worshiped him and nurtured him, doing everything conceivable to create an atmosphere where he could work constantly and without the impediments of the usual family responsibilities. It is difficult for me to imagine that his actual wife and his children were fulfilled in the context of this most self absorbed, narcissistic configuration. In another interesting parallel to the *Mad Men* of the 1960s, Freud also smoked incessantly, and to the very severe detriment of his health.

I suggest that great achievement in any field is likely to come with a dark side, and that some reasonable level of narcissism, mania, and arrogance, and sense of immortality frequently accompanies extraordinary success in the work dimension. *Mad Men* is a dark tale—television noir, if you will. Don and Roger both get divorced; wives and children's and lovers and colleagues hearts are broken; serious health problems stemming from excess develop, and there are major lows and defeats that accompany the magnificent moments of success. The lead characters are charismatic, though they are not very nice. On the other hand, they are extremely talented and creative and at the head of their profession, and if one's value system is not automatically condemning of the advertising industry, one can say that they, too, make a contribution to culture. And, the large cloud of dominant darkness expressed in *Mad Men* is not inherent to the magnificent achievement of the manic and narcissistic leaders of every element of society. Was Freud's narcissism and mania, in sum, more bad for the world than good? If one is inclined to diagnose or to emphasize pathology, it is also necessary to examine the fuller picture—the shades of lightness and darkness. The fictional *Mad Men*, and the real-life mad men to follow in my subsequent illustrations, are best described in all their nuance, with their frailties and strengths, with how they both contribute to society and how they are harmful. These real-life mad men are often both envied by psychoanalysts, and in some instances, are them too. To diagnose and pathologize creates distance—it helps make psychoanalysts' own grandiosity and narcissism a possible, *not me* experience (Sullivan, 1953; Stern, 1990; Bromberg, 1998) and often allows them the illusion that they are more benevolent and altruistic human beings than they are.

To speak most generally, I believe that strong elements of narcissistic grandiosity and mania have always been represented in disproportion in individuals (mostly men) who have displayed the highest level of achievement in the work dimension of life. Of course, some of this achievement, as with, for example, autocratic and violent leaders and thieves, has had profoundly destructive consequences to society. However, as noted with my very brief reference to Freud, much that has moved the world forward has been initiated by highly driven individuals with these characteristics. Qualities that often create difficulty for those who live in intimate quarters may be of enormous benefit to the wider culture. I believe that narcissism, mania, and grandiosity, all too often used either diagnostically or as negative criticism, often can be applied to those whose productive achievement makes the world a better place. I, at this juncture, with no more credentials than my reference to Freud's life, say a few words about charismatic former president, Bill Clinton.

From what I have gleaned from assorted newspaper and magazine articles, Clinton was/is an individual who could work endlessly, apparently without the need for the sleep or rest that most mortals require. His appetites are said to be vast, ranging from voluminous reading and hunger for knowledge and information, to food to sex. His vast store of knowledge and information combined with extraordinary personal ambition and his seeming endless store of energy to make his presence public, led over the years to an assent from a troubled and humble family background to the highest office in the world. Many considered him among America's most brilliant and capable presidents. On the other hand, the same narcissism, grandiosity, and mania that allowed Clinton to achieve what he did—one can call this *good narcissism* (analogous with good and bad cholesterol), precipitated his fall from grace. Although he was said not to use his manic energy to smoke and drink like the *Mad Men*, his sense of immortality expressed in his highly indulgent eating habits nearly killed him. His narcissistic and grandiose sense that he could exercise his sexual appetites with whomever, whenever, and wherever he wished, with no deleterious effect on his career or his family, led directly to his public humiliation and disgrace. His vaunted career was, for some time, derailed, and his much-loved daughter undoubtedly deeply injured. This reflected his *bad narcissism*, the ugly side of mania and grandiosity.

The creative achievements in the advertising industry initiated by the fictional *Mad Men* had more lasting impact on culture than did their heart attacks and the destruction of their respective nuclear families. Few would argue that Freud's neglect of his children in favor of his work, his degradation of his wife in light of his likely long sexual relationship with her sister, and his willingness to neglect the plight of his three sisters who were trapped in Nazi Europe, overshadowed his contributions to the broader culture. Indeed, Freud is barely remembered for his bad narcissism. Clinton has recovered from his profound public humiliation and fall from grace, and with the same manic energy put his life back together. From what one hears anecdotally, he is as fanatic in his pursuit of a healthy diet and exercise regimen as he was when he ate compulsively. His sexual indulgence is rumored still to be prodigious, although he and his wife appear to be unofficially estranged, and the former may cause no harm. His manic capacity for work and his need for public recognition has been translated into becoming the nation's leading and most respected ambassador and advocate for world peace. He is treated with enormous respect and dignity on the world stage, and even by his former political enemies. And, his beloved daughter still appears to adore the daddy who, despite his apparent love for her, had also displayed profound disrespect for her well-being. Don and Roger of *Mad Men*, and the mad men Freud and Clinton, all use the narcissism and manic energy that first catapulted them to success to overcome adversity (note Freud's dealing with his cancer and with Fascism in Austria) and rebound with the same energy with which they began. If they get depressed they do not stay this way for long. Mania is said to be the other side of depression, though even if this is so on an etiologicl level, I have observed with many high-achieving people that the depressive side of the polarity barely emerges with significant consequence.

I believe that the descriptive labels *narcissism, mania*, and *grandiosity*, much less the odious diagnostic labels, have gotten a bad rap in the psychoanalytic profession. As noted, like cholesterol, I believe that there is good and bad in each of these qualities. Neither are usually all-or-none characteristics. All personal qualities, at the extremes, can be troublesome, though most lie on a continuum. Applying diagnostic labels to such qualities is good for the pharmaceutical industry and for those who are more comfortable with black-and-white binary thinking. I blanch at the currently extremely popular diagnostic term, *bipolar*, the most overused diagnosis of our modern time. Most depressed people I have known rarely experience the joys and pleasures of mania and grandiosity, and most manic and narcissistic people I know do not seem to dip into the dull miseries of long depressions. As well, I reiterate an earlier point that depression, too, is usually a highly indulgent state, and the self-absorption involved can readily be described as narcissistic.

I present one brief summary and one more extended one of what Tom Wolfe (1987) called "Masters of the Universe," two men of Wall Street who have been more recent society's mad men. Bradley cannot sit still. He is either working, working out in the gym, engaging in one or another competitive sport or sports instruction, watching his daughters compete in their school sports, traveling for business or recreation, or eating. Notably, he loves business travel and does this almost weekly and, whereas most people I know dread the hassle, stress, and uncertainties of air travel, my patient is energized by this experience. It is very difficult for him to sit still and quiet while watching a movie or television, and to do so he must be ferociously snacking and drinking soft drinks. He cannot read recreationally and reads exclusively for business. He has an enormous appetite and eats too much and complains to me and to others about his weight, and this usually leads to a cycle of even more than normal intense work-outs in the gym and with his personal trainer. He is very close with his two adolescent daughters and engages vigorously with them in mostly sports-related activity. His implicit marriage contract permits him, actually encourages him to spend the bulk of his time traveling and working, although his marriage is more relatively content than most that I see in both my personal and professional life. Bradley is very good-looking, charming, and wealthy, and has much opportunity for casual sex. His relative fidelity in the context of all of his driven behavior and travel has always surprised me, and I sometimes think that he might not be entirely honest with me in around this matter. This said, I do get the sense from him that he and his wife care deeply for one another and that he profoundly values the cohesiveness of his family.

This magnificently successful Wall Street deal-maker and his cohort are the *Mad Men* of today, usually minus the cigarettes and alcohol (except good wine with dinner). Instead of being in constant motion with a cigarette or alcoholic drink passing from hand to mouth, they are likely, like Bradley, to awake between 4 and 5 AM and work-out ferociously before getting to work before 8 AM. Their sense of immortality is more logically earned and literally and consciously pursued. Bradley believes that if he works out with sufficient vigor and controls his diet, he can live near to forever. He does not believe that sleep and rest are relevant, and the absence of these, so far, does not appear to have impact.

Bradley comes to treatment for the imperfections in his life, for the matters that he cannot compulsively control. He does not like that he eats too much, and is deeply worried by factors in the economy that impede his excellent record of investment success. As well, his wife complains that he is insufficiently emotionally present; that he does not listen well, and does not speak with her in a way that reflects personal intimacy, except when he is worried about the business climate. Though he is active sexually with his wife, she argues that he is not sufficiently affectionate. When worried or frightened about work, Bradley can be very dependent on both his wife and on me in the transference. In the normal course of events, I do not feel that I am terribly important beyond being a listener on retainer for those moments when Bradley is scared. His wife probably feels similarly. Bradley argues with me that his wife has little to complain about. He emphasizes his relative sexual fidelity, his love for and devotion to his daughters, and his ability to be a magnificent provider of an extremely luxurious life. He tells his wife, and me, that she cannot expect to have everything—that quiet intimacy is not his strength. He further argues that he is highly generous in other ways to his family, his family of origin, and numerous charitable causes. He is on a number of not-for-profit boards and takes great pride in the considerable amount of time he spends with this and with the prodigious amount of his money earmarked for philanthropy. With his energy, he is always happy to be called upon to help one or another member of his extended family, friends, or business associates. I have the distinct feeling that he would love it if I called on him to be of some tangible help to me.

Bradley is in a profession well suited for him. There is always a high volume of work to do, extensive travel, and much gamble and risk-taking. This fuels his excitement and drives his energy. Although I believe that Bradley is fundamentally ethical, when narcissism, mania, grandiosity and invulnerability get out-of-hand, there is risk that actions taken can cross ethical and legal lines. As seen in recent years, this can be highly destructive to society at large. These potential dangers are exciting to Bradley and to many of his cohorts, the risk of catastrophe to self, family, and society may produce a high. *Mad Men* depicts a life of excess, driven by various degrees of narcissism, mania, and grandiosity, and frames this mostly in darkness—television noir. However, in life, as I have observed with myself and among my more narcissistic and driven friends, colleagues and patients, personal disaster and serious injury to others lies in some juxtaposition with the benefits such qualities may precipitate. Indeed, there are many Freuds, Clintons, and Bradleys whose narcissism and mania, in sum, produce far more good than harm in the world, if not in their immediate familial world, in society at large. Such complexity does not warrant diagnosis.

Another "Master of the Universe," one of our contemporary *Mad Men*, I call Stanley.[1] He was a trim, well-dressed, and vivacious man, 67 years old (I was 55) when we began analysis. Stanley quickly viewed himself my mentor, particularly in the ways of finances, sex, and family life. He perceived me (some dozen years younger than he) as conservative and cautious, and was inclined to share with me much wisdom accumulated from an adventurous and most interesting rags-to-riches life. Brilliant, self-absorbed, and manically driven in all dimensions of life, he emerged from the emotional and economic poverty of his early life to business and personal prosperity. He had accumulated a fortune, largely by taking many risks in his Wall Street career, and had some close brushes and terrified moments with regulators from the securities and exchange commission. He had ambitions toward very high elected office, citing other very wealthy men who have used their own money to

---

[1] I have previously written about this patient using a different pseudonym for him (Hirsch, 2007).

finance national political careers. He shared with me, and impressed me with, many of his well-thought-out political ideas, though he lamented his overriding fear that were he to enter this very public domain, his earlier legal problems could have damaging repercussions. He hated being in this unfamiliar cautious state, and was somewhat depressed about limits that he believed were unfairly placed upon him. Stanley's life was very active. He had many interests and commitments. He was perennially looking for new start-up businesses to invest in; he was always weighing the pros and cons of purchasing a major league sports franchise; he was still active athletically, constantly trying to improve his golf game with frequent lessons; he was very involved philanthropically and seemingly was at one or another benefit or testimonial every other evening; he was consistently looking for new fine restaurants; he saw much of his large family (wife, three children, and many grandchildren) and either totally or partially supported all of them financially; he attended religious services weekly, and had sexual relationships with one particular lover of a number of years and many other younger women in brief relationships. I saw him twice weekly, though he missed or was late to many sessions. Given his level of activity, much of it highly productive (depending on the values of the observer) he never seemed fatigued, and I was both awe struck and jealous his vitality and energy.

He started therapy at his wife's demand—she was not awestruck by his incessant and poorly veiled extramarital sex life and threatened to leave him. He claimed to love his wife dearly, though no longer was able to sustain an erection with her. She, a woman of great beauty and from a wealthy and prominent family, was for Stanley a major step-up in the world. She had originally been unwilling to marry him because of what she felt would be downward mobility, and Stanley employed all of his considerable talents to eventually overcome his rival suitors. He had wanted a large family, but as a parent was far too occupied by his career and extrafamilial interests to be a loving and hands-on father. Although claiming to always have cherished his wife and children, he was largely self-absorbed, disengaged, and in pursuit of a myriad of personal pleasures. However, by age 67, despite his work, avocations, and sexual adventures, he spent far more time with his family than when younger, and appeared to get much satisfaction from being an active grandfather with many grandchildren.

I initially felt as if I were engaging in a grand deception. Stanley placated his wife by visiting me but would rather "be buried" than give up his sexual exploits. However, not too long after beginning treatment, my patient ran into further regulatory problems with his businesses and became quite anxious and somewhat depressed at scrutiny and the various limits that were being imposed upon him. At this point, I became less singularly jealous of him and began to feel that his visits to me were more legitimate. There was a shift in our power relationship. He became less my mentor and more my dependent. I felt an increase in my own strength and, I must confess, relieved that Stanley was having some trouble. Now he alternated between speaking quite openly about his fear that his life would revert to the feelings of dependence, weakness, and oppression that characterized his early years, and enthusiastically informing me of his most recent sexual exploits, his golf conquests, or the latest honor bestowed upon him by some charitable organization. Although I never experienced the latter as boasting, there was an element of dominance-submission as he situated himself as this larger-than-life father, sharing with me a wisdom that might enrich my own pedestrian existence. I often experienced myself as small in relation to Stanley and, in part because of my own lack of a strong father in my development I was receptive to engaging with him in this manner. On the other hand, his sense that he had power in relation to me helped him share his fears with me. As well, his fears and doubts sustained my own narcissistic sense of relative potency. I was also buoyed by having a patient of his wealth and stature, and would regularly read the business and society pages of *The New York Times* to see references to him.

Stanley claimed to regret hurting his wife and children by the all-too-public nature of his sexual infidelities, and by his failure to find his wife sexually desirable any longer or to respond to her overtures. This was not enough to resist sexual opportunity with the attractive and often much younger women seemingly available to him. On the other hand, he underscored the unnatural and counterintuitive property of desiring only one sexual partner, stating that usually the only men who adhere to monogamy are those without opportunity (with the subtext that I might be among those). He argued that it has been unreasonable for his wife to not accept this, pointing out that in no other culture, past or present, are powerful men like him expected to remain monogamous.

I saw Stanley into his early 70s, when barely even able to maintain an erection with the benefit of Viagra, he was still shamelessly seducing much younger women with some frequency. Much of this sex consisted of mutual oral and manual stimulation. By this time, his wife believed that he was too old and impotent for even this, and she created little stir. I believe that our analytic efforts helped Stanley get beyond his overt fears that he would some day lose his esteemed and powerful place in society, and once again be the castrated little boy of his early years, though there remained covert anxieties and angers that still help fuel his driven ways. Stanley did cause considerable pain to his wife, and this marital configuration undoubtedly had repercussions with his children, even though each of them has done relatively well in life. However, by the time our work together had ended his marital strife had ceased and he seemed to me a largely constructive force in his family. He even felt helpful toward the women with whom he was having sex. By his account, they all fully knew it was just casual sex, and took from it whatever benefits they may have received: gifts; help in opening up career opportunities; or simply the pleasure of association with a charming, attractive, and charismatic older man. Of course, it is possible that some of these women felt cheapened or degraded, and one could make a moral argument about Stanley's sexual behavior on a number of accounts. Perhaps I did not because of my greater admiration for and jealousy of his accomplishments, energy, and vitality. However, by the time we stopped treatment, Stanley was more vigorous and satisfied with his life than are the vast majority of people in his age range.

From my perspective, he met most of Freud's original criteria regarding work and love: a rich and involved career; a vital and involved, although ambivalently loving, current relationship with his wife; an affectionate and generous connection to his children and grandchildren; and a contribution to society (often in the form of extensive philanthropy). My experience with Stanley affirms for me how difficult it is, indeed, to reach optimal potential in work and in love, and how everyone, analysts and lay people alike, rarely get close to this ideal despite, perhaps, many years of personal psychoanalysis. Those who, like Stanley, Bradley, Bill (Clinton). Sigmund (Freud), Don and Roger, achieve the very most in the domain of work, often do it at some cost to those who love them. A certain degree of narcissism, along with the mania and grandiosity that sometimes accompany this, may be integral to achieving enormous success in the world of work.

Conclusion

To the extent that analysts diagnose others' narcissism, offer proscribed treatment regimens as if they were physicians treating medical disease entities, or infer standard causalities to such ways of living, analysts are usually unduly emphasizing pathology and failing to attune to strength. And in so doing, in the context of dissociated destructive envy and jealousy, they try to gain an edge over those who tickle their felt inadequacies. This may reflect psychotherapists' own narcissism and weak attempt at manic compensation. Many patients are smarter and more interesting people than their analysts are, have more successful and/or lucrative careers than they do, and may, as well, live richer lives in the context of significant others. Operating on all or most cylinders in both work and love is extraordinarily hard for most people, and I have never observed that psychoanalysts, despite many years of undergoing personal analysis, do this better than their patients who pursue other career paths. It is often tempting to pathologize those "others" who are very wealthy or prominent as either short on morals and principles, lacking in integrity and superficial and mercenary in their values. One may call them pejorative names like narcissist, manic, and grandiose as a way of compensating for one's own felt competitive inadequacies. Analysts often overemphasize the troubled aspects of their lives in priority to their productive contributions. Especially with *Mad Men* or Masters of the Universe, one may be quick to point out the deficiencies in the love side of their life while emphasizing the dark side of their work successes. Implicitly, psychoanalysts and psychotherapists, in their writing of or discussing their patients, imply that they, the therapist leads a fuller life in the dimensions of work and love. Analysts allegedly do not carry the odious diagnoses, patients do. However, for myself and others who truly believe that we are all more simply human than otherwise, and that the therapy relationship is hardly one between one well person and another sick one (see Racker, 1968), this is patently absurd. Analysts only need to look at themselves candidly to see, that if they take the misguided liberty of diagnosing their patients, they must call themselves by the same odious names. And, if they use terms like *narcissism, mania*, and *grandiosity* as descriptive, as I do here, they may sometimes apply to analysts to a greater degree than to their patients. I suggest that what I am describing is more prevalent when working with those patients or public figures described in this article. It hardly takes a psychoanalyst to see the extent that jealousy and envy plays a role in their downgrade of such people. Sometimes the best one can do to sooth one's self is to split off one's feelings of inadequacy and compensate by pathologizing some of the very high achieving people one sees in one's office.

Finally, as briefly noted earlier in this article, psychoanalysts who are the most renown are likely closest in temperament to their narcissistic, manic, and grandiose *Mad Men* and Masters of the Universe. Like Freud, the greatest of all analysts, one must work with considerable ferocity to write and to speak publicly to the extent that it leads to national or international recognition. There are invariable prices to pay in one's love life for such ambitions. One's efforts, indeed, like those whom I have discussed, may lead to much good in the world. This reflects the good cholesterol of narcissism, mania, and grandiosity. However, make no mistake, analysts' motives are very likely be as laden with self-interest (Hirsch, 2008) as those they defensively stereotype from Madison Avenue and Wall Street. I suggest that the psychoanalytic value of self-reflection requires analysts to call themselves the same sort of names they give to their patients, and to recognize that all personal qualities are nuanced, lie on a continuum, and are likely to have both destructive and constructive properties.

REFERENCES

Aron, L. (1996). *A Meeting of Minds*. Hillsdale, NJ: The Analytic Press.

Barnett, J. (1971). Narcissism and dependency in the obsessional-hysteric marriage. *Family Process* 10:75–83.

Bromberg, P. (1998). *Standing in the Spaces*. Hillsdale, NJ: The Analytic Press.

Fiscalini, J. (1993). The psychoanalysis of narcissism: An interpersonal view" In: *Narcissism and the Interpersonal Self*, ed. J. Fiscalini & A. Grey. New York: Columbia University Press, pp. 318–348.

Fosshage, J. L. (2003). Contextualizing self psychology and relational psychoanalysis: Bi-directional influence and proposed syntheses. *Contemp. Psychoanal.* 39:411–448.

Fromm-Reichmann, F. (1959). *Psychoanalysis and Psychotherapy: Selected Papers of Frieda Fromm-Reichmann, ed.* E. V. Weigert. Chicago.: University of Chicago Press.

Gabbard, G. O. (1995). Countertransference: The emerging common ground. *Internat. J. Psychoanal.* 76:475–485.

Greenberg, J., & S. Mitchell. (1983). *Object Relations in Psychoanalytic Theory*. Cambridge, MA: Harvard University Press.

Hirsch, I. (1984). Toward a more subjective view of analyzability. *Amer. J. Psychoanal.* 44:169–182.

——— (1992). An interpersonal perspective: The analyst's unwitting participation in the patient's change. *Psychoanal. Psychol.* 9:299–312.

——— (1993). The ubiquity and relativism of narcissism: Therapeutic implications. In: *Narcissism and the Interpersonal Self*, ed. J. Fiscalini

& A. Grey. New York: Columbia University Press, pp. 293–317.

———— (1998). The concept of enactment and theoretical convergence. *Psychoanal. Quart.*, 67:78–81.

———— (2007). Imperfect love, imperfect lives: Making love, making sex, making moral judgments. *Studies in Gender and Sexuality*, 8:355–371.

———— (2008). *Coasting in the Countertransference: Conflicts of Self Interest between Analyst and Patient*. New York: The Analytic Press.

Jacobs, T.J. (1986). On countertransference enactments. *J. Amer. Psychoanal, Assn*, 34:289–307.

Kohut, H. (1971). *The Analysis of the Self*. New York: International Universities Press.

Lasch, C. (1979). *The Culture of Narcissism*. New York: Norton

Levenson, E. A. (1972). *The Fallacy of Understanding*. New York: Basic Books.

Mitchell, S. (1988). *Relational Concepts in Psychoanalysis*. Cambridge, MA: Harvard University Press.

Racker, H. (1968). *Transference and Countertransference*. New York: International Universities Press.

Renik, O. (1993). Analytic interaction: Conceptualizing technique in the light of the analyst's irreducible subjectivity. *Psychoanal. Quar*, 62:553–571.

Sandler, J. (1976). Countertransference and role-responsiveness. *Internat. Rev. Psychoanal* 3:43–48.

Searles, H. F. (1965). *Collected Papers on Schizophrenia and Related Subjects*. New York: International Universities Press.

Stern, D. B. (1990). Courting surprise—Unbidden perceptions in clinical practice. *Contemp. Psychoanal.* 26:452–478.

Sullivan, H. S. (1953). *The Interpersonal Theory of Psychiatry*. New York: Norton.

Wolfe, T. (1987). *Bonfire of the Vanities*. New York: Farrar, Straus and Giroux.

Wolstein, B. (1954). *Transference*. New York: Grune & Stratton.

Prologue to Chapter 14:
REFLECTIONS ON FERENCZI: ANALYTIC SUBJECTIVITY AND ANALYTIC HIERARCHY

Ferenczi was the first to make efforts to argue that the psychoanalytic process was more humanistic than scientific. He suggested that patients benefitted from what transpired in the analytic relationship more so than from the insight gained in that process. He argued that insight per se was all too influenced by the theory of the analyst and less by efforts to understand each idiosyncratic patient. Though once a favorite of his idealized mentor, Freud, Ferenczi was scorned and often written off as a regressed madman, largely for his skepticism about the universal applicability of Freud's strong and biologically tinged theory and for Ferenczi's experiments with unorthodox way of working with patients in deviation from Freud's theory of therapeutic action.

It should be noted that Ferenczi's psychoanalytic contemporaries as well as those who followed Freudian orthodoxy many years later, shared a concern that conceptualizing psychoanalysis as humanistic and not scientific led to the worry that the public reaction to psychoanalysis would be more critical than it already was. Addressing matters sexual was central to the psychoanalytic process and unless this inquiry was conducted by alleged medical scientists, it risked universal condemnation as prurient and at risk for sexual boundary violations.

Ferenczi eschewed behaving with his patients as either a alleged objective scientist or an authoritative medical doctor, adopting a far less authoritarian and more personal manner. Without the benefit of the future conceptualizations of Sullivan (1953) and Racker (1968), Ferenczi engaged as more human than otherwise, not viewing the therapeutic relationship as that between a well analyst and a sick patient. Like Sullivan who followed, Ferenczi was largely disrespected by the psychoanalytic mainstream, who held on to the view that insight proffered by an objective and scientific analyst was the sole vehicle for meaningful analytic change. As noted, the contemporary view that the therapeutic action of psychoanalysis had much to do with the evolution of the patient-therapist interaction per se, begins with Ferenczi.

Ferenczi can be seen as both the forerunner of the British middle school of Object Relations and the American Interpersonal tradition. In short summary, the Ferenczi who lovingly nurtured his developmentally arrested or deprived patients back to health formed the basis of the emotional tone of the British school. The Ferenczi who embraced his subjectivity, his unconscious participation and his authentic engagement, minus specific therapeutic strategies, had enormous influence on the development of the Interpersonal tradition. As anyone who has read this book up to this point can see, the latter more egalitarian and less parental Ferenczi has greater resonance for me.

REFERENCES

Racker, H. (1968). *Transference and Countertransference.* New York: International Universities Press.ad

Sullivan, H.S. (1953). *The Interpersonal Theory of Psychiatry.* New York: Norton.

Chapter 14

REFLECTIONS ON FERENCZI, ANALYTIC SUBJECTIVITY, AND ANALYTIC HIERARCHY*

For the most part, contemporary psychoanalytic theorizing situates the analyst as a subjective other in the analytic dyad, implicitly reducing the hierarchy seen in earlier conceptions of the psychoanalytic relationship—analyst as objective observer, patient as subjective participant. The seeds of this revolution begins in the 1920s with Ferenczi's recognition that the quality of the two-person analytic relationship usually carries more weight in successful analyses than does insight per se. Albeit in quite different ways, the roots of both interpersonal psychoanalysis and middle school object relations theory can be traced to Ferenczi's emendations of the classical Freudian Model.

Since the 1980s, what has been called the postmodern or relational turn has effectively shifted prevailing psychoanalytic thinking away from the theretofore dominant view that psychoanalysis is or can ever be an objective science. How any given psychoanalyst tends to work with patients, and/or think theoretically, is inherently a function of the subjective personhood of that unique individual. Each major psychoanalytic tradition or "school" has core theoretical suppositions about both the nature of human development and an ideal clinical process to which most adherents subscribe. I suggest, however, that each unique clinical psychoanalyst engages with patients in ways that reflect at least as much the person of that analyst as membership in any of these particular schools of thought. In the negative, this may be seen as anarchy and, in the positive, as creativity. Either way, for better or for worse, I see this as inevitable and reflective of the irreducible subjectivity (Renik, 1993) of both analytic theorizing and of clinical process.

The decline of the view of psychoanalysis as a science, as well as the possibility of the analyst serving as an objective observer, begins not with the relational movement in the 1980s but with its forerunners: the influence of Sandor Ferenczi in Europe (see, e.g., Ferenczi, 1924; Dupont, 1932/1988), and the development of interpersonal psychoanalysis

*Hirsch, I. (2016). Reflections on Ferenczi: Analytic subjectivity and analytic hierarchy. *Contemporary Psychoanalysis* 52:383–390.

in the United States in the 1940s (Sullivan, 1953; Thompson, 1950). Ferenczi's contributions were dramatic and nothing short of revolutionary, eventually changing the face of contemporary psychoanalysis. However, like Sullivan after him, it took a long time for his ideas to be recognized, respected, and incorporated into the broader corpus of psychoanalysis. Indeed, both seminal figures were either ignored or scorned for many years by the hegemonic body of traditional classical psychoanalysis and their wish to have psychoanalysis publically perceived as an objective medical science. In the beginning, this was understandable—there existed the great risk that this new enterprise of psychoanalysis and its stark focus on sexuality would be seen by both the public and the medical establishment as prurient and essentially pornographic in motive. And often the "science" was not helped by European prejudice toward the largely Jewish practitioners of this strange new profession. One can say that, at the time, it was in the best personal interest (Hirsch, 2008) of analytic practitioners to both view themselves and market themselves as objective medical scientists.

In this environment, as well as in the United States of the 1940s through the 1960s, where psychoanalysis was trying to establish a respectable foothold as a medical profession, it is understandable that any embrace of Ferenczi's revolutionary ideas or those of the interpersonalists who were influenced by him, would be most disruptive. As I see it, Ferenczi's most elementary and essential paradigm-shifting idea was that the relationship between analyst and patient had more mutative power than did insight produced by the analyst's interpretive interventions alone. Although in current times most analysts from a range of traditions believe that therapeutic action can evolve from both a new and salubrious personal experience with a subjective yet professional "other," and emotional insight derived from that relationship, in Ferenczi's era the former was seen as apostasy—a profound threat to a relatively new and still marginal profession.

There are fundamentally two ways to think about the mutative action of psychoanalysis as a function of a new experience with a professional yet subjective other. Ferenczi (1924) introduced both of these concepts (see below), and each has had a seminal impact in the development of different analytic traditions or schools, all now under the contemporary relational umbrella. I will designate one as the notion to consider the analyst as replacement object in the context of repairing the patient's developmental deficiencies, and the other as the analysts unwitting co-participation in the repetition of the patient's core relational patterns and the evolution of this mutual enactment into something new and, it is hoped, better. In each paradigm, analytic success depends on the patient's internalization of an emotionally significant and enriching personal analytic experience. The former can be seen as the forerunner both to the middle school of object relations and self-psychology, and the latter to the interpersonal tradition. Who the analyst is as a person and his or her esthetics has much to do with the embrace of one school or another (Hirsch, 2008, 2015; Kuchuck, 2013), as well as the often subtle ways in which each analyst tends to interact with others (Wolstein, 1975).

According to Thompson (1950), who was Ferenczi's on-and-off patient, and Harris and Kuchuck (2015), Ferenczi's personality had everything to do with his theoretical and clinical emendations. This is not a unique idea and is relevant to all of the psychoanalytic icons who have originated major new ideas and/or schools of thought. Ferenczi is described in these volumes as someone far more interested and immersed in literature, anthropology, and sociology than in the biology and neurology of his mentor, Freud. He is portrayed' consistently as an egalitarian and democratic soul with a strong distaste for hierarchy and authoritarian pretense. These personal features alone can account for his relative rejection of traditional doctor-patient hierarchy and skepticism about strong theories that sound scientific, tend to pigeonhole people into categories, and call for prescribed technical interventions. Ferenczi was the first to conclude that Freud's theories of mind too often led to patients being seen as less than unique individuals and more as pawns to be used to validate current theoretical conceptions. He is described as enthusiastic, inexhaustible, and experimental on the one hand, and empathic, loving, and warm on the other, engaging with patients more as an equal and a friend than as a distant and scholarly medical authority. He was critical of the use of psychoanalytic theory to create what he felt was excessive asymmetry between analyst and patient. One crucial aspect of Ferenczi's more democratic professional attitude was his recognition that who the analyst is as a person and the values that reflect this will invariably affect the ·way that the analyst engages with patients, and even more dramatically for his time, he recognized that the patient has the ability to perceive who the analyst is as a separate subjectivity (Aron, 1996). It is evident that the now widely accepted idea that the analytic process consists of an interaction between two subjective co-participants originates with Ferenczi.

Ferenczi's more symmetrical and interactive psychoanalysis looked very different from that of his contemporaries and, as noted, can be seen to bear the seeds of different traditions that converge under the heading of relational. I suggest here, as have others (e.g., Harris & Kuchuck, 2015), that Ferenczi's analysis of Michael Balint and, in turn, Balint's influence on Donald Winnicott, formed the essential basis of the "middle school" of object relations as it exists today. Ferenczi seemed personally predisposed to be particularly sensitive to the suffering of others and even to consider what others might consider the normal range of the inevitable slings and arrows of life as "traumatic." Of course, what deserves the designation of trauma and what does not is often in the eye of the beholder, though some contemporary analysts are more likely than others to use this designation liberally. In essence, Ferenczi's prevailing view, as reflected in the literature of the middle school of object relations (see Winnicott, 1958), is that deficiencies in early engagement with mothering figures lead to developmental arrest. The liberal use of the term "trauma" can support this. However, a key way that any analyst must participate is to engage in what Winnicott calls a holding environment in the context of serving as a good enough mother, i.e., a better maternal environment than the original. This distinctly developmental model situates the analyst as one whose main task is to compensate for what was missing for the patient earlier in life and, in so doing, in essence restart dormant development. One can readily see Ferenczi in this context, described by Thompson, 1950) as one who both looked to be loved and was very warm, loving, and nurturing to his patients. Ferenczi went further in this regard than do most contemporary analysts influenced by him. He often had maternal-like physical contact with patients and he expressed verbal and sometimes even physical affection far more frequently than was the norm then, and now as well. He often advocated analysts' willingness to admit mistakes and errors, a level of symmetry that one could interpret as very giving to patients, in contrast to the cooler, withholding, and aloof demeanor of most of his contemporaries and prescribed by traditional classical psychoanalysis.

Traditional self-psychology as originally articulated by Heinz Kohut (1984) has much in common with the emotional tenor of object relations thinking and, as well, can be seen as another of Ferenczi's legacies. This is also a developmental model with the prevailing view that emphasizes patients' developmental arrests and prescribes the role of the analyst as a better object than the original ones. The emphasis here is on patients' suffering from a lack of being truly known—a deficiency of empathy from early significant others. The analysts' consistent effort at empathy, though inevitably imperfect, is viewed as the fuel for igniting patients' further development and for the emergence of a sense of self. In both this tradition and that of object relations, analysts are advised to withhold their subjective otherness until the judged to be ill-equipped patient is strong enough or has enough "self" to embrace the analyst as subjective other. Here, too, one can see the precursor of Ferenczi, though Kohut never made this especially clear in his writing. Ferenczi, apparently, was nothing if not striving to be empathic toward his patients, eschewing theory-based interpretations in favor of consistent efforts at attunement to patients' experiences. Indeed, many years later, the same criticism was leveled by Kohut, criticizing psychoanalytic understanding for being dominated by analysts' cherished theories rather than efforts to understand the unique experience of each patient.

In tracing Ferenczi's impact on interpersonal psychoanalysis, one need not go further than Harry Stack Sullivan having dispatched his closest friend and colleague, Clara Thompson to undergo an analysis with Ferenczi in Budapest and to bring back to him what she had learned and, as well, do a little bit of analysis with Sullivan as her patient. Sullivan was an autodidact, introducing the idea of analytic subjectivity ("participant- observation") to America, although he was never a patient nor a student in a psychoanalytic institute. Though the embrace of psychoanalysis as a relationship between two subjectivities begins with Ferenczi, it was Sullivan who brought this to the United States and who recognized his sympathy with Ferenczi's ideas. Thompson, who was formally trained as an analyst, integrated the key concept of transference into what had been Sullivan's "interpersonal psychiatry," a subjectively tinged inquiry into the external life and life history of the patient. Thompson (1950) elaborates an interpersonal psychoanalysis that situates the analyst as a unique person in inevitable conscious and unconscious interaction with each patient (Fiscalini, 2004). Those American analysts who paid attention to Thompson's work learned about mutuality (Aron, 1996), the impact that the analyst as a person may have on the patient and the material produced in the analysis, as well as, of course, the impact that the patient has on the analyst. Thompson's assertion that the subjective analyst is always countertransferring, both as a function of the unique person of the analyst and what is evoked by each patient (Wolstein, 1975), led analysts in the United States to pay close attention to the concept of countertransference. The central importance of attention to the countertransference experience in order to understand patients, now a part of the repertoire of most analysts, was first espoused in America by Thompson, and an integral ingredient in her embrace of this idea came from her first-hand exposure to Ferenczi. Thompson's emphasis on all aspects of the countertransference experience can be seen vividly in the writing of some of her prominent colleagues and students (e.g., Levenson, 1972; Searles, 1979; Wolstein, 1975).

Interpersonal psychoanalysis embraces somewhat different elements of Ferenczi than that of the relational colleagues who are more identified with Donald Winnicott and Heinz Kohut. Interpersonalists emphasize analysts' unwitting participation, i.e., ways of engaging that emerge in the natural flow of analytic engagement. There is no prescribed role—the analyst does not aim to be a reparative object, either a "good enough" mother or an exclusive empathizer. The analyst is viewed as a flawed other who will be unconsciously drawn into relational patterns that both reflect the personality of the analyst and the relational and patterned pull of the patient. There is normally an effort *not* to be in a particular role (e.g., holding, empathizing, interpreting) but to respond to patients with a reflective but spontaneous authenticity—questions based on curiosity, observations, reflections spoken out loud. The origins of the now analytically central concept of mutual enactment (Levenson, 1972) emerge from the view that, in a way that is not premeditated, analysts unwittingly live out with patients their key internalized relational configurations. Once again, this phenomenon emerges out of an effort toward authentic relatedness—the absence of assuming, for example, a premeditated reparative role.

Thus, the interpersonal perspective is a reflection of somewhat different aspects of Ferenczi than exist with some relational colleagues. For one, the analyst as a distinct reparative object can be seen as hierarchical and may lend itself to the potential configuration of analyst as healthy, robust parent and patient as damaged and deficient other. The "more simply human" analyst (Sullivan, 1953) implicitly acknowledges any analyst as possibly as or more flawed than any given patient

(Hirsch, 2008, 2015; Searles, 1979). In addition, patients are usually encouraged to openly speak about perceptions that they have about their analyst, again with the implicit acknowledgment that patients may be just as or even more perceptive about aspects of the unique person of the analyst as analysts are in their observations about the patient. In this vein, Ferenczi went so far as to experiment with mutual analysis.

Ferenczi, like most of us flawed human beings, had his contradictions. Chief among these is, in my view, the question of how an analyst can be spontaneous, authentic, and nonhierarchical while at the same time assuming a defined role as an exclusively loving and reparative and parental object to patients who are conceptualized or diagnosed as either deficient or selfless? Moreover, the consistent description of Ferenczi as a powerful giver of love and hungry receptacle for the love of others likely placed strictures on his willingness to address and experience the angry and ugly aspects of his patients – and, indeed, we all have many ugly aspects (Harris & Kuchuck, 2015; Thompson, 1950). My own bias toward the interpersonal Ferenczi is probably clear to any reader by now, though of course this is a function of who I am as a person, and is not by any means an objective assessment of what tradition is superior. Indeed, we all like our own analytic traditions more than others and this is as it should be. That is, we are all more likely to practice more effectively in the context of a medium that we embrace. Ferenczi's painful and intrepid flight from the orthodoxy of his mentor and his colleagues is but one illustration of the extent to which the unique person of each analyst affects both theoretical preferences and clinical practice.

REFERENCES

Aron, L. (1996). *A Meeting of Minds*. Hillsdale, NJ: Analytic Press.

Dupont, J. (1988). *The Clinical Diary of Sandor Ferenczi*. Cambridge, MA: Harvard University Press. (Original work published 1932).

Ferenczi, S. (1924). Confusion of tongues between the adults and the child. *International Journal of Psychoanalysis. 30:*225–230.

Fiscalini,]. (2004). *Coparticipant psychoanalysis*. New York, NY: Columbia University Press.

Harris, A., & Kuchuck, S. (2015). *The legacy of Sandor Ferenczi: From ghost to ancestor.* New York, NY: Routledge.

Hirsch, I. (2008). *Coasting in the Countertransference: Conflicts of Self-interest Between Analyst and Patient.* New York, NY: Routledge.

——— (2015). *The Interpersonal Tradition: The Origins of Psychoanalytic Subjectivity.* New York, NY: Routledge.

Kohut, H. (1984). *How Does Analysis Cure?* Chicago, IL: University of Chicago Press.

Kuchuck, S. (2013). *Clinical Implications of the Psychoanalyst's Life Experience: When the Personal Becomes Professional.* New York, NY: Routledge.

Levenson, E. (1972). *The fallacy of understanding.* New York, NY: Basic Books.

Renik, O. (1993). Analytic interaction: Conceptualizing technique in the light of the analyst's irreducible subjectivity, *Psychoanalytic Quarterly* 62:553–571.

Searles, H. (1979). *Countertransference and related subjects.* New York, NY: International Universities Press.

Sullivan, H.S. (1953). *The interpersonal theory of psychiatry.* New York, NY: Norton.

Thompson, C. (1950). *Psychoanalysis: Evolution and Development.* New York, NY: Hermitage.

Winnicott, D.W. (1958). *Collected Papers: Through Pediatrics to Psychoanalysis.* New York, NY: Basic Books.

Wolstein, B. (1975). Countertransference: The psychoanalyst's shared experience and inquiry with his patient. *Journal of the American Academy of Psychoanalysis* 3:77–89.

Prologue to Chapter 15:
SUBJECTIVITY AND ANALYSTS' PERSONAL FREEDOM

There are a number legitimate theories that evolve out of the different psychoanalytic traditions and there is no way to say that one is universally better than another. Practitioners and devotees of the various theories evolve largely through matters that are personal, in particular, esthetic sensibilities and identifications with revered personal analysts and teachers. And even within each theoretical tradition, there is a wide range of ways that each *member* theorizes and practices. The unique person of each analyst has much do to with the way he or she works and I believe that this is largely for the good. Working in one's own idiom and within a certain comfort level is likely to lead to working at our best.

In this article I attempt to outline 9 of the important underlying dichotomies that exist among analysts who embrace different sensibilities. What follows is a very brief presentation of each.

(1) Psychoanalysis as hard science vs. psychoanalysis hermeneutic and part of the humanities. Controversy about the value of diagnosis is very relevant here.

(2) The analyst as very quiet and reserved vs. the analyst as relatively interactive.

(3) A basic view of patients as resilient vs. a basic view of fragility.

(4) A view of patients largely as victims of bad past experience vs. a view of patients as agentic, unconsciously structuring life to repeat and conform to past troubled experience.

(5) Adherence to traditional analytic ritual vs. the value of spontaneous engagement.

(6) The very controversial issue about the advantages and disadvantages of analysts' use of deliberate self-disclosure.

(7) Personality as endogenously based (biology and neurology) vs. personality as exogenously developed via the internalization of key personal relationships.

(8) Analysts' reveries as an invariably useful vehicle in the effort to understand patients vs. the possibility that reverie can also reflect analysts' personal self-absorption.

(9) Analytic practitioners as more altruistic breed than seen in other professions vs. analysts as selfish and flawed as most everyone else.

It should be noted that these stark dichotomies usually do not capture the ways that most analysts think. Indeed, while most of us lean one way or another, these leanings usually are not binary and tend to lie on a continuum.

Chapter 15

Subjectivity and Analysts' Personal Freedom[*]

What has been called the "Relational turn" or the "post-modem turn" has, since the 1980s, effectively shifted prevailing psychoanalytic thinking in the United States away from the theretofore dominant view that psychoanalysis is an objective science. How any given psychoanalyst thinks, and what he or she believes, is inherently a function of the subjectivity of that unique individual. From this perspective, a belief in psychoanalysis' objectivity can be just as subjective as the belief that this is impossible. Each major psychoanalytic tradition or school has core theoretical suppositions about both the nature of human development and what constitutes an ideal clinical process. And while it is commonly assumed that most adherents of a given school subscribe to its beliefs and ideals, I suggest in this paper that each psychoanalyst engages with patients in ways that reflect as much the person of that analyst as membership in any of these particular schools of thought. In the negative this may be seen as anarchy, and in the positive, as creativity. Either way, I see this as inevitable and characterizing what Renik (1993) has called "the irreducible subjectivity" of analytic theorizing and of clinical process.

Critiques of psychoanalysis as science and the deconstruction of analytic objectivity began not with the Relational movement in the 1980s but its forerunner, the Interpersonal psychoanalysis of the 1940s. Sullivan's (e.g., 1953), replacement of the analyst as objectivist, blank screen with one whom he termed "participant-observer" was the first and most important step in identifying analytic process as a relationship between two subjective co-participants (see Fiscalini, 2004). Sullivan and his colleagues drew upon anthropology, sociology, and social psychology, swerving away from what had remained for many years an identification with the hard sciences and with medicine. Participant observation is largely based on Heisenberg's principle of uncertainty. Heisenberg was a physicist declaring that, since the observer inevitably influences what is observed, subjectivity reigns, even in the hardest of sciences, and we cannot ever be absolutely certain about what is concluded.

*Hirsch, I. (2017). Subjectivity and analysts' personal freedom. In: J. Petrucelli & S. Schoen (Eds), *Unknowable, Unspeakable and Unsprung: Psychoanalytic Perspectives on Truth, Scandal, Secrets and Lies*. New York & London: Routledge. pp. 124–133.

In addition to reconceptualizing psychoanalytic process as intrinsically mutually subjective, Sullivan and his colleagues posited a view of human development based less on universal principles like fixed psychosexual stages (e.g., Oedipal conflict, castration anxiety, sibling rivalry, guilt over masturbation) and more on examining the unique interpersonal history of each individual. With fewer theoretical preconceptions to lean on, it became more difficult not only to know how to proceed clinically but how to understand each unique individual patient. Wolstein (1959) captured this best with his simple credo: "Each patient is unique, each analyst is unique, each dyad is unique." Sullivan's pursuit of analytic work with psychotic patients exemplified the point that one must be careful about making *a priori* judgments about people based on universal ideas about symptoms, diagnoses, and developmental histories. One great value of uncertainty, as disruptive as it can be, is that it will more likely lead to the supreme analytic asset of curiosity (Stem, 1997).

This profound paradigm shift introduced by Sullivan and his colleagues, most prominently Erich Fromm and Clara Thompson, existed, with minor exceptions for many years only in the margins of psychoanalysis. It was not until 1983 when Jay Greenberg and Stephen Mitchell, two analysts trained at the White Institute, which was the first and one of very few prominent analytic institutes in the Interpersonal tradition, published their now classic text, *Object Relations in Psychoanalytic Theory,* that Interpersonal thinking became known to the wider world of psychoanalysis. Though Greenberg and Mitchell's new and broader term, "Relational," was more influenced by the Interpersonal perspective than any other single tradition, the inclusiveness of this term as well as the ways in which it incorporated other traditions (e.g., Object Relational), made it appealing to a far wider audience (Greenberg and Mitchell, 1983).

Greenberg, Mitchell, and a host of writers, some self-identified as Interpersonal though most as Relational, effectively elaborated Sullivan's participant-observer analyst as an irreducibly subjective co-participant, and concepts such as intersubjectivity, two-person psychology, and dialectical constructivism flourished. Assuming that analysts were always countertransferring, this concept drew intense analytic focus. Traditional conceptions of transference distortion evolved into mutual transference-countertransference enactment, with an emphasis on the significance of the analyst's conscious and, most significantly, unconscious involvement in psychoanalytic process. The inherently subjective concept of mutual enactment was embraced by a wide range of analytic traditions in and out of the large Relational umbrella,[1] though distinctive elements of the history of various traditions remain evident in both theoretical/ developmental ideas about the origins of enactments and in recommended ways of engaging clinically. Certainly some historically meaningful overlap and divergence can be found among "schools" in their use of this concept, and I have little question that there are different emphases between Mitchell's largely Interpersonally influenced thinking and, for example, middle-school Object Relations theorists, contemporary Kleinians, Self-Psychologists and post Self-Psychologists, and liberal contemporary Freudians.

However, for the most part it is my sense that most interpersonally identified thinkers are indistinguishable from what have now become mainstream Relational ways of conceptualizing and working[2] (Mitchell, 1988). And further, whatever distinctions can still be drawn between schools, no theoretical tradition, set of narratives, or preferred way of engaging with patients will ever be proven to be superior to others. Essentially, practitioners think in ways that are most personally resonant to them. We all like our basic ways of theorizing and working better than alternatives and privately think these superior, though upon reflection they can be said to be superior *only for us.*

I have suggested elsewhere (Hirsch, 2008, 2015) that analysts' preferred ways of thinking and working are based on a combination of personal and intellectual aesthetics, unique individual personalities, and identifications with personal analysts and/or teachers. Though many of us do remain at least somewhat loyal to the traditions in which we were raised, there may still be vast differences among members of each tradition, since personality and taste will always prevail, especially with regard to the way we engage with patients. In what follows I will articulate and briefly discuss nine dimensions of subjective preference that distinguish analysts, often somewhat independently of their identified traditions, from one another. While I will try not to, I will inevitably resort to a degree of "either/or" thinking. Further, while I am aware that

---

[1]The Interpersonally identified Levenson (1972), gave birth to this concept, referring to this phenomenon as "transformation," and asserting that the analyst must *unwittingly* become part of the patient's problem in order to help resolve it. It was Jacobs (1986), unaware of Levenson's writing, who first used the term "mutual enactment."

[2]For a more thorough discussion of the juxtaposition Relational and Interpersonal perspectives, see Hirsch (1998).

some of these dimensions may seem to capture undesirable splits that would ideally be bridged or integrated, I also believe that our personal biases often outweigh our attempts to transcend them, and to some degree we will all, at times, fall into categories. Further, along each of these dimensions, I suspect that my own personal biases will be quite evident.

First, some of us are attracted to the hard sciences and to matters technical, while others find the humanities and social sciences more appealing. For the former there is greater likelihood of interpretive understanding and explanations of patients' development that can be very complicated and abstract. In the latter, there is usually more emphasis on description than explanation, and interpretations are more likely to sound commonsensical and pragmatic. Patients are thought about more novelistically - that is, in the way novelists may capture people. The first group may criticize the second for being superficial and insufficiently deep, while the latter may accuse the former of intellectualization and science or physics envy (see Levenson, 1972; Mitchell, 1988). I have suggested elsewhere (Hirsch, 2008, 2015) that the psychoanalytic profession from the beginning seemed to be burdened with a self-consciousness about being insufficiently scientific, often resorting to convoluted, explanatory conceptions that are unnecessarily complicated.

Second, some of us are temperamentally quiet and reserved and others more expressive and gregarious. Independently of theoretical prescriptions, this dimension alone may lead to vast differences in ways of engaging with patients. Individual practitioners may find theoretical reasons why one way is better than another in order to reduce conflict about one's own interpersonal strengths and weaknesses. Very reserved analysts may be critical of the intrusive elements of more active engagement, seeing it as interfering with the analytic ideal of patients expressing themselves without influence. Active verbal engagement may be viewed as narcissistic, self-centered, and competitive. More verbally engaged analysts may dismiss very quiet colleagues as cold and emotionally distant - hurtful to patients in this respect and too rigidly wedded to traditional analytic protocol. They may claim that excessive reserve sets a bad example for patients, discouraging them from being more emotionally expressive and verbally open (Renik, 1993).

Third, some analysts are inclined toward viewing patients as fragile and easily injured, while others see them as resilient and not benefiting from being treated as if they were delicate. The former group may try overtly to be gentle in manner and be very careful about broaching sensitive topics. Conceptions of timing may be central, along with the proclivity to judge that patients may not be ready to address certain material. Dealing with themes that emerge in the transference is more likely to be put on hold, and the patient tends to be assumed not to welcome the observations of the other. The term "need" is likely to be invoked, e.g., the patient "needs" to be held or contained. The latter group will often pay less attention to issues of timing, assuming that if a patient raises something explicitly or implicitly, this indicates a readiness to address it (Singer, 1965; Gill, 1982), and the same is true for the tendency to address issues in the transference as they appear. In this context there is no attempt for the analyst to engage or to speak in a manner that is not of normal tone. The term "need" is less likely to be invoked and the term "wish" is more likely to be used, e.g., the patient wishes to be held but this may or may not be the best thing for the analyst to do at this moment (Mitchell, 1988). Fundamentally, those analysts with this latter vision do not view well-intentioned interventions as likely to be profoundly damaging. The former group criticizes the latter for being insensitive to vulnerability and, because of this, more likely to retraumatize patients. The latter group is critical about the former's tendency to pathologize patients and, in so doing, treat them as even weaker than they may already feel. There also exists the charge that many analysts have a stake in seeing patients as "sick" as a way for the analyst to feel in a stronger and "healthier" state him or herself.

Fourth, and closely related to the above, is the conflict between emphasizing the degree to which patients have been hurt by important others and, conversely, viewing patients as unconsciously orchestrating and repeating in contemporary life the very hurts they sustained earlier in life. One view focuses on patient as almost exclusively a victim, the other on patient as unconscious agent in recreating a troubled future destiny. The former group may be more inclined to be empathic with patients' wounds and not at all actively question what the patient may be doing to invoke these wounds currently. To do otherwise would amount to blaming the victim, and piling new hurt on to old injury. Patients are not seen as healed enough to hear that they may be active agents in their current life in ways they were not when they were children.

The latter group believes that it is pathologizing for patients in most life situations to experience themselves in current life primarily as victims, since this implies that they have little control over life at it exists now. This group argues that, although patients may feel soothed and comforted by analysts' exclusive empathy for their victimization, they will not likely change unless they can recognize how they unconsciously recreate their past miseries in their current lives. Further, this group of analysts posits that people may be all too comfortable in familiar unhappiness, and excessive empathizing with this misery can reduce the desire to move on from this well-known, albeit unhappy, state. These analysts are more likely to resonate with what Freud originally identified as the domain of psychoanalysis—not inevitable and ubiquitous sadness, tragedy, and unhappiness, but the misery that we ourselves unconsciously bring on. This said, every analyst knows that empathy with patients' subjective experience of their own lives is an absolute necessity. Conflict between respective points of view arises when one subgroup of analysts perceive the other as putting excessive emphasis on either empathy or on challenge of patients' experience of themselves.

Fifth, as Hoffman (1998) has thoroughly discussed, each analyst attempts to strike some balance between adhering to the more conservative tenets of historically standard psychoanalytic rituals, on one hand, and the injection of spontaneous commentary on the other (see also Tublin, 2011). Though we invariably engage differently with each unique patient, we all lean one way or another along the continuum of ritual and spontaneity. Those of us who adhere more closely to ritual may criticize the embrace of spontaneity as a form of analytic self-indulgence. They may view such analysts as insufficiently willing to take a contemplative back seat to patients' freedom to express themselves, perhaps even suppressing this freedom by usurping the expressive dimension. Those analysts who embrace spontaneous expressiveness are likely to see an excess of adherence to ritual as too rigid—perhaps reflecting a need to live by rules and regulations.

Sixth, along somewhat similar lines is the controversy over analysts' deliberate disclosure of affective states. However, spontaneous commentary is not synonymous with deliberate self-disclosure, though these can be conflated. One may make spontaneous comments or observations to patients without deliberately disclosing affective states. Indeed, the latter phenomenon remains the most controversial issue in analytic practice. Many analysts who embrace the value of spontaneous commentary are still reluctant to disclose affective states. One reason, not commonly acknowledged explicitly, is that the expectation that we will answer patients' questions about what we are feeling may leave us unduly exposed and anxious.

Just as the use of the couch and thus not being visually observed has been calming and liberating for many analysts, so too has the ritual of not being expected to talk about one's feelings. And of course, as with other forms of spontaneity, there is the argument that analysts' expressions of feelings are likely to exert excessive influence on patients and reflect narcissistic indulgences. Those who advocate a "judicious" use of deliberate disclosure claim that outlawing this mode of expression is too restrictive: Patients often know what we are feeling in any case and it is too *gamey* to withhold confirmation of what patients sense and perceive. Such withholding of verbally expressed affective states is seen as creating undue asymmetry in the analytic relationship.

Seventh, some analysts view many personal problems as endogenously based and may focus on the alleged biological and neurological roots of personality. This belief is most clearly present when dealing with patients who function less effectively, e.g., people with long-standing depression, those considered Aspergian, or borderline, or in any way psychotic. For such practitioners the value of diagnosis is obvious, not only because it places a limit on what can be expected from analytic work, but because it can dictate technical application, i.e., prescribed ways to treat such categories of patients. This follows from a medical model of psychoanalysis, and its proponents argue that failure to acknowledge the endogenous bases of personality not only avoids awareness of research literature, but is naive and grandiosely quixotic. On the other end of this controversy are those who eschew biology and neurology as important factors in personality development. Rather, who we become is a function of our history of relationships with others and the internalization of life experiences. Viewing even severely dysfunctional individuals as predestined to be this way is far too limiting of human potential and can take the easy way out of what is a very difficult analytic task. While it is usually acknowledged that analytic work with more severely troubled people is more difficult than with high-functioning patients (see Searles, 1979; Hirsch, 2015), this is seen more as a function of entrenchment and adaptive self-protection than it is the result of anything endogenous. Analysts who view things in this way are likely to accuse their conceptual adversaries of being overly dependent on clear structure (e.g., diagnostic certainty) and may be envious of the "real doctors" in the medical profession.[3]

Eighth, some analysts place great value on retreat into private reverie during sessions, believing both that the occurrence of the retreat and the content of the reverie will be invariably informative about the patient. Others believe that, although the nature of the analytic interaction may provoke retreat, the content of the retreat and the amount of time spent there may often have little to do with any given patient. The former subset of analysts accuse the latter group of having insufficient faith in unconscious-to-unconscious communication and of adhering too rigidly to rational modes of analytic engagement. The alternative argument accuses the reverie celebrators of rationalizing their self-interested retreats, while simultaneously assuming that they reflect an unconsciously influenced profound connection to patients (Hirsch, 2008).

Ninth, an extension of this difference is the view that psychoanalysts by and large are an altruistic breed, in contrast with what may correspond with Sullivan's (1953) long-ago declaration that we are all more simply human than otherwise. Some analysts, for example, tend to be highly nurturing in ways that may lead them to feel that they are abandoning self-interest and only responding to what is best for patients. Others may not be especially nurturing, but may believe that they can uniformly stay pointedly attentive and engaged as consistent servants of the analytic process. Those more skeptical of a dominant altruism point out that holding such a self-deceptive view elevates analysts to a higher personal and moral plane than their patients. This, in turn, is unconsciously communicated to patients, and as well, reflects an element of denial that contrasts with the analytic ideal of acceptance of *all* facets of self-states and personal shortcomings.

I have noted elsewhere (Hirsch, 2008, 2015) that psychoanalytic process is best served when analysts are intensively and affectively engaged with their patients and are comfortable with the theoretical

---

[3]Parenthetically, the value of medication is less of a controversy than one might expect. Many analysts who eschew endogenous explanations of personality may be sanguine about medication because this can temper noxious symptoms. They would argue that psychology provokes biology and neurology. In other words, our biology or neurology have not caused our personality but are profoundly influenced by our affective states. For example, low serotonin levels do not cause depression; rather, when we are depressed, serotonin declines. Of course, this whole arena remains an area of profound difference among clinicians.

narratives and theories of therapeutic action that most resonate personally. Each of us is likely to have strong feelings about the advantages of our preferred theories and ways of working and this is as it should be. Try as we might to be flexible and reflect on our own preferences regarding the dimensions I have outlined above, who we have become as people and as professionals will inevitably prevail. As long as we are not excessively rigid in our beliefs and willing to try adapting to the idiosyncrasies of each individual patient, our personal commitments lead to both comfort and involvement. They are part of what puts us in a position to be productive. Indeed, each of our unique ways of working *is* superior to some alternative precisely because it best suits each of us as individuals. This degree of subjectivity creates muddle and confusion for those looking in from the outside, though I believe that it creates the basis for an important sense of security for those of us on the inside, and thus probably for our patients as well. Subjectivity reigns in every dimension of this most unscientific profession and it can be no other way. If this is thought to be a shortcoming in our field, we can only make the best of it.

REFERENCES

Fiscalini, J. (2004). *Coparticipant Psychoanalysis.* New York: Columbia University Press.

Gill, M. (1982). *Analysis of Transference (Volume 1).* New York: Inter-national Universities Press.

Greenberg, J. & Mitchell, S. (1983). *Object Relations in Psychoanalytic Theory.* Cambridge, MA: Harvard University Press.

Hirsch, I. (1998). Further thoughts about interpersonal and relational perspectives. *Contemporary Psychoanalysis,* 34:501–538.

———— (2008). *Coasting in the Countertransference: Conflicts of Self-Interest between Analyst and Patient.* New York: Routledge.

———— (2014). Narcissism, mania and analysts' envy of patients. *Psychoanalytic Inquiry,* 34:408–420.

———— (2015). *The Interpersonal Tradition: The Origins of Psychoanalytic Subjectivity.* New York: Routledge.

Hoffman, I. (1998). *Ritual and Spontaneity in the Psychoanalytic Process.* Hillsdale, NJ: The Analytic Press.

Jacobs, T. (1986). On countertransference enactments. *Journal of the American Psychoanalytic Association,* 34:289–307.

Levenson, E. (1972). *The Fallacy of Understanding.* New York: Basic Books.

Mitchell, S. (1988). *Relational Concepts in Psychoanalysis.* Cambridge, MA: Harvard University Press.

Renik, O.D. (1993). Analytic interaction: conceptualizing technique in the light of the analyst's irreducible subjectivity. *Psychoanalytic Quarterly,*

62:553–571.

Searles, H. (1979). *Countertransference and Related Subjects.* New York: International Universities Press.

Singer, E. (1965). *Key Concepts in Psychotherapy.* New York: Basic Books.

Stem, D.B. (1997). *Unformulated Experience.* Hillsdale, NJ: The Analytic Press.

Sullivan, H.S. (1953). *The Interpersonal Theory of Psychiatry.* New York: Norton.

Tublin, S. (2011). Discipline and freedom in relational psychoanalysis. *Contemporary Psychoanalysis,* 47:519–546.

Wolstein, B. (1959). *Countertransference.* New York: Grune & Stratton.

Prologue to Chapter 16:
FROM FAMILIAR AND FAMILIAL REPETITION TO THE ANXIETY OF LIVING DIFFERENTLY

This final chapter can be seen as sort of a credo. It represents, in a pithy fashion and accompanied by a clinical illustration, my fundamental view of how human personality evolves from internalized life experience with significant others and how wedded we all are to this familial and familiar experience. As troubled and unfulfilled that these internalizations may make us, I argue that they reflect both a loyalty to significant others and an adaptive equilibrium that is likely to trump the pursuit of a liberated happiness. Indeed, I underscore the point made by many, that we are all unconsciously motivated to repeat earlier life configurations and that we similarly organize our lives to conform to the known and relatively comfortable past. Potential personality change leads to the anxiety of separation and to the sense of aloneness that inevitably accompanies this.

The existentialist Freud proclaimed that the domain of psychoanalytic therapy is the addressing of the problems that we make for ourselves. That is, problems and symptoms cannot be attributed to the past per se, but to the unconscious wishes to shape our current existence to conform to the familiar and familial past. Psychoanalysis as a therapy can be effective in two dimensions: the insightful recognition of the power unconscious motivation and as well, the mutual enacting, in the transference-countertransference matrix, of what each patient has internalized. The analysis of these mutual enactments in vivo offer the opportunity to engage differently with one's analyst and then possibly in the larger world of others.

Chapter 16

FROM FAMILIAR AND FAMILIAL REPETITION TO THE ANXIETY OF LIVING DIFFERENTLY*

This article attempts to summarize the author's view of what is generative in the psychoanalytic process. Included in this discussion are reflections on the ideal aims of psychoanalysis and a perspective on mutative action. One clinical example is used to illustrate the author's theses.

As a brief introduction, I believe that the essential domain of psychoanalysis is addressing the problems that we make for ourselves, i.e., paraphrasing Freud when he was asked about the purpose of this enterprise. He distinguished this "addressing the problem" from the unavoidable sadness, loss, and tragedy that befalls all of us and that we cannot control. In this regard, Freud was the ultimate existentialist, suggesting that when we can be made affectively aware of our unconsciously motivated, yet burdensome, repetitions of past troubles—and the possible reasons for such repetition, we become more capable of exerting our conscious agency and our choice and will to live life somewhat differently. Of course, we now know that emotional awareness is not the singular key to leading a richer life than heretofore. Our repetitive patterns are as enduring as they are because they have been internalized in the context of self-other life experience with our most cherished others and our identifications with these most significant others, what Stephen Mitchell (1988) called internalized relational configurations. The psychoanalytic relationship, as a new and potentially significant relationship, offers the opportunity to internalize relational patterns that differ from the formative ones in the past, at least those earlier internalizations that continue to generate the problems we make for ourselves (Hirsch, 2015).

I will try to be more specific. I believe that all psychological problems are adaptive and develop as the best possible compromise to life circumstances. This is antithetical to any medical or diagnostic model of illness. Our problems in living, ways that we fail to reach potentials

*Hirsch, I. (2018). From familiar and familial repetition to the anxiety of living differently. *Contemporary Psychoanalysis, 54:*290–298.

in work and in love, reflect configurations of what we learned in order to create an equilibrium of minimal possible anxiety, both within ourselves and with our most significant familial others (Sullivan, 1953). Indeed, such equilibrium becomes familiar and comfortable—it is what we evolve to know best and any change at all creates anxiety (Fromm, 1964; Singer, 1965). In this context, I believe that, we are far more motivated to repeat the familiar and the comfortable than we are driven toward any notion of happiness per se, particularly when the comfortable conflicts with happiness. Familiar misery trumps the pursuit of personal fulfillment. In this vein, we are always in great conflict about giving up the equilibrium-producing problems that we have unconsciously made for ourselves in order to adapt to life circumstances. Our problems, indeed, are unconsciously motivated and always have developmental meaning; as Harold Searles (1979) suggested, we love our pathology. This said, and obvious to all readers, just because we are deeply attached to the troubled aspects of our internal objects does not mean that we have not been truly wounded by hurtful past experience. As all analysts know, it is imperative that these wounds be fully faced and grieved during the course of any analytic experience.

Clara Thompson, Harry Stack Sullivan's closest colleague and founding progenitor along with Erich Fromm, of the interpersonal tradition in psychoanalysis, elaborated the existential side of Freud. Paraphrasing Thompson (1950), our problems in living lie not in our past, but in the way we unconsciously shape our current life and relationships to conform to that past. She suggests, as did Freud, that we are inclined to evoke the same type of unhappiness and or failure that we experienced originally. Of course, we also evoke or repeat the rich and loving life experiences that have been internalized. For better and for worse, we are unconsciously motivated to live in the manner we know best and to which we are most wedded; thus, living differently creates the anxiety of aloneness—a sense of disconnection and disloyalty to our cherished internal objects.

In this context, in order to initiate analytic therapy, patients must have some conflict about their familiar patterns of living life, and it is the analyst's job to help generate uncomfortable and unfamiliar, but expanded and hopefully richer ways of engaging this life (Greenberg, 2001; Stern, 2006). Our task as analysts begins with trying to understand patients through their own eyes. However, even in the beginning of therapy I have found that most patients are receptive to hearing my observations about them, and these observations are often in contrast with patients' view of themselves. As analysts, we come to know our patients through what they tell us about their present and past experience and by the way that they engage with us, otherwise known as transference. This latter way, of course, reflects a more experiential knowing. I don't think that I need to say to this readership that all "knowing" is subjective, as is any given transference observation.

What makes psychoanalysis stand apart from any other therapeutic model is this emphasis on experiential knowing—the interplay between transference and countertransference as a lived-out parallel to the way patient's shape their lives in general. Levenson (1983) has referred to the analyst's ability to recognize repeated patterning as perhaps our greatest potential skill. He and Racker 1968) before him were first in the psycho-analytic literature to identify and clearly articulate that analysts not only observe patients' transferences but mutually and unwittingly live-out the role of the "other" in patients' lives. That is, we unconsciously engage with patients in parallel patterns to their past and present lives outside, e.g., we will likely be sadistic with masochistic people and we will often be bored by those who engage us in ways that reflect the lack of expectancy to be an object of interest. Levenson (1972) called this phenomenon "transformation," though. it has become known and widely embraced by analysts of many stripes as "mutual enactment." Paraphrasing him, we must become part of the problem in order to help solve it.

In this context, I view patients as agentic, unconsciously shaping their adult lives to conform to the familiar past and shaping the trans-ference-countertransference matrix in parallel pattern. Of course, each unique individual analyst will enter this matrix somewhat differently and moreover, the unique person of the analyst has some impact on the way patients live out who they are. The analytic relationship is mutual, as Aron (1996) has made clear, yet mutual influence does not imply sym-metrical engagement. I believe that analysts are obliged to be the more recessive partner in the relationship and allow patients to fundamentally shape the relationship between patient and analyst.

For me, what can be generative in psychoanalysis is basically twofold. For one, it is the patient's evolving recognition of pattern between transference and external life, the way life is unconsciously shaped to repeat what may be a troublesome but all too familiar and com-fortable equilibrium. Indeed, I believe that subjectively tinged narrative insight is still a relevant part of psychoanalysis, if for no other reason than it helps to highlight that the problems in our past influence the present but do not need to eternally dictate currently lived life. I believe it crucial that patients recognize that they are not simply victims of past wounds but are active, albeit unconscious, agents in repeating these wounds (Wolstein, 1954). When psychoanalysis is generative, it transforms passivity into activity and resignation into choice.

Second, with respect to the theme of generativity, what is probably even more important, although inseparable, is the evolution of the analytic relationship from a repetition of the old and familiar to something new and more unfamiliar. In unwittingly becoming part of the problem in order to solve it, we analysts aim to recognize how we invariably hurt our patients in order that we can ultimately become somewhat different than the hurtful elements of those internalized past and current others. To the extent that we can do this, we not only offer a new and unfamiliar experience to our patients as a contemporary significant other, but, ideally, our patients internalize elements of our relationship that contrast with the more troubled aspects of earlier internalizations.

One important caveat: I believe we must be warned against demonizing patients' earlier internalizations, parents in particular, and proffering a selfishly motivated binary between the noble and good therapist and the thoroughly deficient parent. I prefer to think of what we do as generative of new experience and not only reparative of bad older experience. Though the difference is subtle and the analytic relationship certainly can be viewed as reparative, the connotation of this term ("reparative") often lends itself to the "good us, bad them" binary, as I note above.

Clinical Illustration

Susan's mother called with much urgency—her previously high functioning daughter, recently diagnosed as acutely paranoid schizophrenic, was about to be released from her brief psychiatric hospitalization and she was still paranoid and delusional. There was talk of a possible longer-term hospitalization in an expensive private facility, but Susan's parents and husband hoped to avoid this, although they feared otherwise. Susan, a 32-year-old lawyer, had given birth to her first child, a daughter, six months earlier and had been in her third month back at work as an associate in a law firm, after a three-month maternity leave with some part time legal work woven in.

Susan's husband was at the time an advanced doctoral student earning little money, and Susan's salary basically supported her family unit. Although Susan mostly enjoyed her baby during her time off, she felt unproductive and a bit bored. Nonetheless, she was anxious about what her life would be like when she returned to full-time work at what was apparently an unstintingly demanding law firm with a reputation for treating associates in an other-than-humane manner. Her husband, from what I gathered, was a fundamentally caring man, though he considered his career in medical research ultimately more important than his wife's lawyerly ambitions. He had spoken pragmatically about the need for her income, viewing Susan as strong and stalwart, as she always had been. He saw her work as a lawyer as a vehicle for economic security, less noble than his own work. In this context and under financial pressure, he overlooked both Susan's anxiety and conflict about integrating motherhood and a demanding career. He felt sanguine about the arrangements they had made for a daily drop-off at a day care facility associated with his university and Susan's parents promise to help out in a pinch.

Susan had always been an ambitious and independent person but she had been frightened about going back to that particular law firm while maintaining a satisfactory relationship with her infant daughter. She did, however, love being a lawyer, did not share her husband's dark view of this profession, and feared being bored as a stay-at-home mom. Her own professional mother was responsible, but chilly and demanding. Susan was raised to be strong and independent and to not expect much luxury or help. She had an inordinate number of responsibilities growing up, including being expected to do considerable parenting to a much younger sister. Her father was softer, but a bit of a head-in-the-clouds academic, the recessive partner in a marriage dominated by his wife. Susan never faltered—she had rich friendships, excelled academically and athletically, and had hopes for a successful career in a field that she truly enjoyed. She was upbeat in temperament, rarely got down, depressed, or angry. She moved forward seamlessly and with little self-reflection. Although smart and well educated, she was more of a doer than a contemplator.

Susan had never met a challenge that she could not readily handle until this one. She could not get in touch either with her degree of helplessness and dependency or her anger. She could not keep up with her work and was criticized by her seniors. She did not seem to have the psychological vocabulary to articulate to herself, or to anyone else, that her situation in this particular law firm, with an infant child, was just too much for her and that she was furious at her superiors for their cruelty, at her husband for not recognizing the degree of her stress, at her mother for never allowing her to relax and let herself be more dependent on others, and at her sweet father for not protecting her.

This constellation of feelings was translated into a series of delusions. Susan felt that her law firm partners were accusing her of illegal doings and intended to report her to the bar association, while being in correspondence with her husband in some vague and undefined way. These delusions led to her leaving her law firm and she ended up in the hospital and on anti-psychotic meds. In my first meeting with Susan, she made it clear that she believed that I was hired by, and in contact with, her law firm. She was polite, tentative, and friendly, with a nonaggressive manner and trying hard to be reasonable—a good and respectful girl in spite of my collusion with the "enemy."

I relished this opportunity and challenge, for I have seen in recent years only one other patient who had gone acutely mad after always functioning at least reasonably well in the world. Early in my career, I spent four years working psychoanalytically with acutely psychotic and suicidal people in a day hospital setting and I missed this work enormously. There has been nothing more gratifying than helping patients reconstitute in the face of being perceived by family and other mental health professionals as on the way toward chronic dysfunction. Susan reminded me of these patients and I felt both confident that I could help her and comfortable with her paranoia. With Harold Searles as my academic guide, I readily told her when I thought that she was talking in a delusional way and that, although her manner was not at all aggressive, I conveyed to her that she must be angry at all of those who were insensitive to her incredible stress. I also suggested that she must be angry at her little girl for messing up her life like she did, and challenged her to see how out of touch she was with her dissociated dependent self—actually with her whole range of affective states. I suggested to her that part of her going crazy was a way to say "enough," and part was to exact revenge on those guilty others who took poor care of her. Now, Susan was forcing those in her world to nurture her.

Within two to three weeks at three sessions per week and reduced medication, Susan was no longer delusional and seemed, according to her report, a bit shaken and humbled by what had happened, but pretty much back to normal. She was grateful to me for being so candid with her and

I felt like a hero. Nonetheless, Susan was still not self-reflective and although my comments about her anger and her neediness made logical sense to her, she claimed to not really feel those feelings. Indeed, I had expected her to not only be sane again but to be a good, reflective analytic patient. She was not the latter at all—she was too damned upbeat and optimistic and ready to reassume life as it had been, albeit with another law firm. She had no intention of stopping therapy and I felt a distinct mutual father-daughter attachment, but she insisted that she was ready to "get on with things and not dwell or feel sorry for myself."

We argued, first teasingly and sarcastically, about the manifest absence of the feelings I was convinced were there, although Susan did eventually become angry at my stubborn persistence. She told me I also expected her to be a good obedient and hard-working girl in a way that paralleled her mother, husband, and former bosses. The only difference was that I expected her to be a good patient—to be the way I wanted her to be, a way that would make life easier for me. Indeed, I selfishly wanted to ride my success in ridding her of her acute madness into the success of character change, a change in character that was in harmony with my own personal and professional values.

We are still meeting, albeit now twice per week. I have stopped pushing her to meet my expectations and pace, and indeed, she is becoming a more overtly angry and demanding person, more sensitive to her own unmet desires for varieties of nurturing dependence. My interactive tone has evolved from clearly communicating high expectations to one that has a more nurturing timbre.

Summary

I have attempted to articulate my personal internalization of the interpersonal perspective with respect to the key question of what is generative in our psychoanalytic process. Because this is difficult to do without some background conceptualization of how problems in living a fulfilled life develop and stubbornly persist, I have also theorized about this question. Finally, I have offered a brief clinical presentation that I believe illustrates my essential point of view about the development of troubled patterns of living and one way that the psychoanalytic process may intervene in a generative fashion.

REFERENCES

Aron, L. (1996). *A Meeting of Minds.* Hillsdale, NJ: Analytic Press.

Fromm, E. (1964). *The Heart of Man.* New York: Harper & Row.

Greenberg, J. (2001). The analyst's participation: A new look. *Journal of the American Psychoanalytic Association,* 49(2): 359–398
doi: 10.1177/00030651010490020801

Hirsch, I. (2015). *The Interpersonal Tradition: the Origins of Psychoanalytic Subjectivity.* New York: Routledge.

Levenson, E. (1972). *The Fallacy of Understanding.* New York, NY: Basic Books.

———— (1983). *The Ambiguity of Change.* Northgate, NJ: Jason Ironstone.

Mitchell, S. (1988). *Relational concepts in psychoanalysis.* Cambridge, MA: Harvard University Press.

Racker, H. (1968). *Transference and Countertransference.* New York, NY: International Universities Press.

Searles, H. (1979). *Countertransference and Related Subjects.* New York, NY: International Universities Press.

Singer, E. (1965). *Key concepts in psychotherapy.* New York, NY: Basic Books.

Stern, D.B. (2006). States of relatedness: Are ideas part of the family? *Contemporary Psychoanalysis,* 42(4):565–576.
doi: 10.1080/00107530.2006.10747129

Sullivan, H.S. (1953). *The Interpersonal Theory of Psychiatry.* New York, NY: Norton.

Thompson, C. (1950). *Psychoanalysis: Evolution and Development.* New York, NY: Hermitage.

Wolstein, B. (1954). *Transference.* New York, NY: Grune & Stratton.

www.ingramcontent.com/pod-product-compliance
Lightning Source LLC
Chambersburg PA
CBHW051712020426
42333CB00014B/956